Rodney McMillian

Landscape Paintings

Rodney McMillian

Landscape Paintings

Aspen Art Museum

Director's Foreword **6**

Painting the Domestic **21**
Heidi Zuckerman in conversation with Rodney McMillian

Rodney McMillian: Beside Himself **61**
Thomas J. Lax

Wildseedling: there are veins in these lands **103**
Rodney McMillian

Artist Curriculum Vitae **126**

Installation Views **133**

Contributors Biographies **142**

Exhibition Checklist **143**

List of Illustrations **144**

Director's Foreword

Rodney McMillian creates disruptive landscape paintings that locate the body in space, primarily through its absence. For his Aspen Art Museum exhibition, all of the paintings are made on discarded bedding. The works are emotional and urgent, characterized by darkness and filled with messiness. Abstractly and poetically referencing the ploughed landscape as a body to be known, McMillian's paintings are grown, with a sense of honesty, out of the American South and serve as sites for the acknowledgment of trauma as well as the sustained wear and tear of human existence.

It is with immense honor and pride that the Aspen Art Museum presents *Landscape Paintings*, the first comprehensive exhibition and publication focused on the painting practice of the artist. Conceived in close dialogue and through numerous studio visits with McMillian, the exhibition has a specific, defined focus, while the book contains images of almost every painting produced by the artist since, and including, his graduate thesis exhibition, demonstrating a fuller comprehension of the impetus of his work.

I am deeply grateful to the staff of Susanne Vielmetter Los Angeles Projects and to Susanne personally—her gallery along with the artist are the primary lenders for this exhibition and her staff was integral in sourcing imagery and other resources for the catalogue. In addition, I want to express my gratitude to the Kadist Art Foundation as they have generously lent work to the exhibition. Michele Maccarone, as well as the team at her gallery, also graciously supported the artist, the exhibition, and the publication in many ways and in many forms.

My profound gratitude is due to Toby Devan Lewis who has permanently endowed our essential Publications Fund and shares our value and knowledge of how important the power of print is. She has forever ensured that our good work will be seen the world over, and the opportunity to provide a book for a young artist is an incredible and sustaining gift.

I also want to acknowledge the generosity of both my colleague and friend, curator Thomas Lax, as well as McMillian for contributing revelatory essays to the catalogue. Without such scholarship, this catalogue would not possess the gravitas that the work commands.

I am grateful for the commitment of Peter Eleey and Mia Locks of MoMA P.S.1 in bringing McMillian's work to a broader audience and participating as a venue for the exhibition.

I would like to thank AAM Editor, Sarah Stephenson, who carefully edited all of the texts and provided essential insight with grace and subtlety, as ever. Sara Fowler, AAM Junior Graphic Designer, again designed a catalogue that elegantly captures the emotive richness inherent in McMillian's work.

At the Aspen Art Museum, we work as an extremely close and committed team and there are numerous individuals who have worked to make the exhibition and catalogue a great success, including: Michael Aberman, Design Director, who oversees the production of all of our catalogues; Sherry Black, Curatorial Associate and Archivist, who worked closely with Susanne Vielmetter Los Angeles Projects to ensure that an image of almost every painting be included in the book and coordinated myriad details with McMillian; Courtenay Finn, Curator, whose insight I have come to rely on and whose collaboration and follow-through helps make our exhibition programming the success that it is; Jonathan Hagman, Chief Preparator, and our crew who facilitated the installation of the exhibition and continue to be lauded by the artists with which we work; Amelia Russo, Executive Coordinator for the Director, who offered crucial support throughout the process; John-Paul Schaefer, Deputy Director, whose essential feedback and encouragement is unwavering; and Luis Yllanes, Director of Exhibitions and Registration, who handled all the loan negotiations, served as our lender liaison, and ensured the work's timely and safe transport.

Enormous thanks go to Susan and Larry Marx who have created an endowment to fund our exhibitions in perpetuity, allowing the museum to continue to present exhibitions of the highest quality. Thank you also goes to Toby Devan Lewis for funding our visiting artist endowment so artists may engage with our audiences and create exhibitions unique to our museum. Allison and Warren Kanders funded the exhibition and I am incredibly grateful to them for their continued generosity to the museum. The exhibition is also funded in part by the Aspen Art Museum National Council and I am grateful for its continued financial assistance. One hundred percent of its contributions go to support our exhibitions.

The magic and electricity of being in an artist's studio is one of the most addictive parts of curating exhibitions. The opportunity for frank and raw dialogue about why art gets made and why it matters to the greater world is essential. Rodney welcomed me numerous times not only into his physical space, but also into the depths of his creative efforts. I feel very grateful to have his trust, which thus allowed for this highly specific, curated exhibition as well as the recording of one of our conversations that has become part of this book. We hope both will have the desired impact on the understanding of Rodney's work.

Heidi Zuckerman
Nancy and Bob Magoon CEO and Director

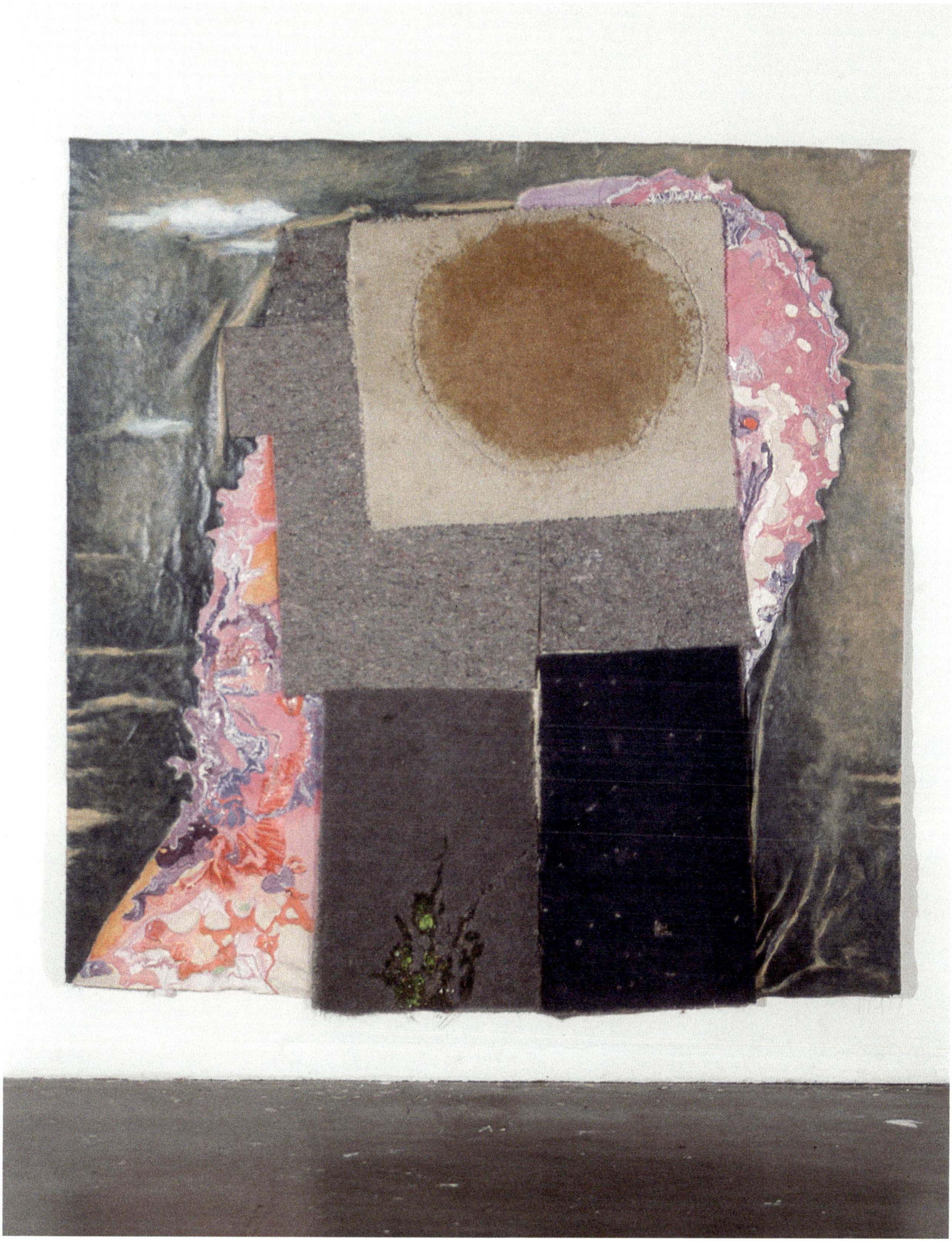

Untitled, 2001

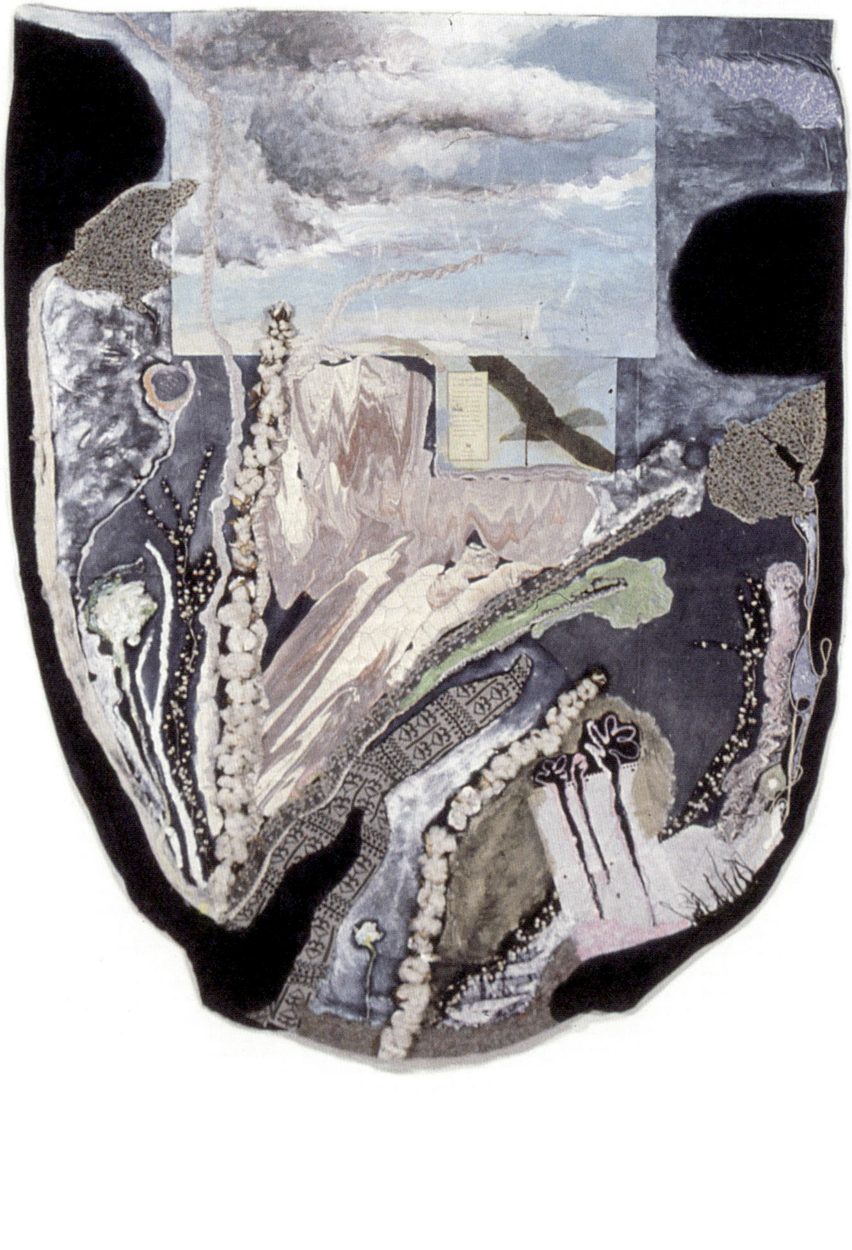

Untitled, 2001

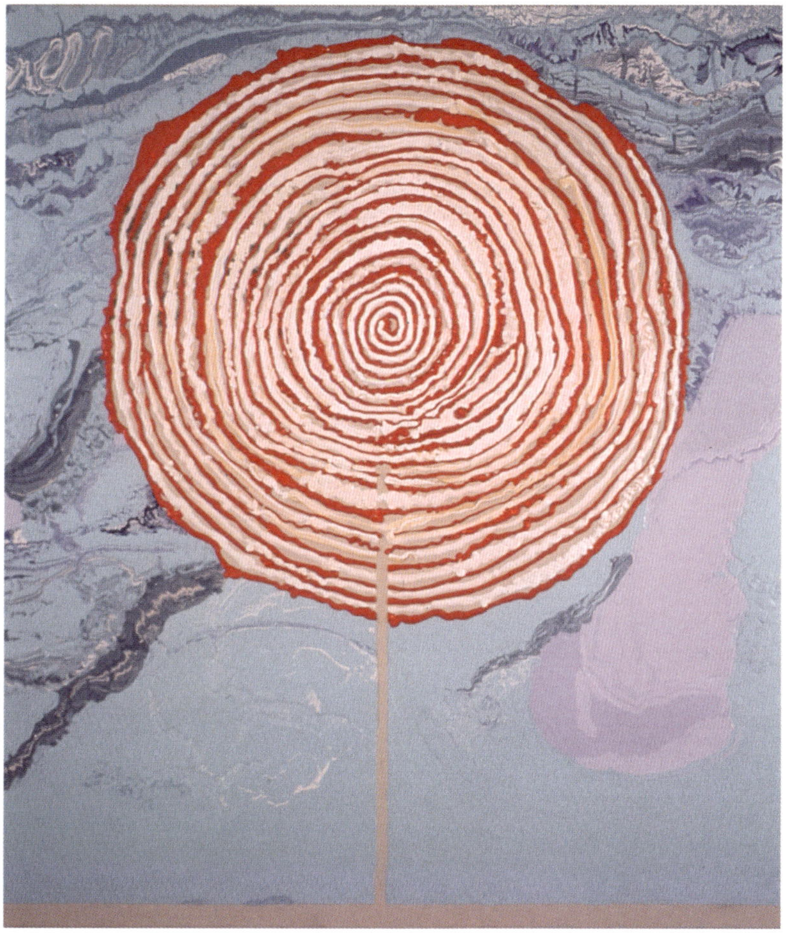

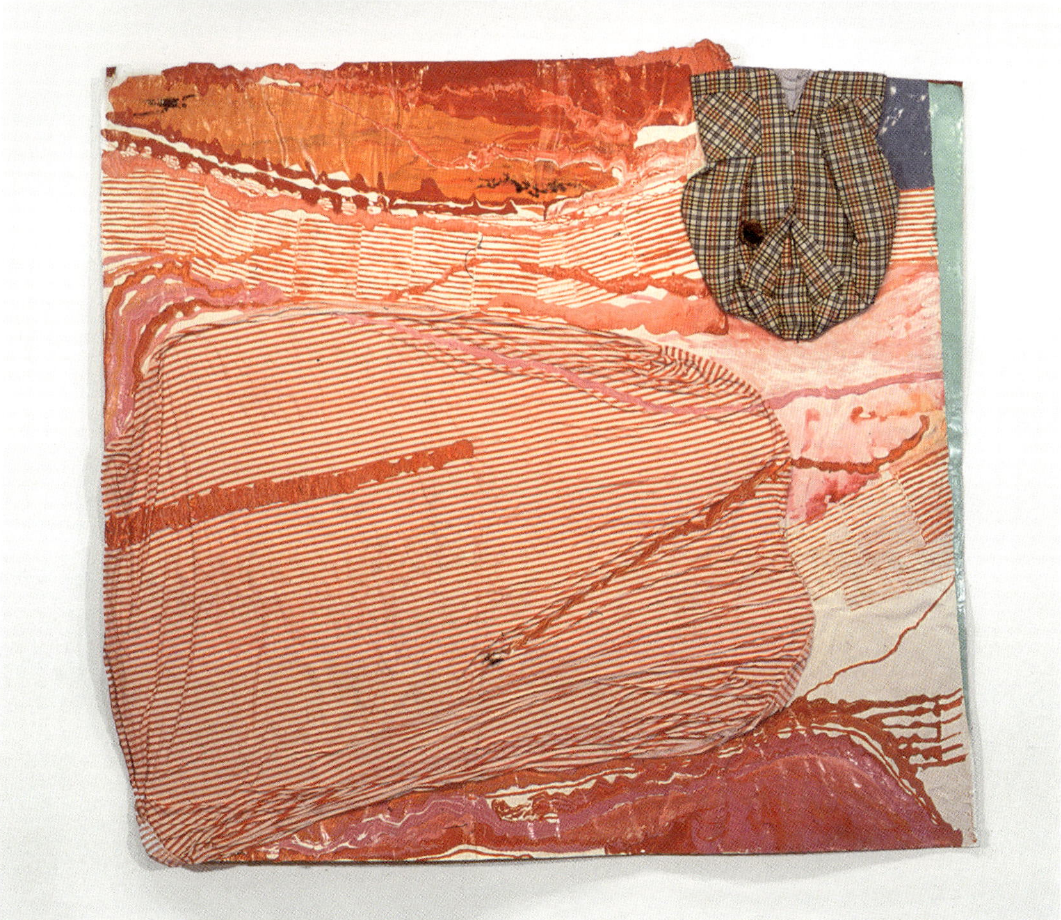

Untitled (lollipop), 2002
Untitled (flag), 2001

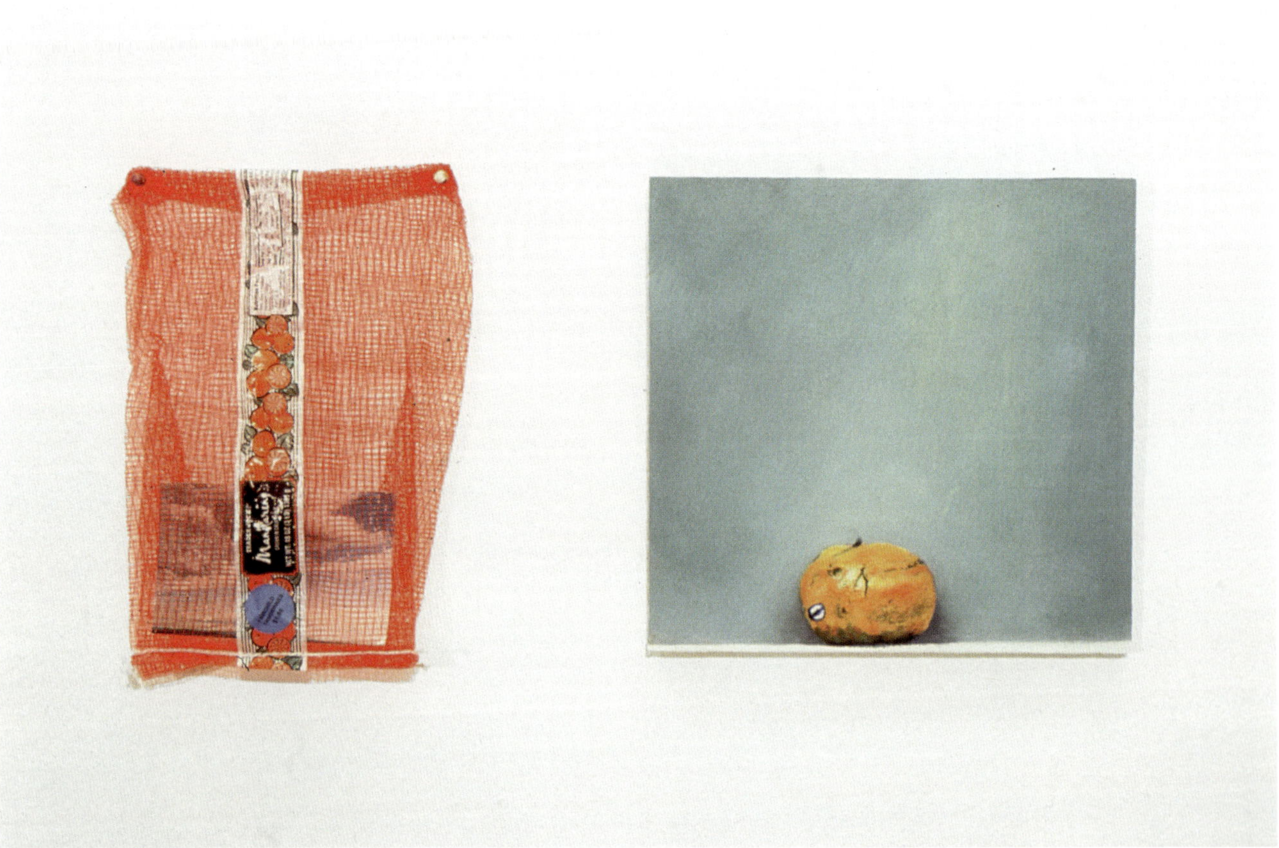

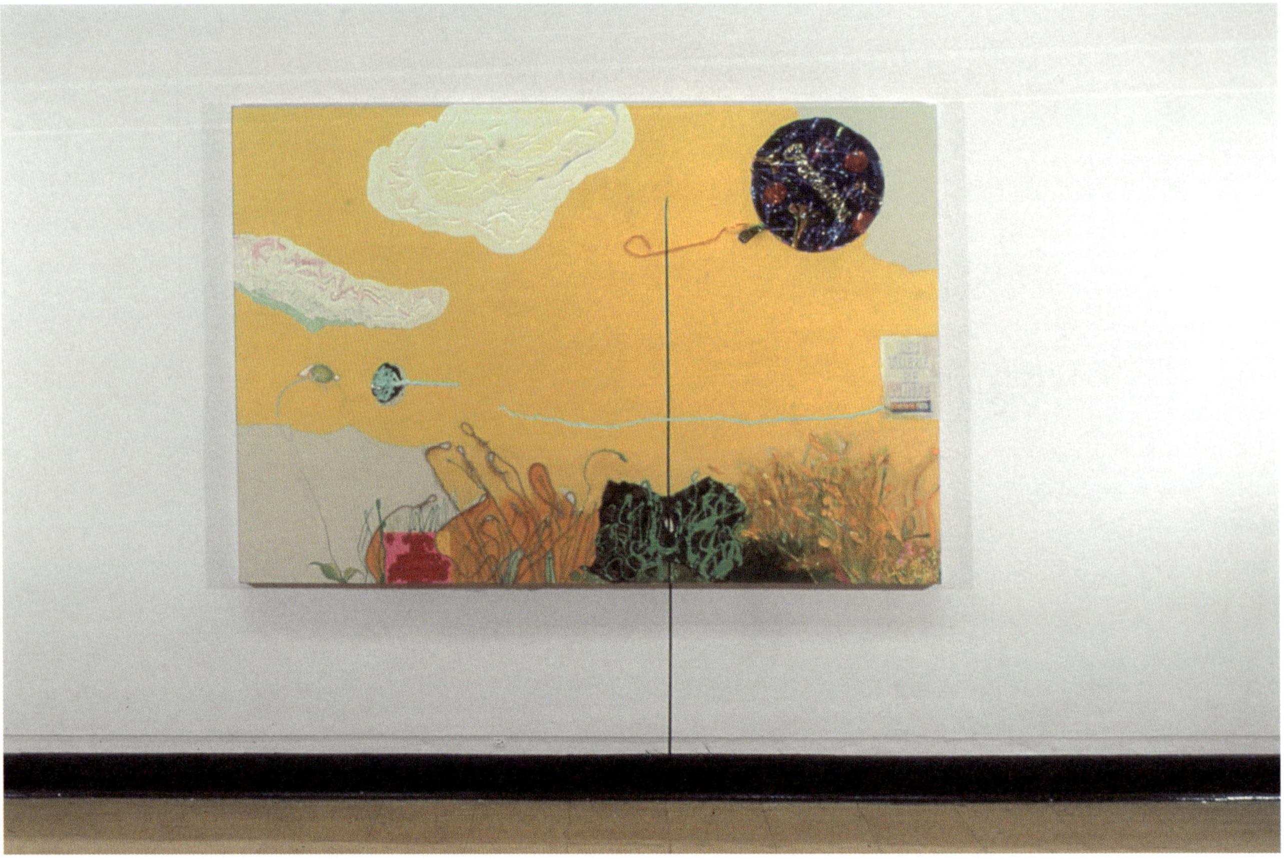

$ 0.42, 2001
Untitled (flag) II, 2001

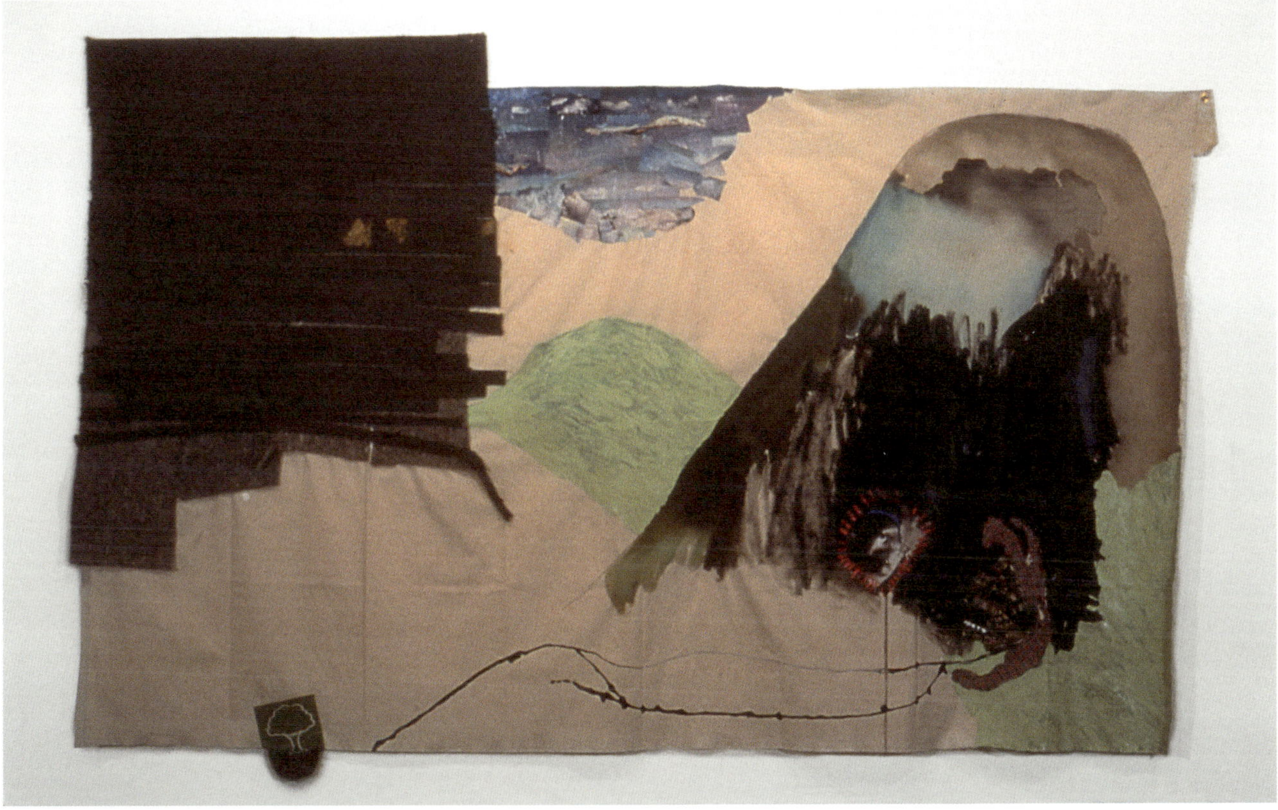

Untitled (flag) I, 2001

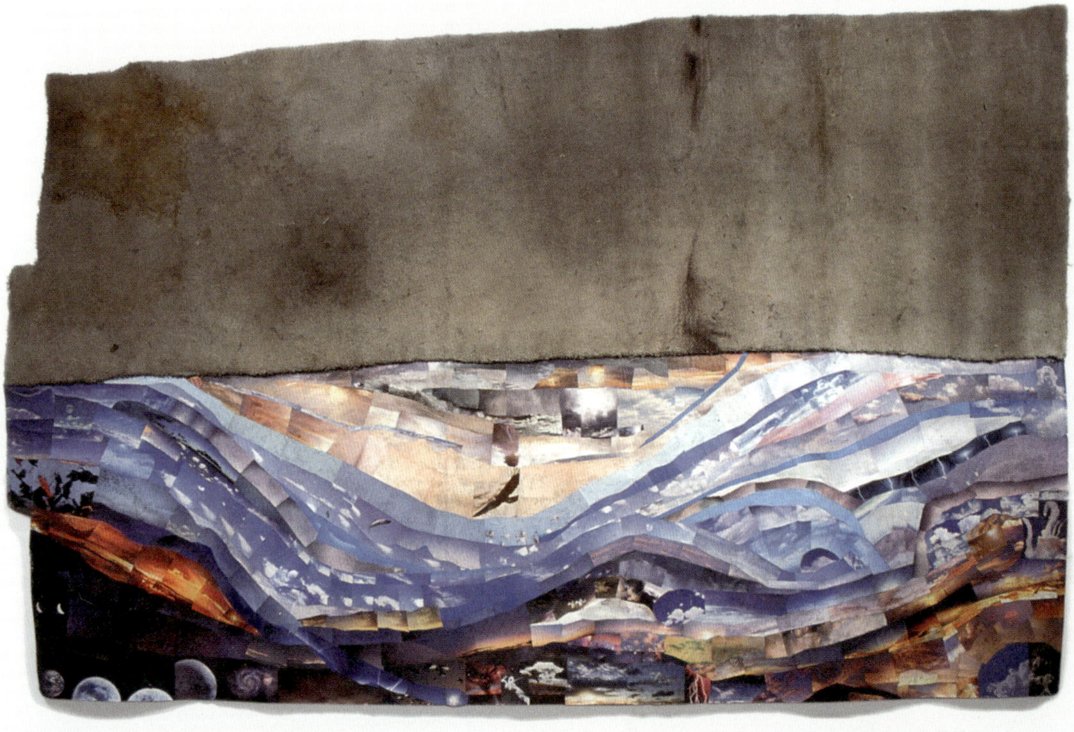

Untitled, 2003

Untitled, 2001
Untitled (bald eagle), 2002

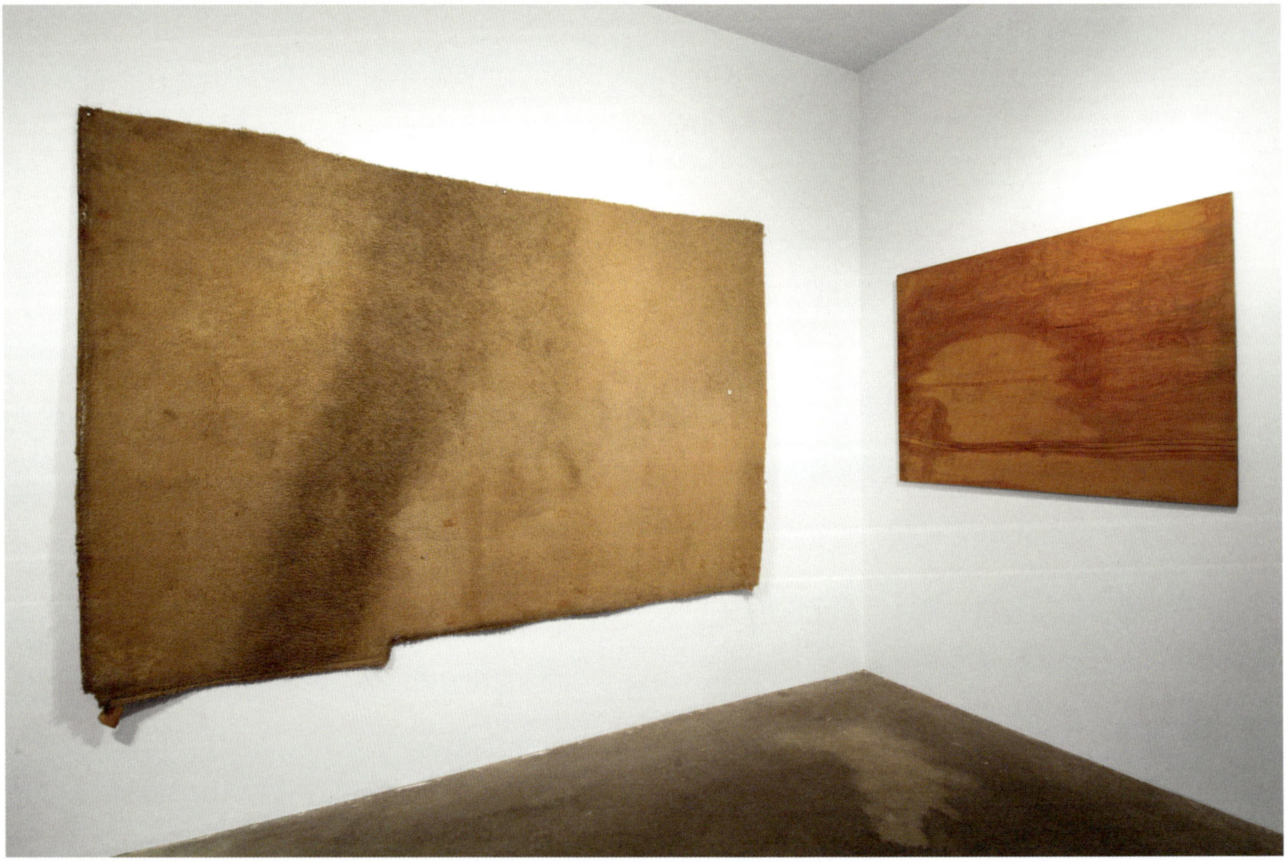

Ascension (From the church on the corner of Prospect Ave and Rodney Dr), 2005

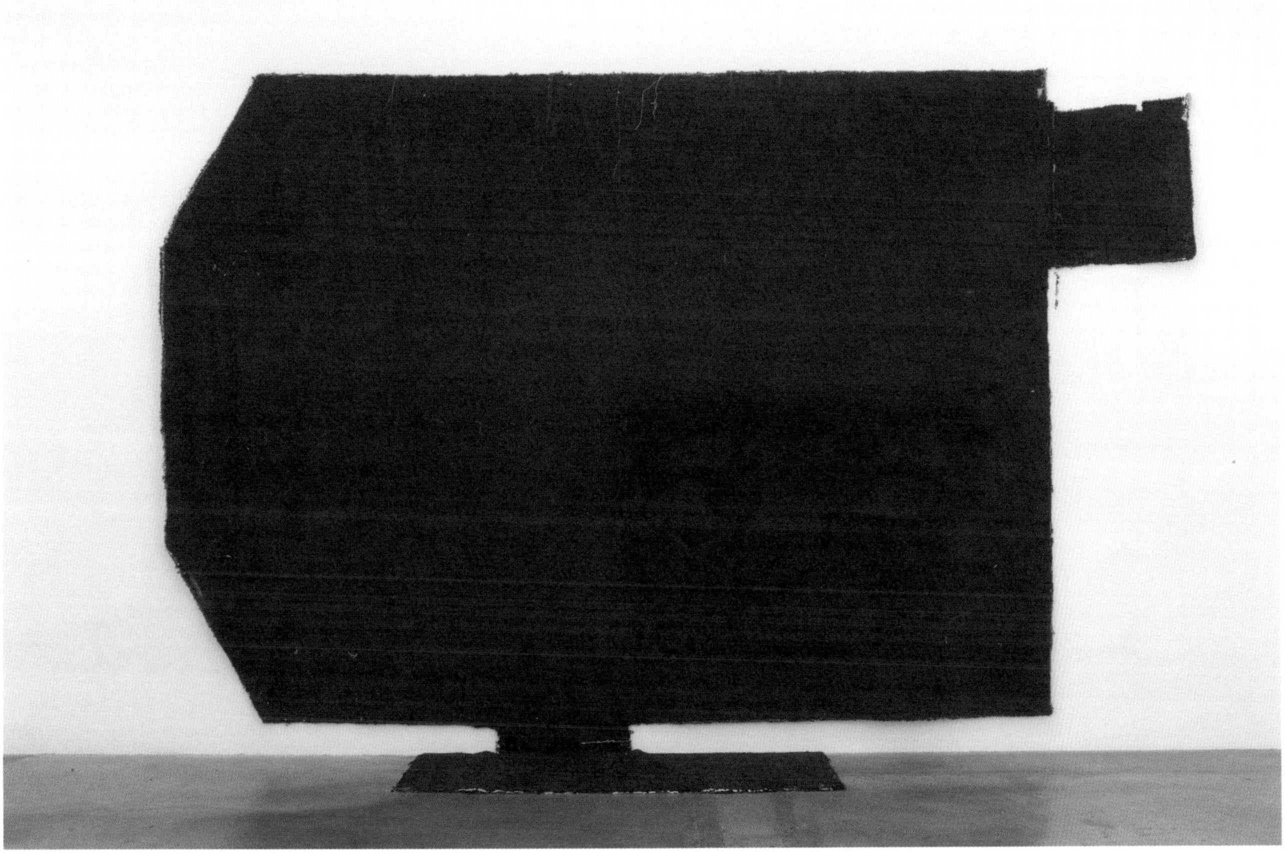

Untitled, 2011

18

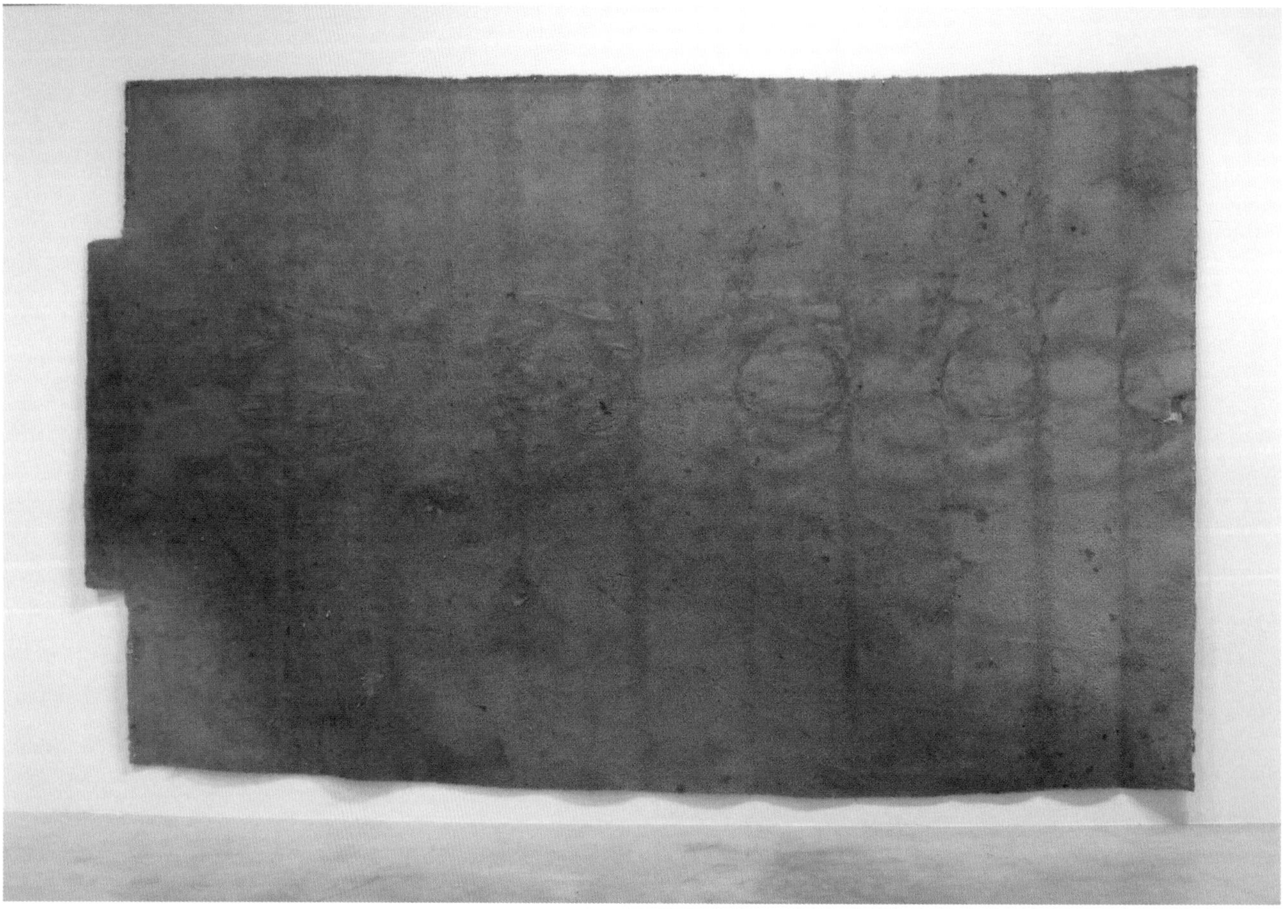

Untitled, 2004

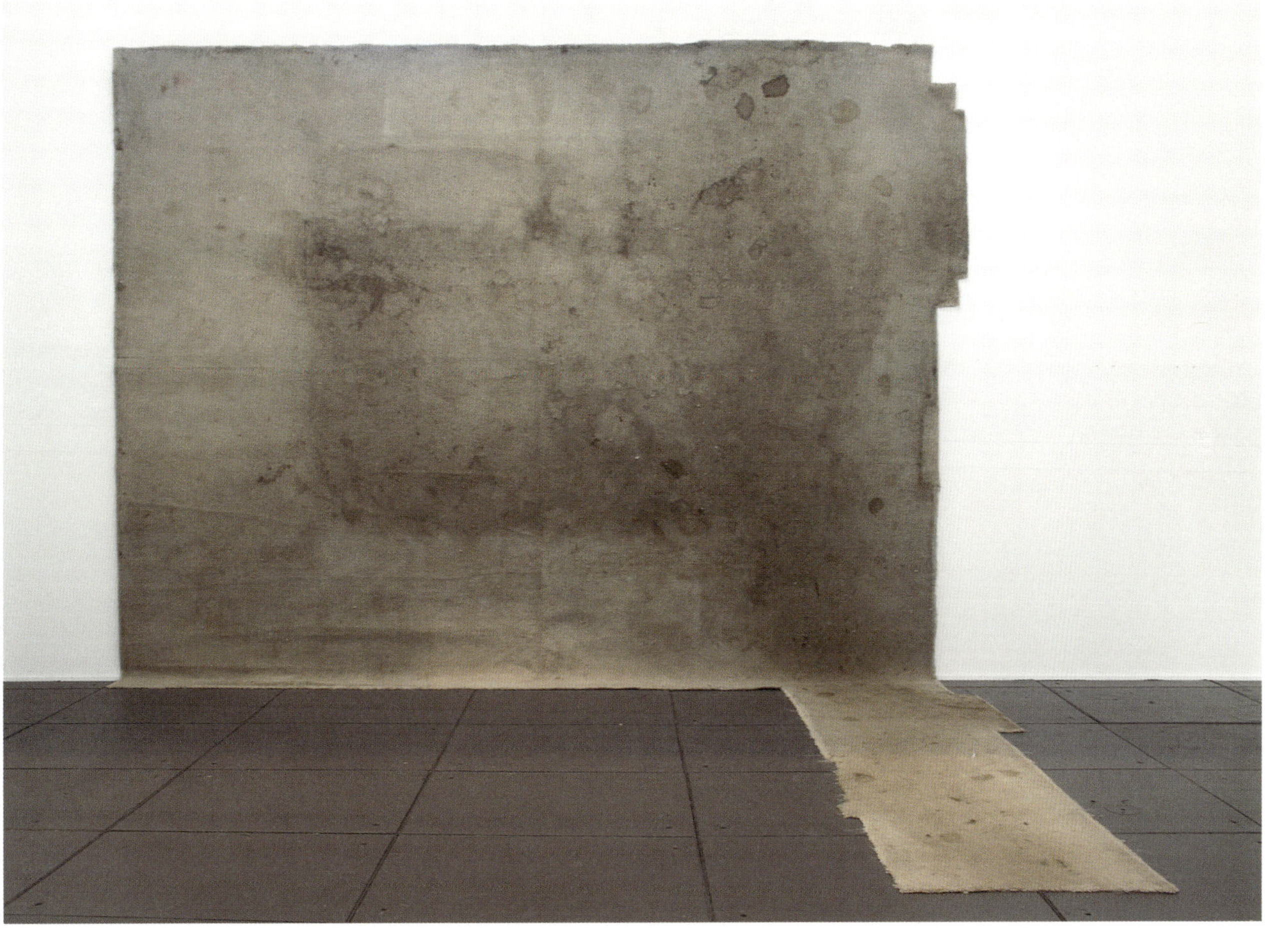

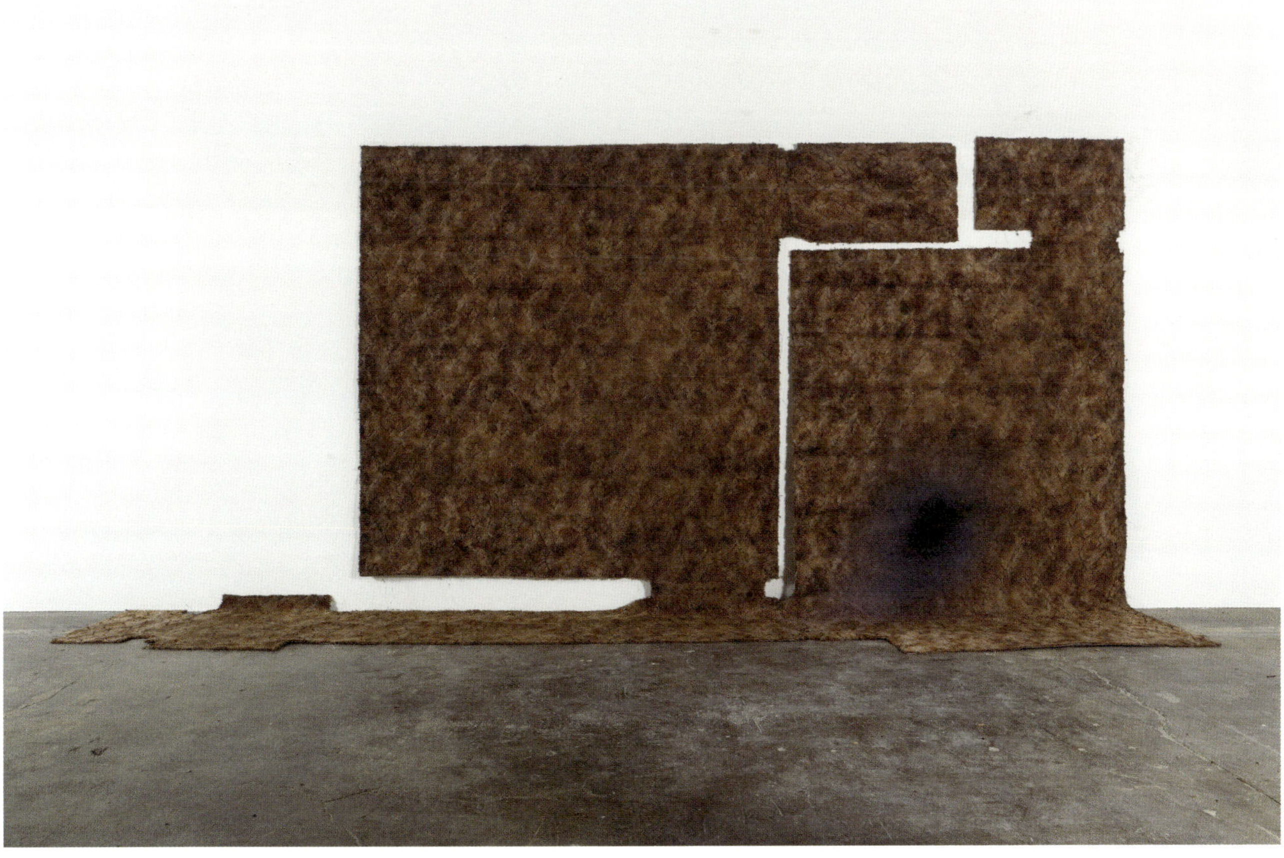

Untitled, 2005
Carpet Painting (Bedroom and TV Room), 2012

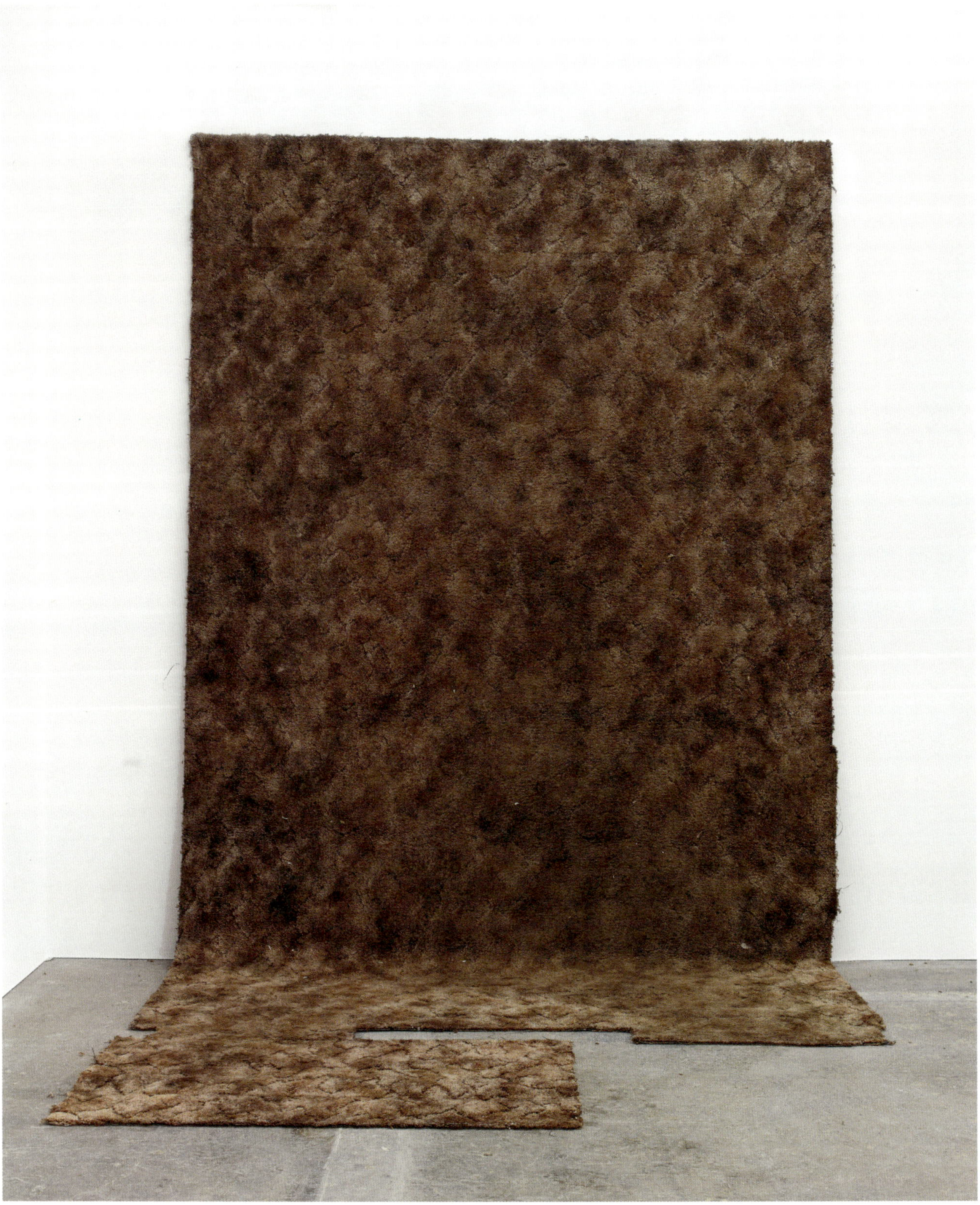

Carpet Painting (Office and Ollie's Room), 2012

Painting the Domestic

Heidi Zuckerman in conversation with Rodney McMillian

HZ

I wanted to begin by talking about your practice in general, which is particularly diverse. As we were starting to put the book together, I decided that I wanted to include all the paintings you have made. Sherry Black [AAM Curatorial Associate and Archivist] asked in response to this, "If the work incorporates paint on carpet and it's on the floor, does that constitute a painting? Or if it has paint on a couch?" I wanted to initiate our conversation with this idea of what painting is for you and how you think about it within the context of your own practice.

RM

It really is just a medium. It's also a history. Often, when I decide to paint, it's about a type of representation or thinking about representation in relationship to history. But it's also about it being in relation to either the image or the materials with which I'm working. Painting is like a brush. It's like a camera. It's a form that communicates a specific type of thing in a specific type of way.

HZ

Do the paintings have to have paint in them?

RM

No. I consider the carpet pieces to be paintings. I'm thinking about painting history and about the frame and the paint. I'm thinking about them being carpet, and that they have the trace of human presence. There's often illusionistic space within those carpets.

HZ

Do you intentionally select that material and its placement on the wall to create the illusionistic space? Or is it there prior to you selecting it, and it's only through your enhancing or naming it that it's further defined?

RM

The illusionistic space is already there. Once the pieces are hung vertically, the history of painting or the way that people look at paintings comes into effect. The works are also definitely antagonistic to certain modernist tropes and tenets.

HZ

Because of their physicality, grittiness, or denial of purity?

RM

Definitely. There's no purity there. But also in the sense that they present a different idea of a subject. They deal with class in a way that a lot of modernist painting, at least American modernist painting, didn't really want to. It focused mostly on the materiality of painting and excluded a lot of other art practices as well as political, social, and cultural voices through the reduction of what painting could be, the reduction of painting to its material constructs.

HZ

I always associate a lot of modernist works with these very formal aspects, whether it's shape, color, line, or composition. If you are pulling from the everyday, the domestic, and the grittiness of human existence, it inevitably becomes antithetical to modernism.

In some of your early works, the domestic took the form of the couches, carpets, or rugs. For our exhibition, the focus is on bedsheets and bedspreads. What draws you to those objects and what do you hope to imbue the work with by using those structures?

RM

The domestic has been a strong focus for me because it's easy to cite. It's an interesting place in which to have a conversation around issues of class, race, identity, or belief systems, which are indoctrinated in the home. These objects are great signifiers for talking about indoctrinations, presumptions, or aspirations. I refer to the home so much because some of my own understanding of, or at least formation of, myself was formed and shaped there.

HZ

People rarely talk about class in America. They don't talk about race that much either, but they talk more about race than they do about class. How intertwined are the two in the context of your work?

RM

They are definitely quite intertwined. There are aspects of my work where it's clearly specifically about class. I don't think the components about race are as discernable, although there are works that are definitely concerned with this. It's interesting that we don't talk about it so much because it's so glaringly present.

HZ

Right. When I think about class, I think about it as extending beyond the home and into the neighborhood, which I don't think about as much in terms of race.

RM

Interesting. That might be a luxury. I definitely think of it as an extension because people of a certain class are usually grouped together, since that's where it's affordable, and it's all systematized. Because of the history of this country with the systemic economic oppression, when you factor in race, many black people have often been relegated to a specific neighborhood or community because that's all they can afford.

HZ

Tying that into the materials you use, where did the sheets come from?

RM

They're from different second-hand stores in California.

HZ

They're all local?

RM

Yes. I went to St. Vincent de Paul, which is huge and right down the street. They have a whole section of bedding materials.

HZ

When you are shopping for them, what are you looking for?

RM

I'm looking for different colors and patterns. Some of it's based upon what I already have. It's also based upon the ideas I've been formulating for the image or the material, and what kind of density and type of paint I want to use on the sheet.

HZ

Am I right in understanding that none of them are singles?

RM

You're right, yes. Most of them are at least doubles or queens. I like that it's a space for more than one person. Especially because I've been thinking about ideas around the landscape and science fiction so there needs to be more space as well as this idea of bodies on them.

HZ

Do you mean in terms of the ability of bodies to inhabit space and both be awed by it as well as potentially conquer it?

RM

Exactly, and in terms of the bedding in a space of repose and comfort.

HZ

Sal Khan, the founder of Khan Academy, recently gave a talk about how he likes to read history books, but that he also reads a lot of science fiction, and he explained how they are essentially the same. One considers what has already happened, the other is about what's coming. Do you have a similar relationship to science fiction?

RM

I have a relationship to science fiction and history, but it's a little bit different—I consider them both to be fiction. They're also both present tense in that our interpretation of them is through the prism of us projecting onto or gleaning information from them. Granted, there are histories that are real in terms of having material, consequential effects on all of us, but the way that those histories are told, the way that we understand the nuances during the complexities of those periods, that's the fiction.

HZ

There is some contemporary thinking that dystopic science-fiction writing on machines and cyborgs has informed our negative notions of the future. If we see sci-fi as a way of foretelling what people will create in terms of science and technology, there is now an effort to ask science-fiction writers to construct more positive futures and thus see how that might affect technological developments.

RM

I like the idea, but when I think of science fiction, or the science fiction that I read, it seems to be more about the present tense. I don't really buy the future aspect—it's about now. Of course, there are some texts that infer a hope for the future, maybe that's a strategy. We need as much hope as we can get.

HZ

In terms of something like *Blue sun* (2014–15; page 115), you have talked about this as being a landscape painting. Can you expand on what the landscapes are?

RM

Many of them are about abstraction, but there are some that are more figurative. They address what's absent in most landscape paintings. Often, it's a body. It's also an abject history of toil or the spillage of blood. When I'm making these pieces, I'm thinking about the landscapes that I've encountered here in America—they are complex sites. They aren't pastoral—I can't visit a national park and be awed by the beauty of it. Not because I don't see it, but because it's a space deliberately constructed for that moment of awe. My interest in landscapes and these materials is not only in locating them through a different historical lens, but also from a type of bodily perspective—as opposed to the shock and awe of the sublime or the godly.

HZ

What I understand from this and from your work as a whole is an intention to communicate some of the complexities of things that are taken for granted if people do not ask questions.

RM

Yes. That is the attempt.

HZ

When I look at *a Mouth: and the galaxy within* (2012–15; page 116), I also see a lot of expanding and contracting organic forms—everything from lava and volcanic eruptions to a comet to a black hole and the universe.

RM

Definitely. There are multiple organic forms and I see this as a type of comet orifice, an access to a universe. What was exciting about this piece, in terms of the title and how it formally came together, was that there was this bridge between a body, or a body part—there aren't any bodies in the work, but there is a suggestion of them—with outer space, and I was interested in that interior space of the mouth. It's really quite shallow, but it suggests a lot more depth.

HZ

The mouth is an interesting body part because it both expels and inhales. Do you have a perspective on what is happening in *a Mouth*?

RM

I think of it as doing a bit of both. I was reading Mladen Dolar's book *A Voice and Nothing More* recently and it has a really interesting paragraph on Munch's *The Scream*. Dolar discusses whether the scream is coming out of the mouth and suggests that what could actually be coming out is the land being sucked through the mouth. It's hard to discern exactly where the voice is or what's activating it, but one thing is clear: there is a voice, even if it can't be heard, and there's a type of silence that's really loud because it goes directly to the idea of voice. With *a Mouth*, there is some of that happening, but pictorially, it's more of a cosmic space.

HZ

What do you hope viewers will feel or think when they are in front of your work?

RM

I hope that they think about the way these are made materially, about the layering and density of certain aspects, and take this all into account in relation to the ideas—for example, where one finds a gravitational pull because of an aesthetic choice and where one finds the opposite of that. I want to create a space where there is a desire to think about what's missing or to understand those aesthetic choices in relation to viewers' ideas about the landscape.

HZ

One of the things I really like about your work is that it isn't precious and it speaks the truth. Part of it doing this is an unapologetic embrace of the grittiness of life. Some of that is because of its physicality, your choice of paint type, and how it is hung—an acknowledgment of gravity, where sometimes the works are singing for the heavens and sometimes they are weighed down like everyone is pulling on them. How intentional is this?

RM

That sense of gravity or lift is what's motivating a lot of the choices I make and what that means in terms of teasing out aspects of being a vessel in this world.

HZ

Do you mean that in terms of being alive, it is partly about getting dirty—not just physically, but also emotionally?

RM

Right. It's emotionally and intellectually messy, complex, nuanced, and unresolved. That's what I'm hoping is in this work.

HZ

Do you think that through your paintings, you are stating that they are "the truth" or that it is OK to be in that space?

RM

It's more the latter—about that being the space to occupy. So much of painting is about taste and a type of beauty that can be mindlessly consumed. That ability to consume "mindlessly" has been trained. When I paint, I'm able to articulate this conversation through the medium or material itself. It is a history with a platform that's already engaged in the conversation, even though some are unaware that it's being had.

HZ

I read a quote today about how courage is being who you know you want to be in the world, despite the world telling you to be something different. It seems to be what you are talking about, too, in terms of taking empowerment and thinking differently from the people who have done it and that you admire.

RM

Right. The writers, musicians, and artists who have influenced me all offer perspectives on how one can be in the world in a way that is irreverent to indoctrinations and status quos. They are wonderful role models for how we can use whatever abilities we have to exist in a way that feels true to our own belief systems. They provided a great road map for me and there are many different paths to choose from.

HZ

That goes back to one of the primary reasons for the existence of art in the world, which is an alternate means of communicating.

RM

Yes, it's one of many, and it's fantastic.

Untitled, 2013
Untitled, 2013

Untitled (from *The Clampetts*), I, 2011

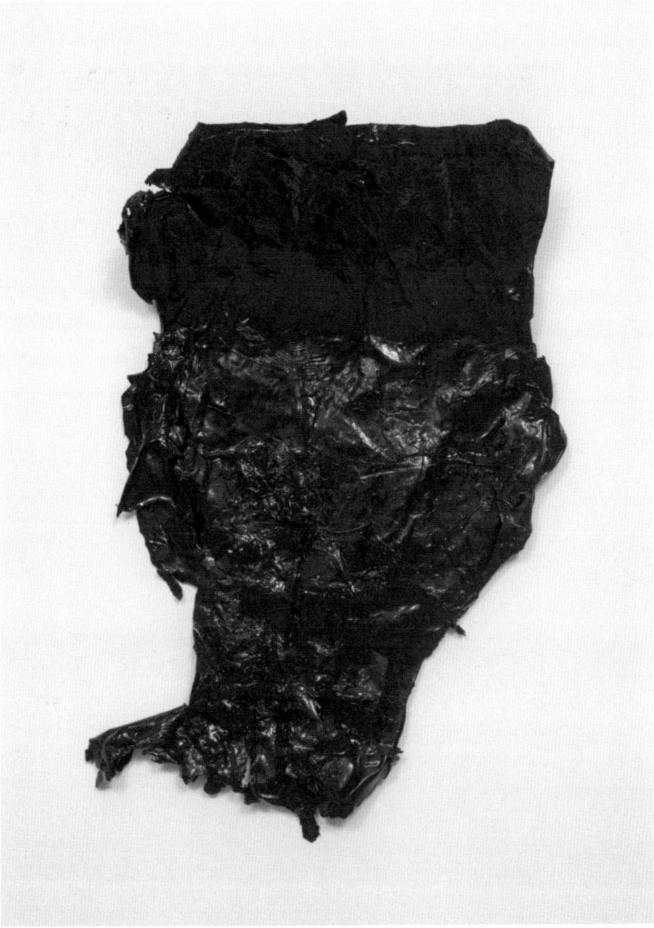

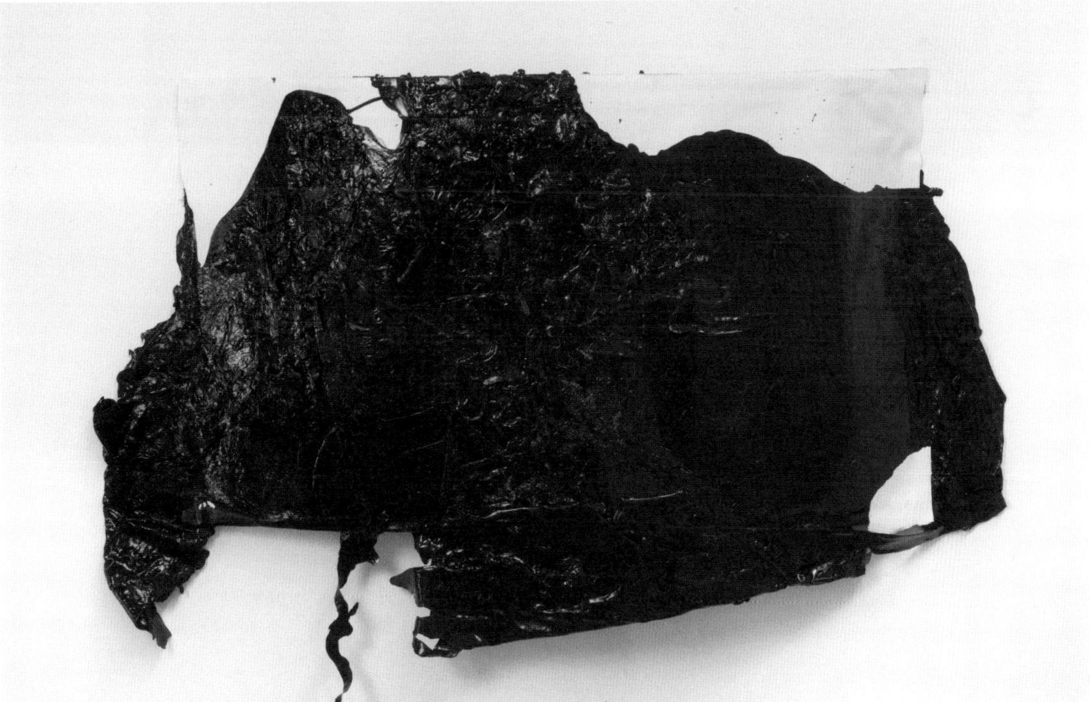

Untitled (from *The Clampetts*), II, 2011
a slow drip (from *The Clampetts*), 2010

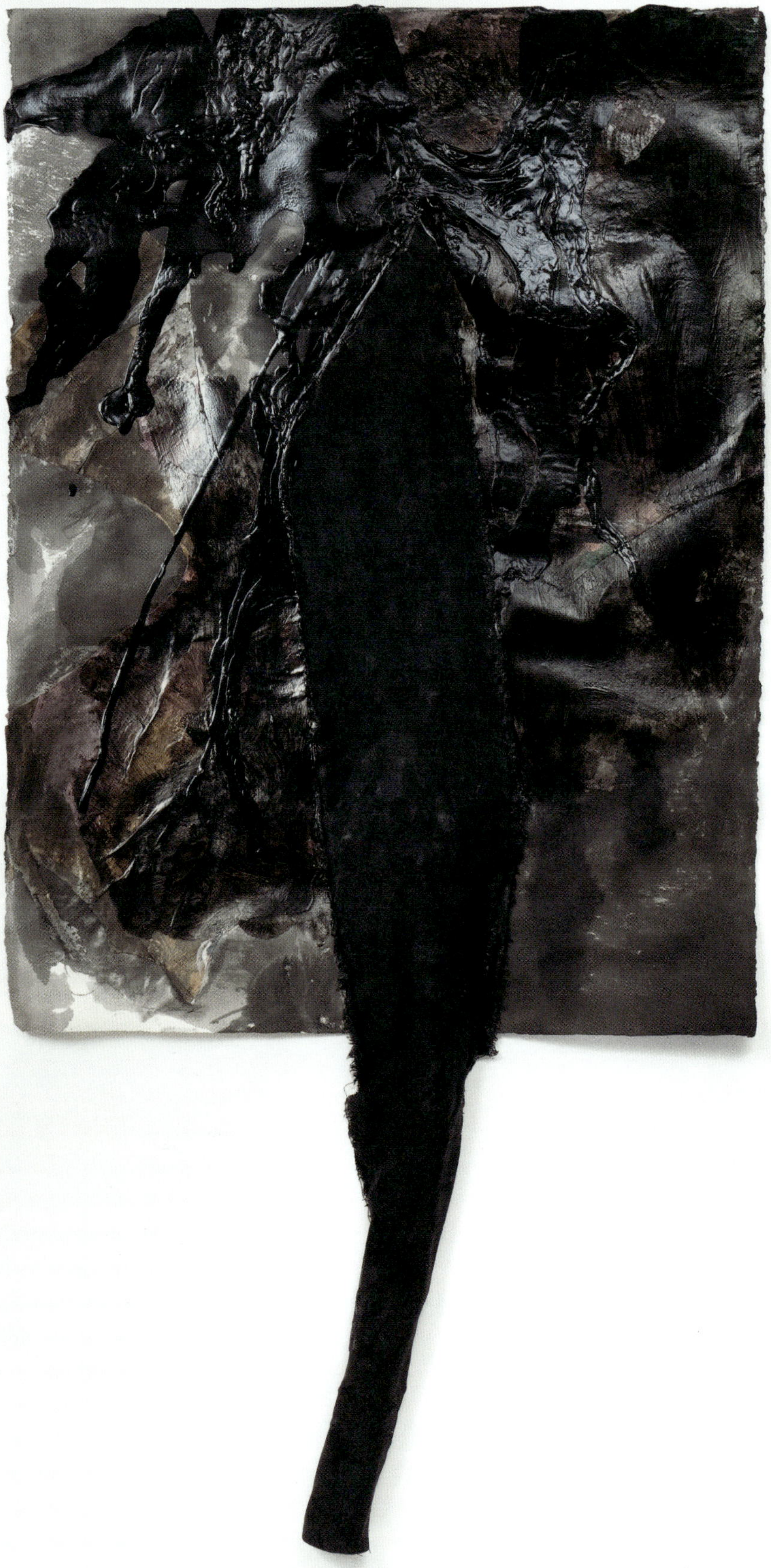

untitled (from the nipple to the bottle...still), 2013

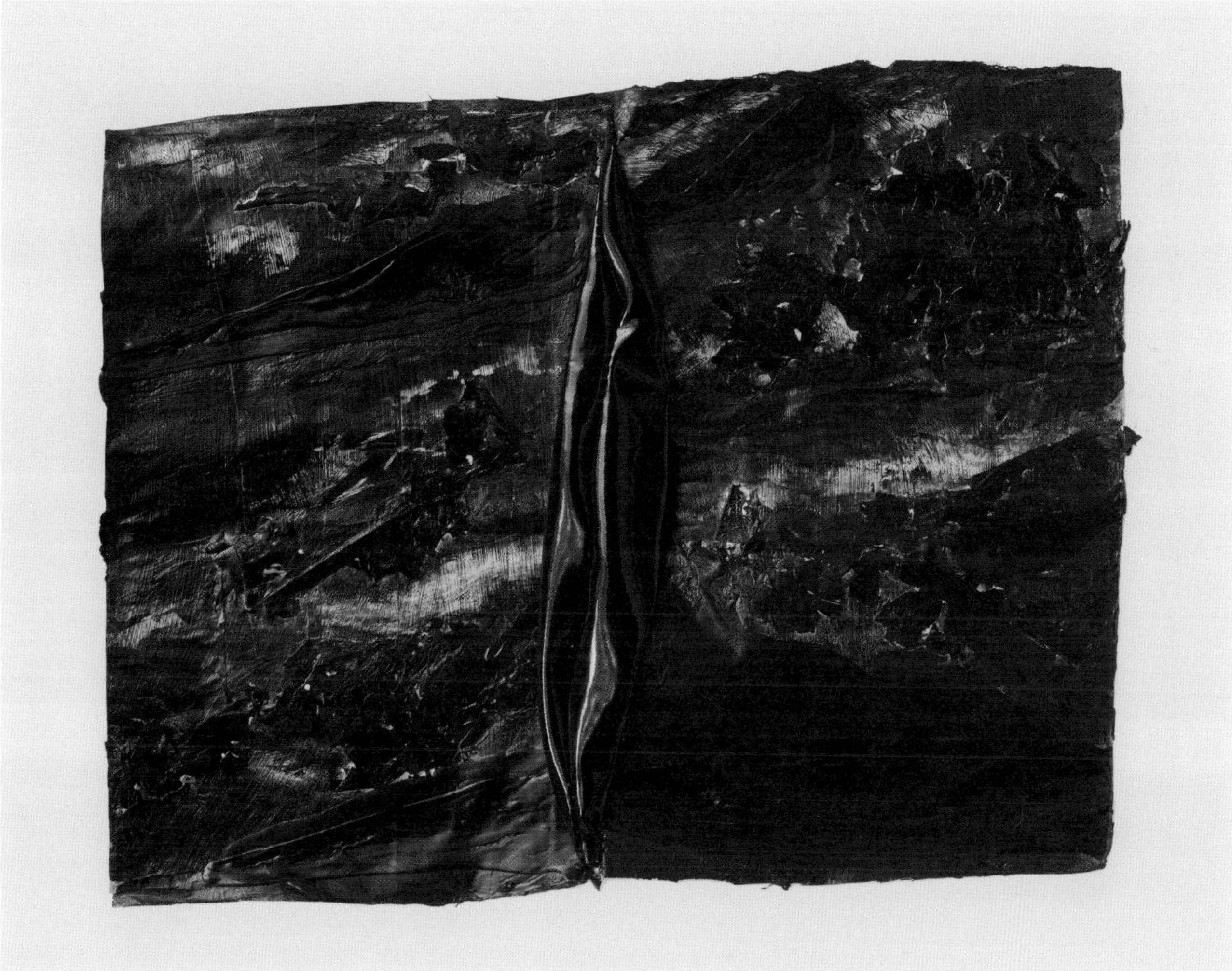

Untitled (Northern Lights), 2011

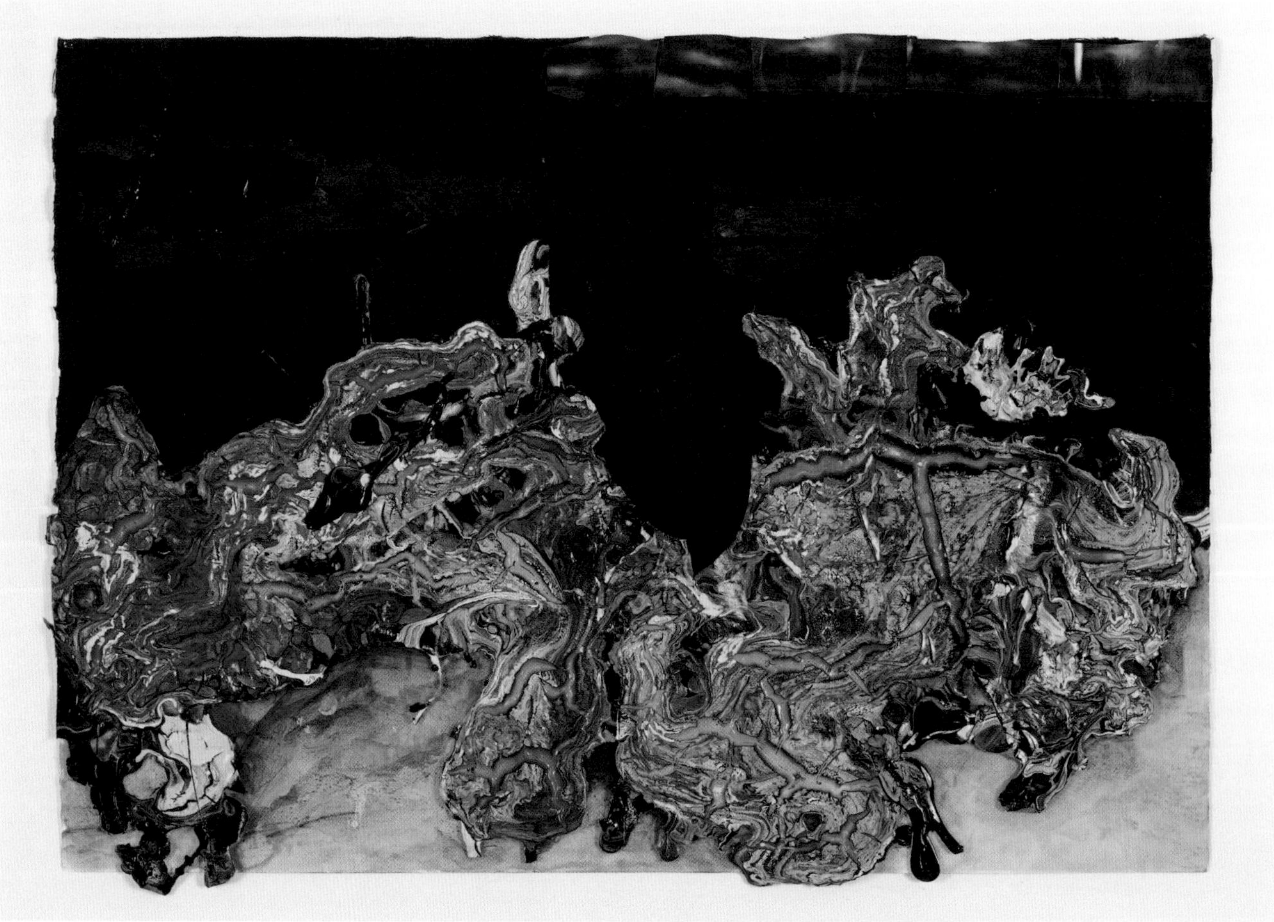

Untitled, 2012

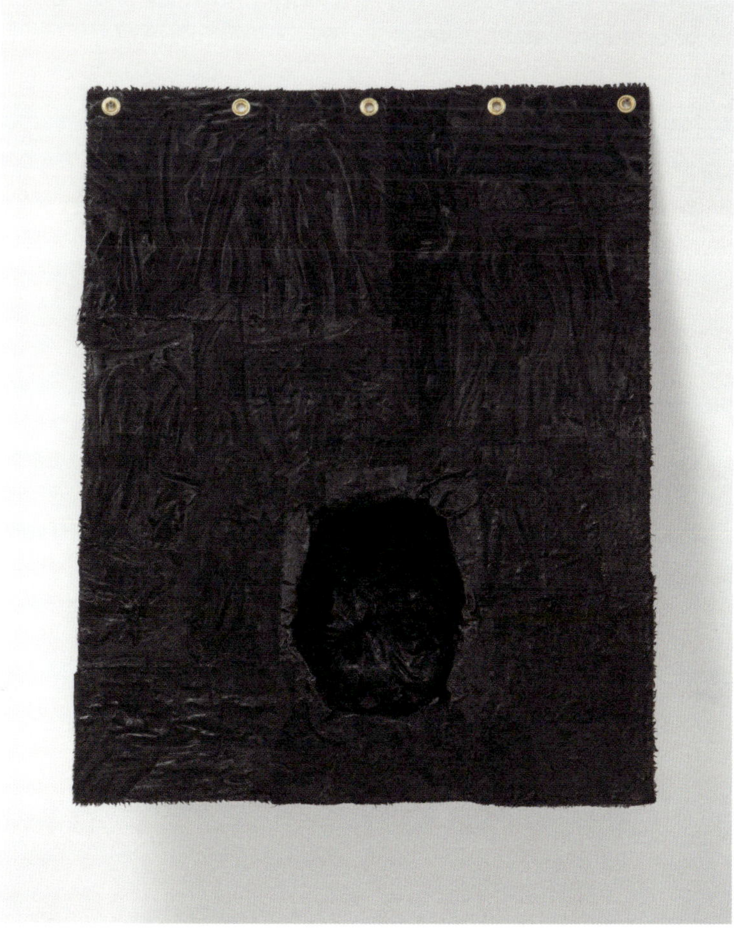

Sleepy Time Down South (landscape with moon), 2011
a kemmering, 2013

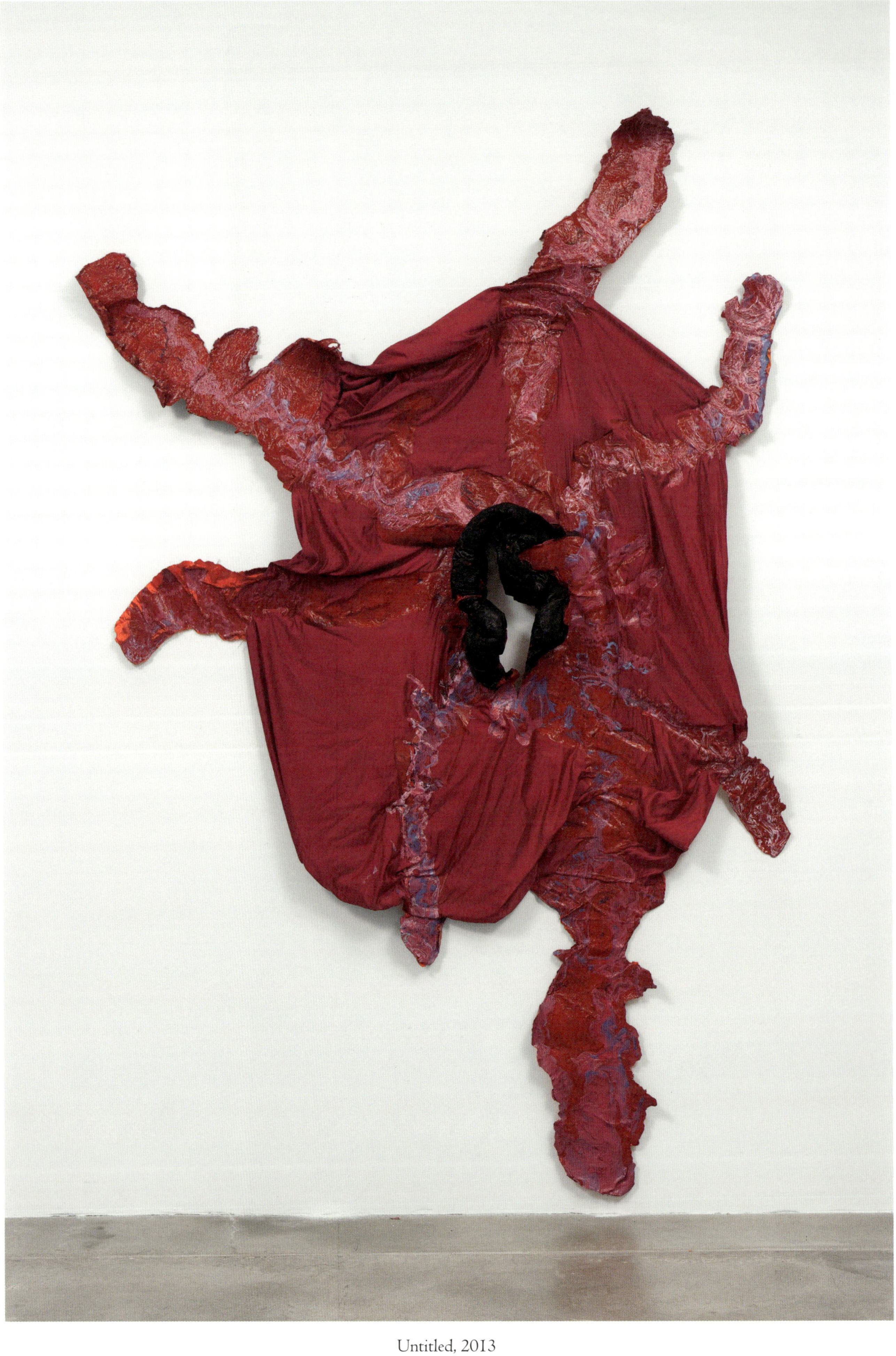

Untitled, 2013

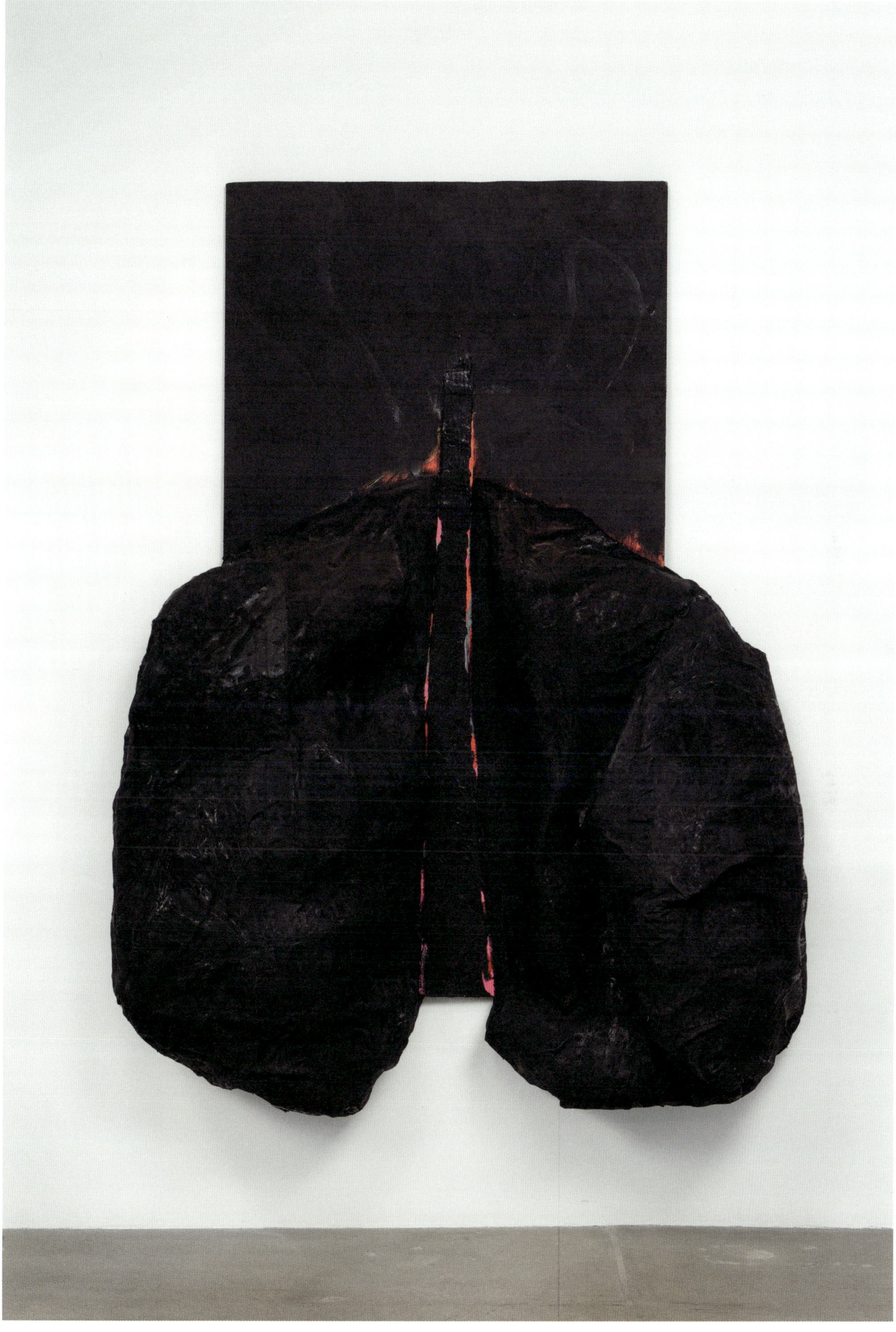

Untitled (lungs), 2006–13

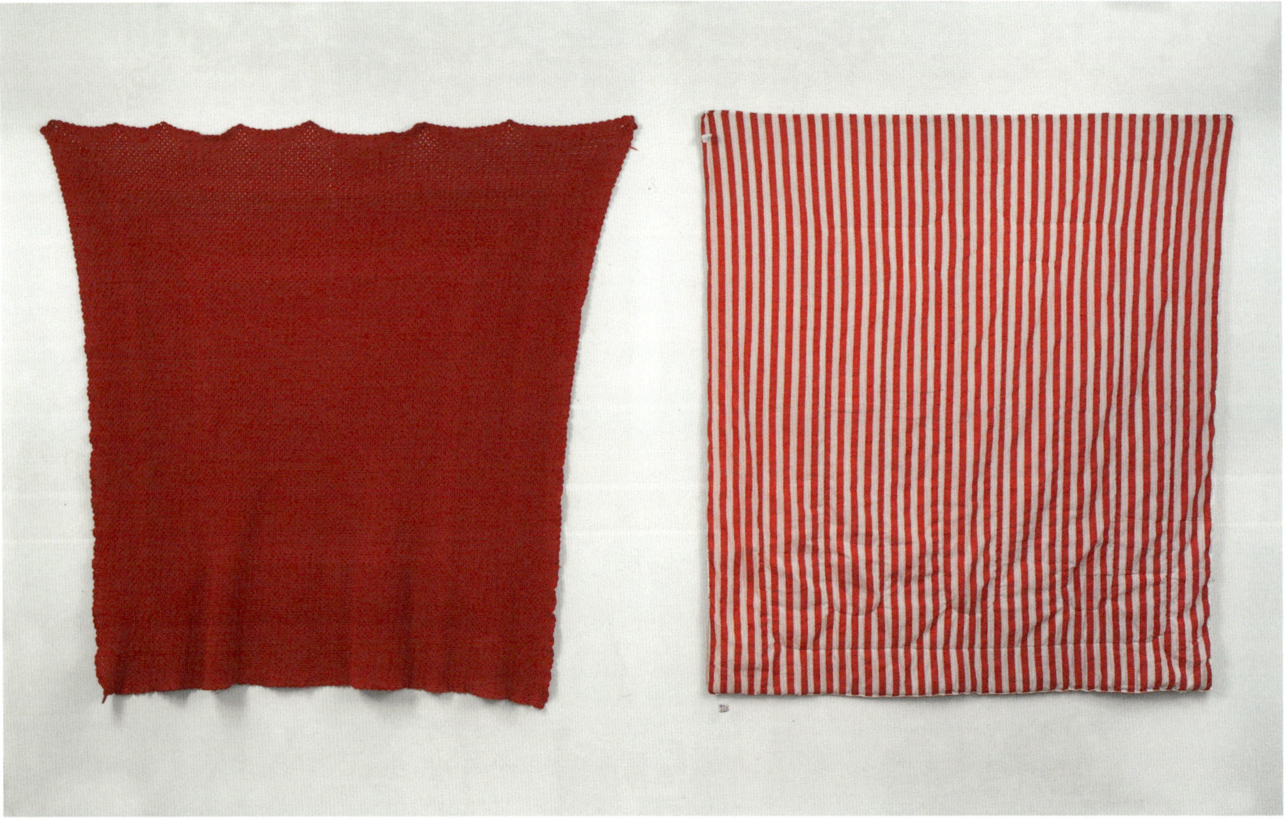

Untitled (flag) V, 2007–08

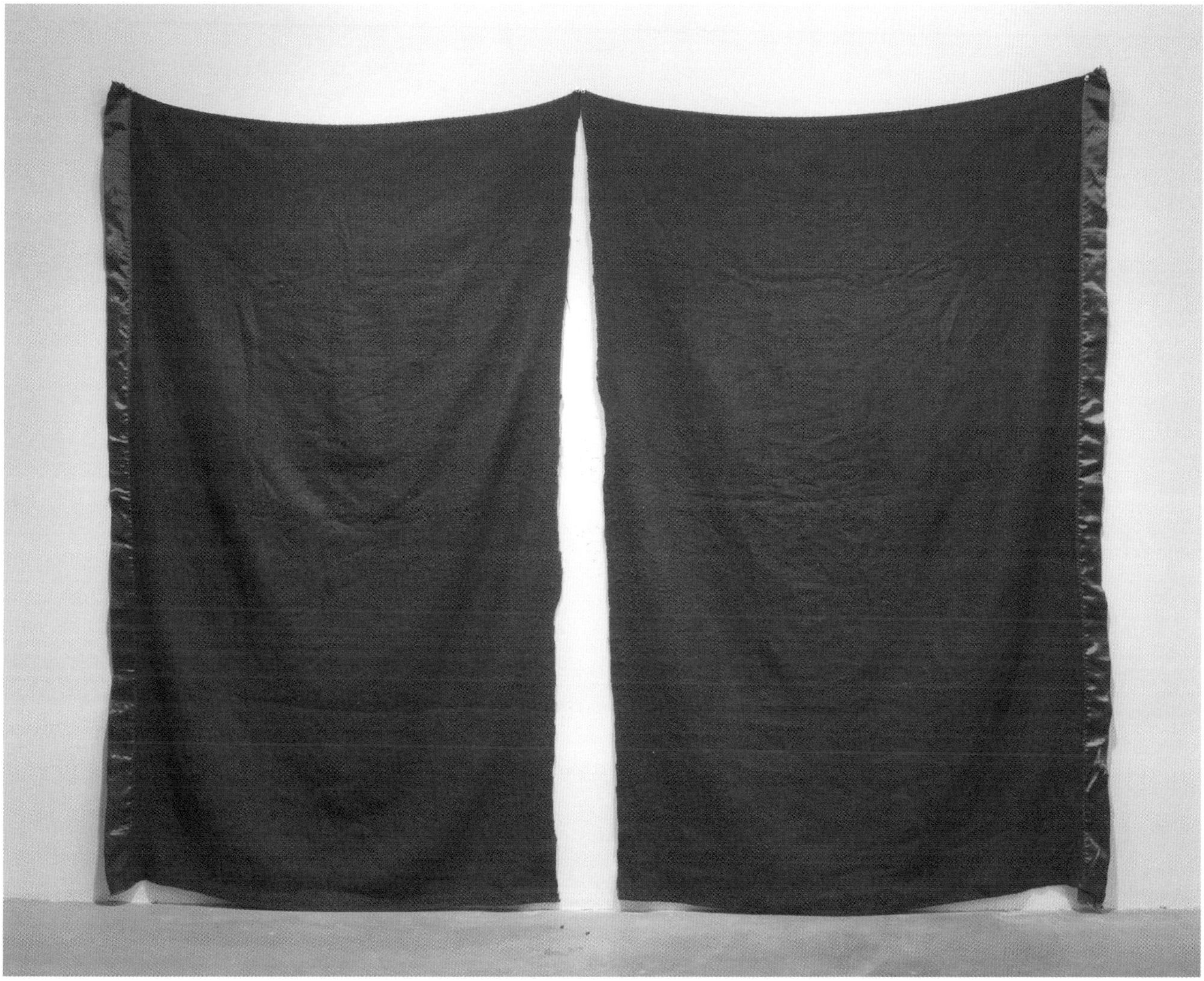

Untitled, 2005

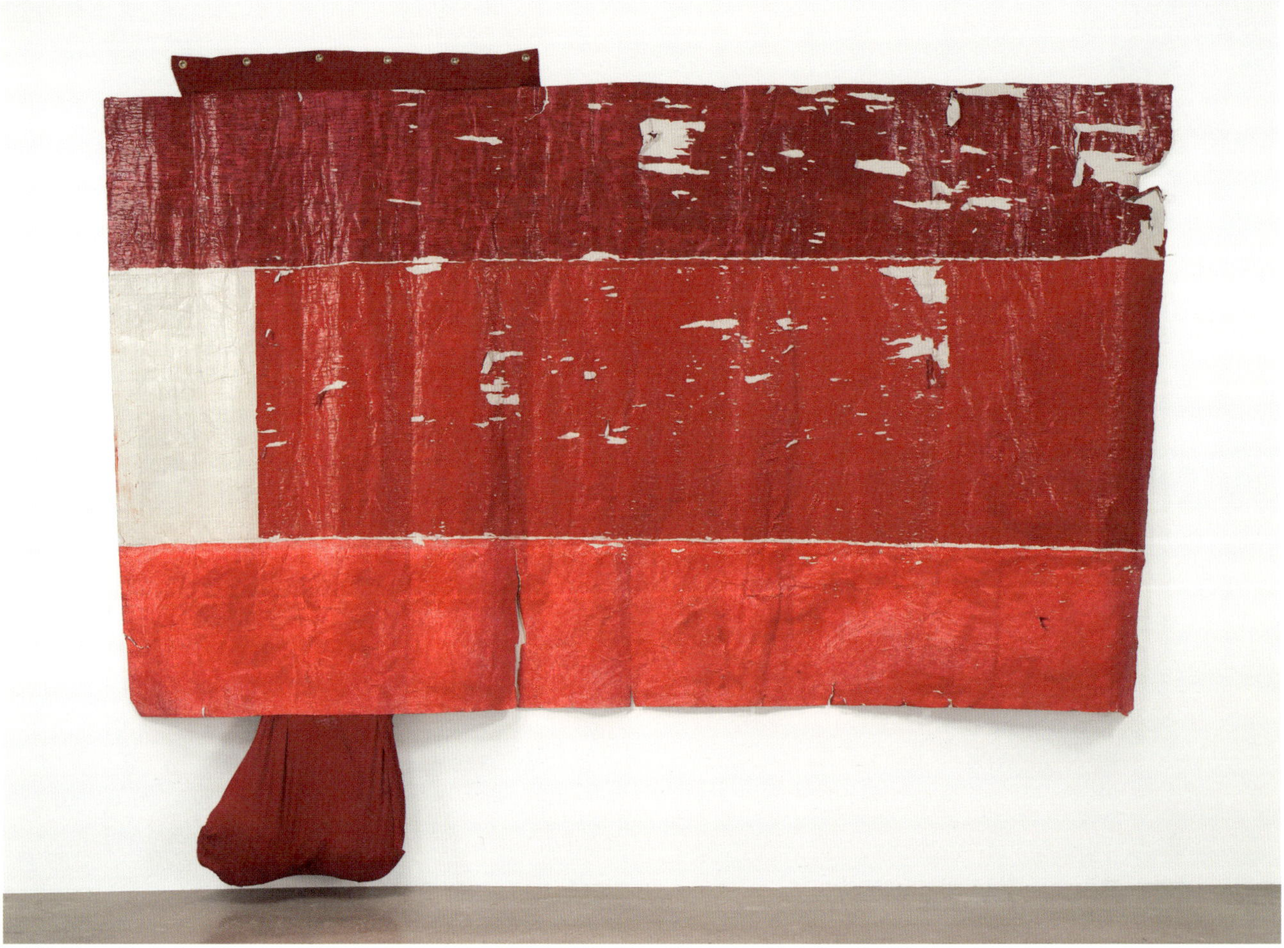

Untitled (flag) IV, 2006–08

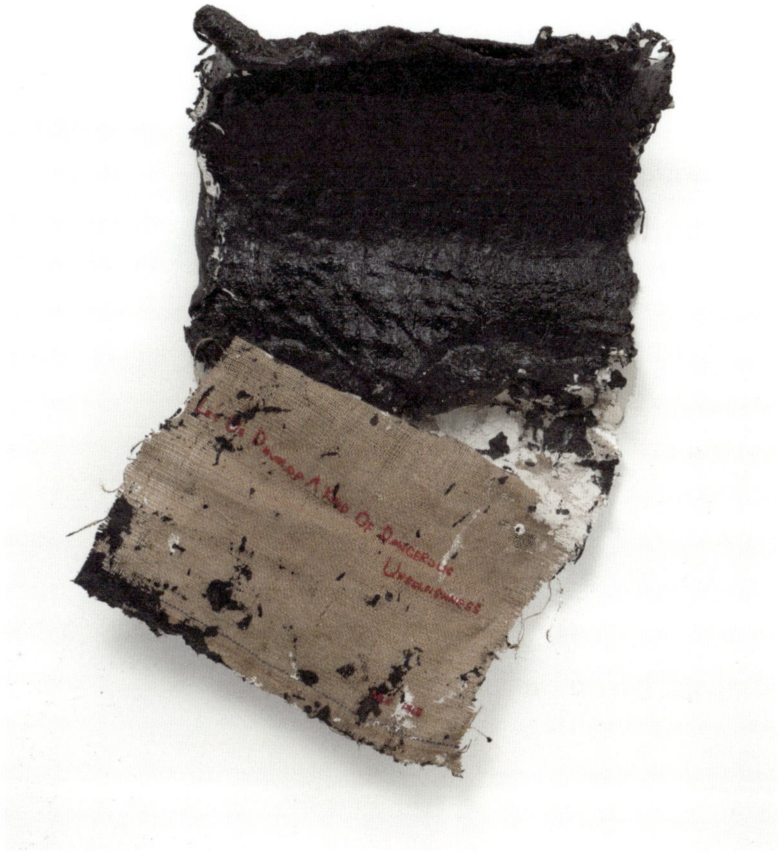

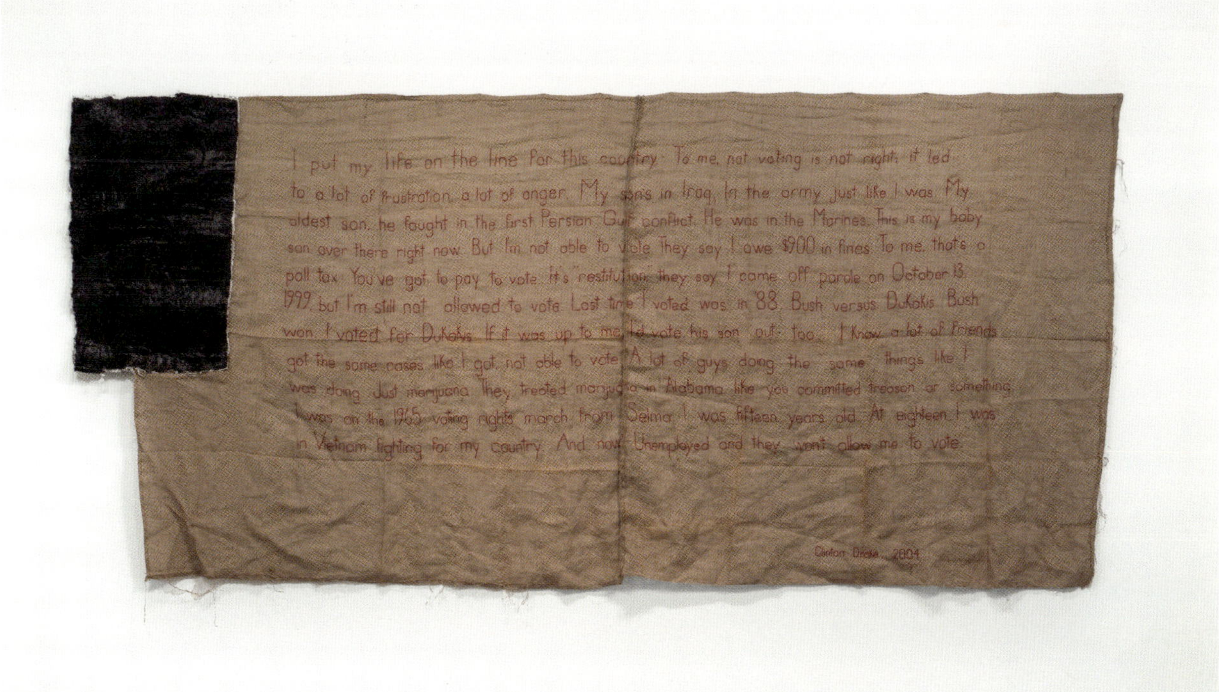

Untitled, 2012

Untitled (flag VI), 2012

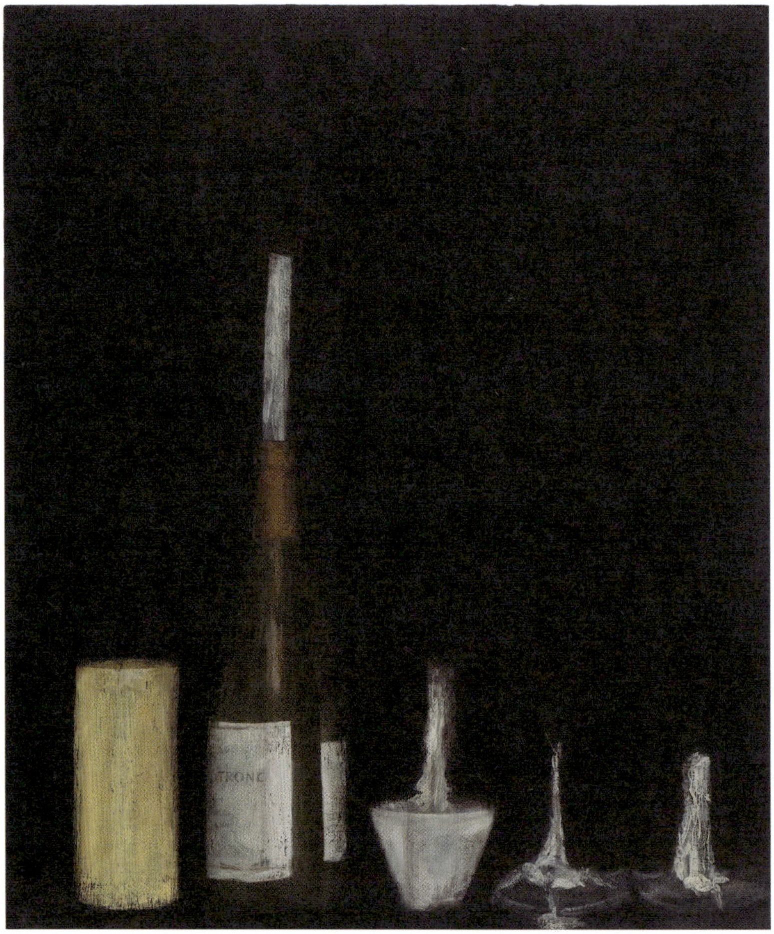

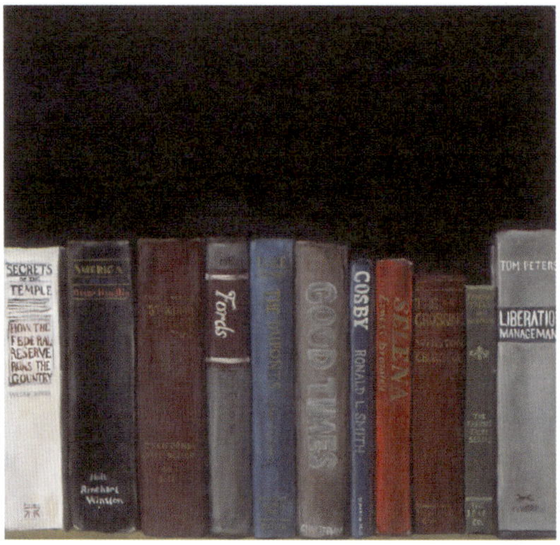

Untitled (candles), 2006–10
in progress, 2003

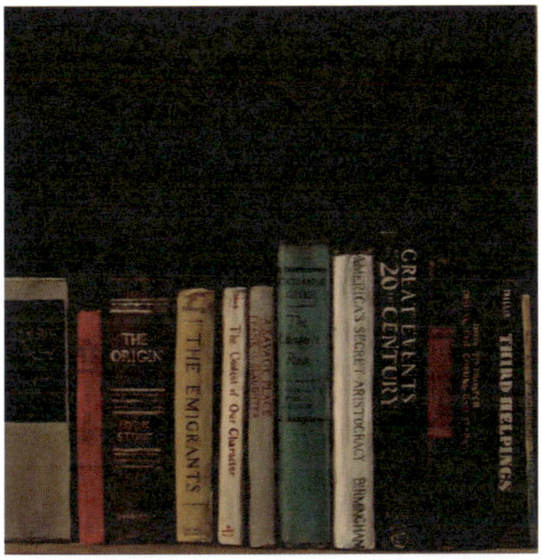

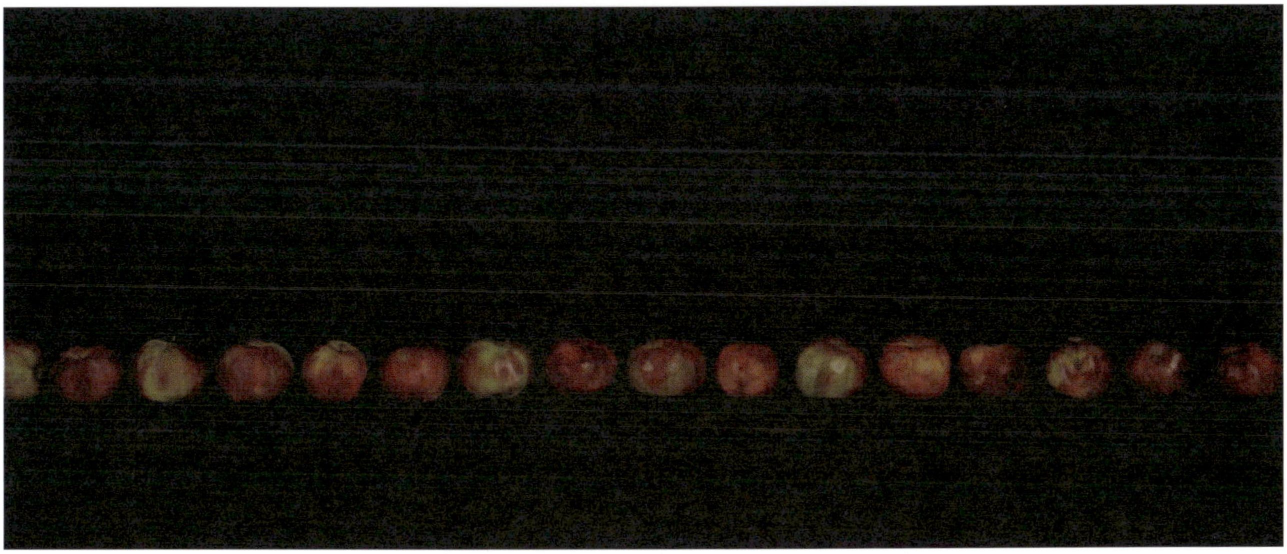

Untitled, 2003
Untitled (In progress), 2005

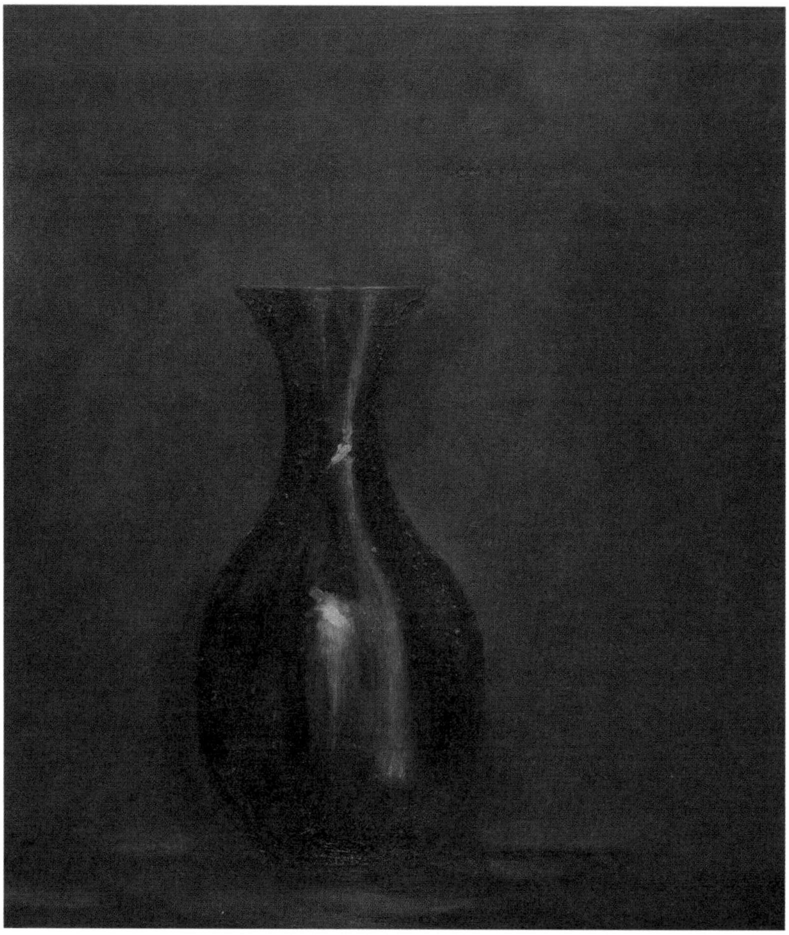

The Vessels (a clear glass vase spray painted and painted again), 2011–14
25¢, 2012

Untitled, 2003
Apple (stretching and yawning) for G. Jones, 2004

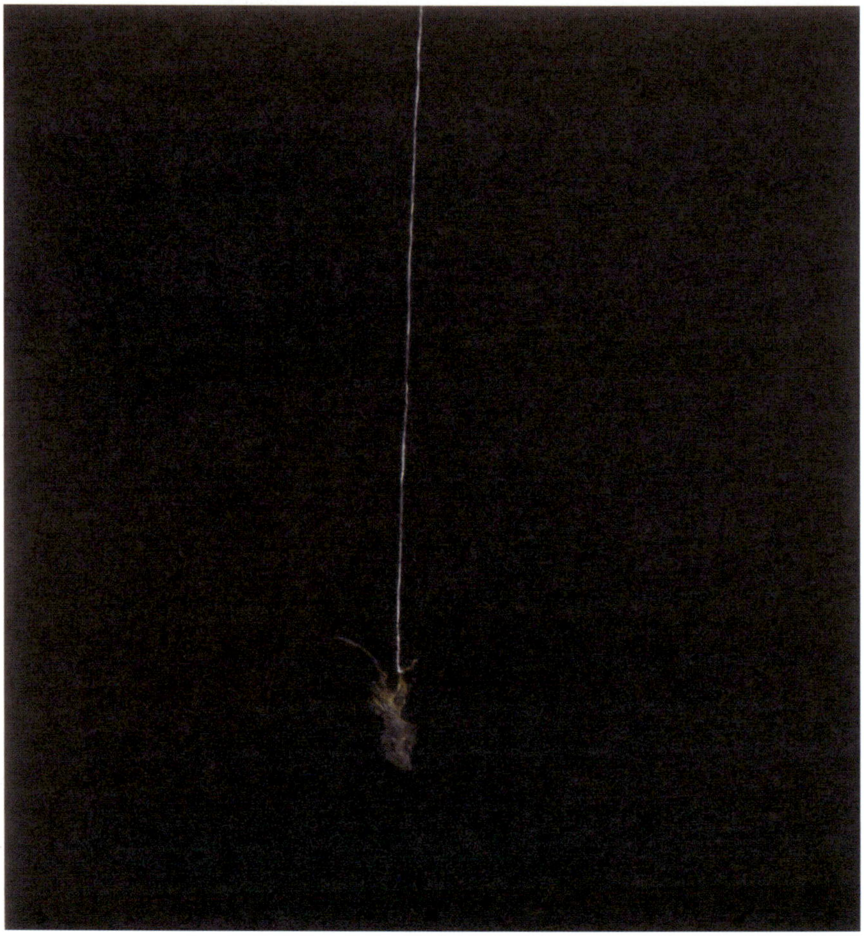

a lemon, 2006–12
Lily, 2004

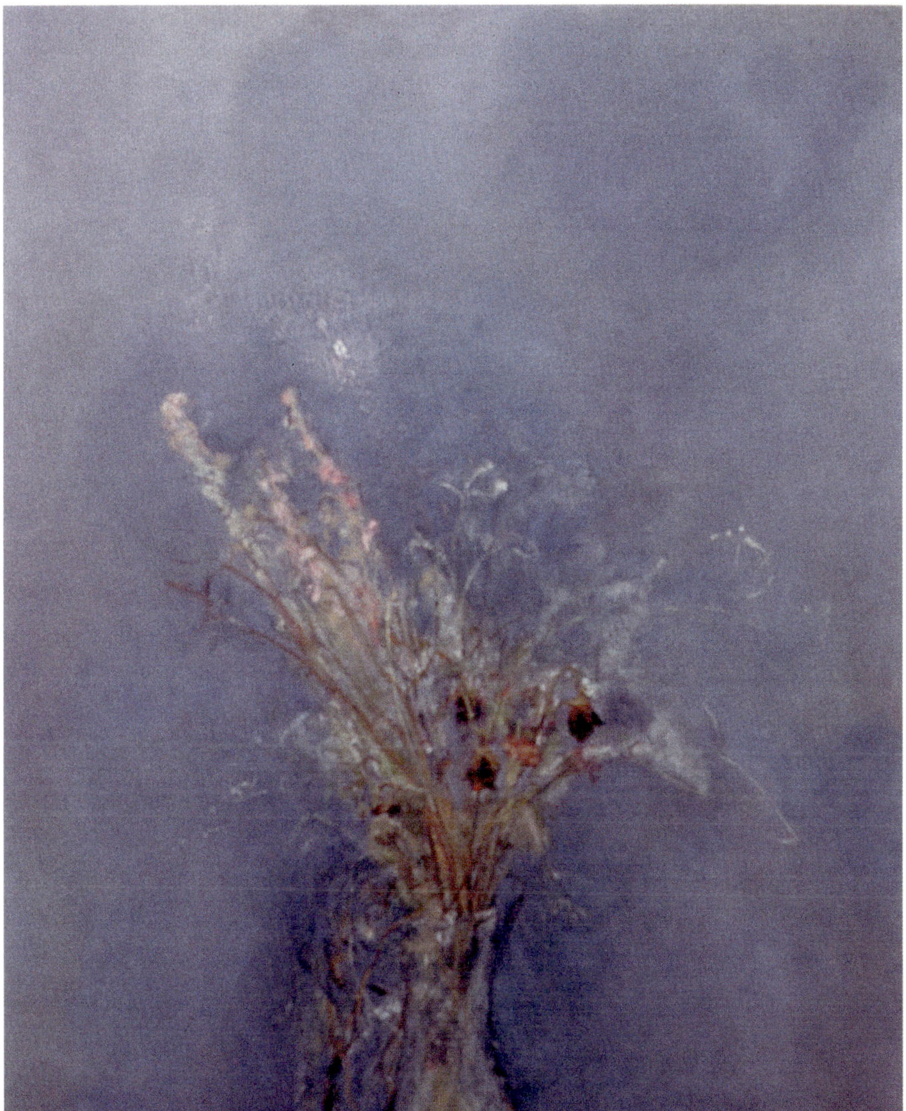

Unfinished (it's easier to get something new right than something old) for Laurie Nye and Martha Eknars, 2002–03

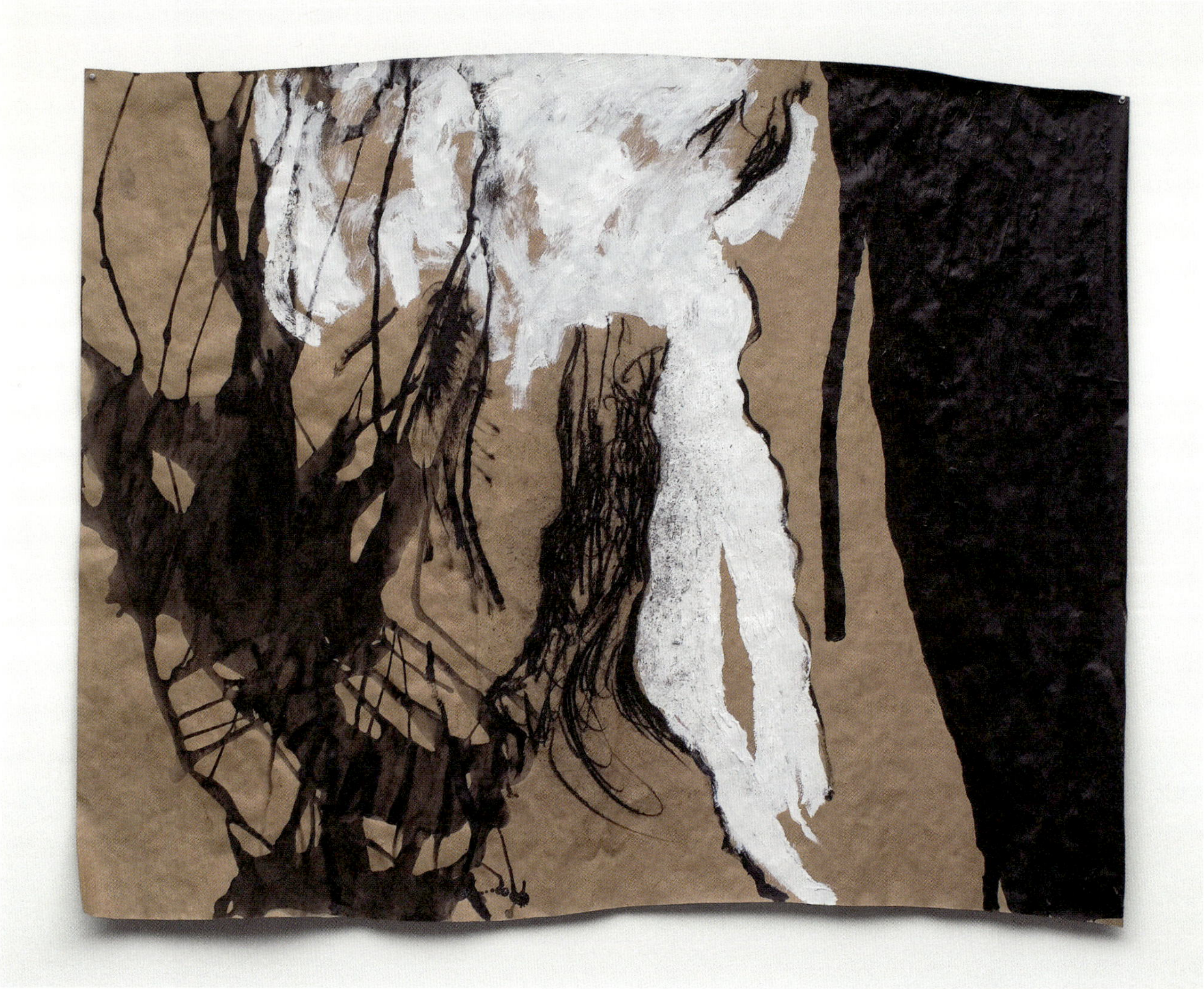

Untitled (Part II), 2008

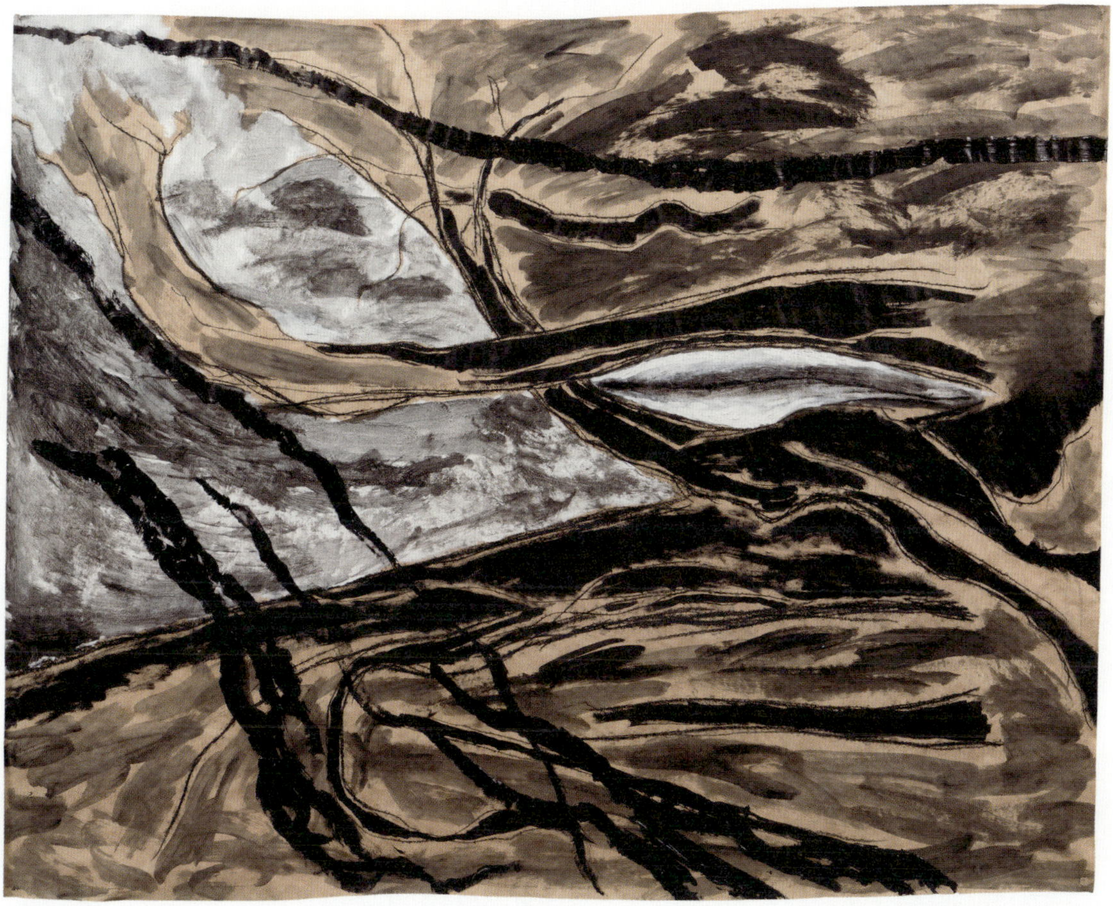

Untitled (Part I), 2008

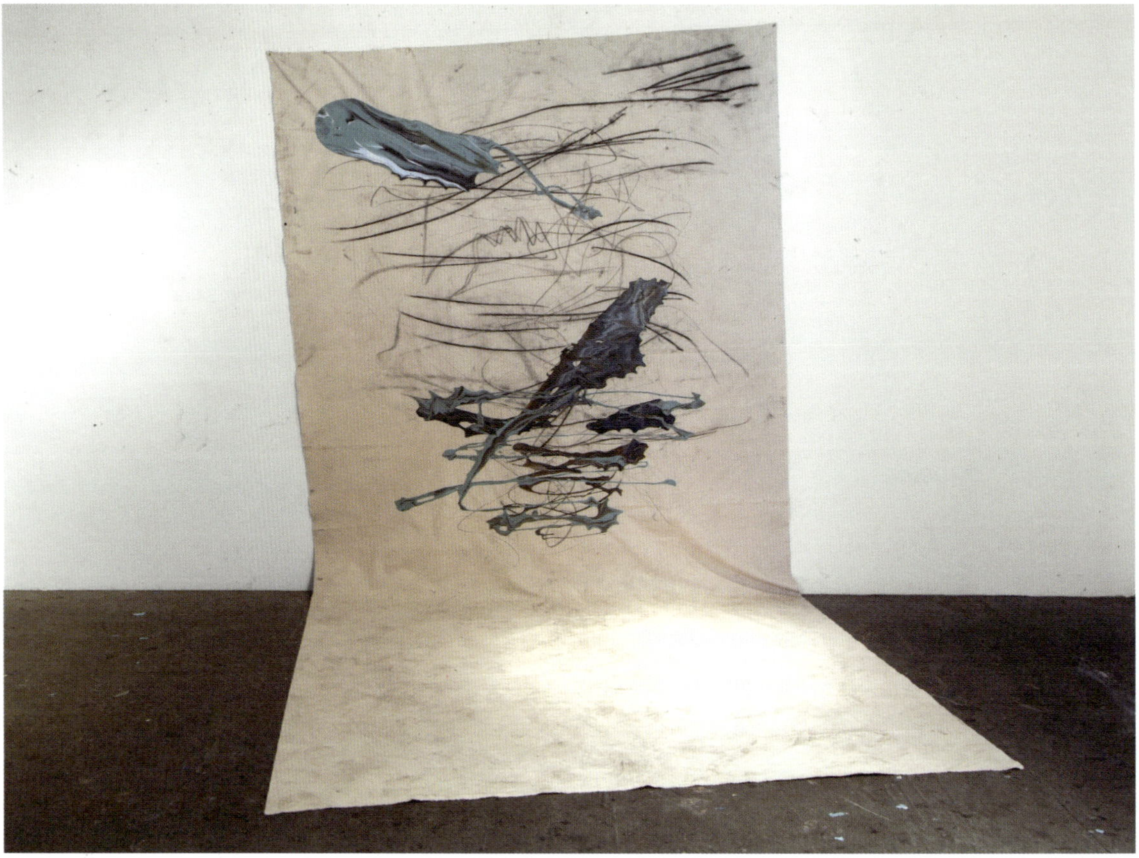

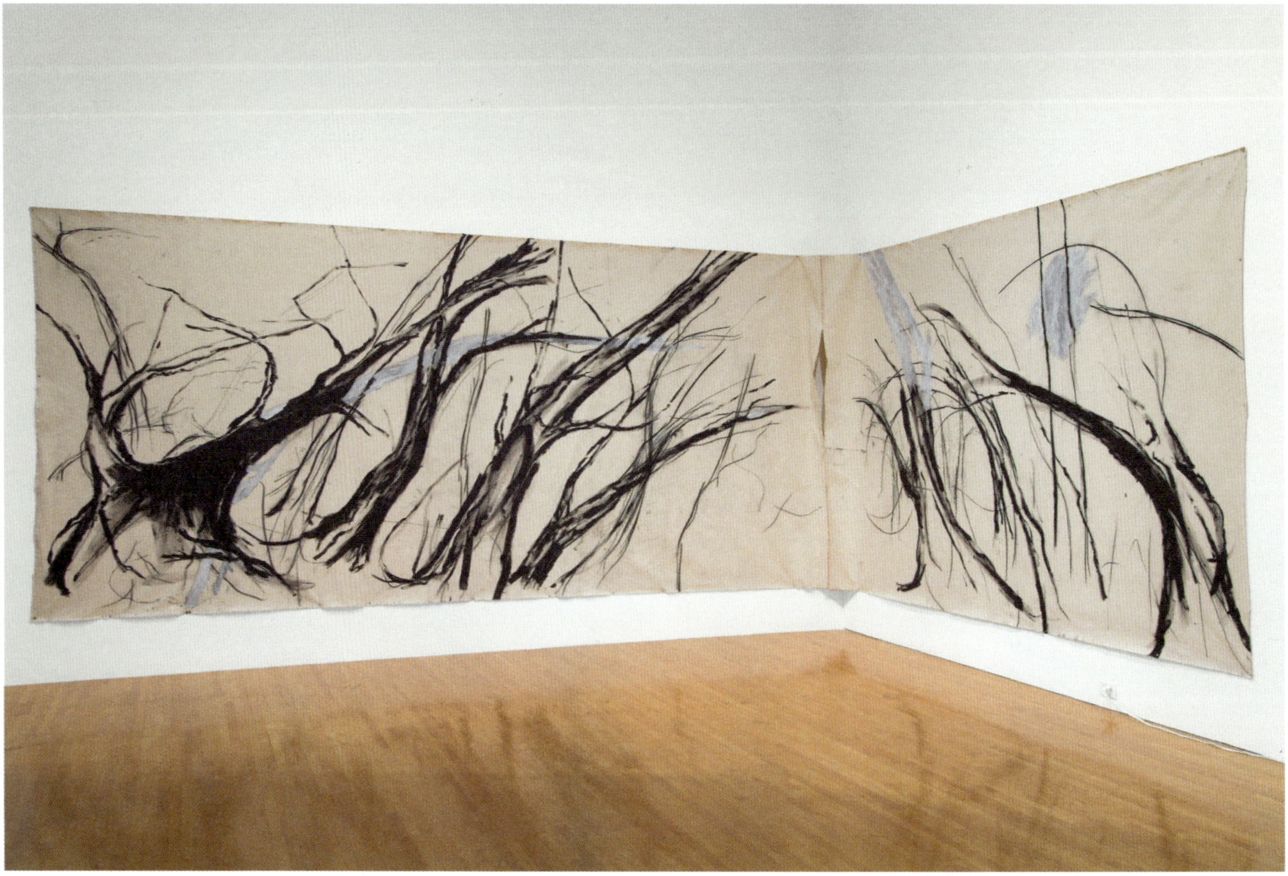

Untitled, 2004
Untitled (Landscape), 2005

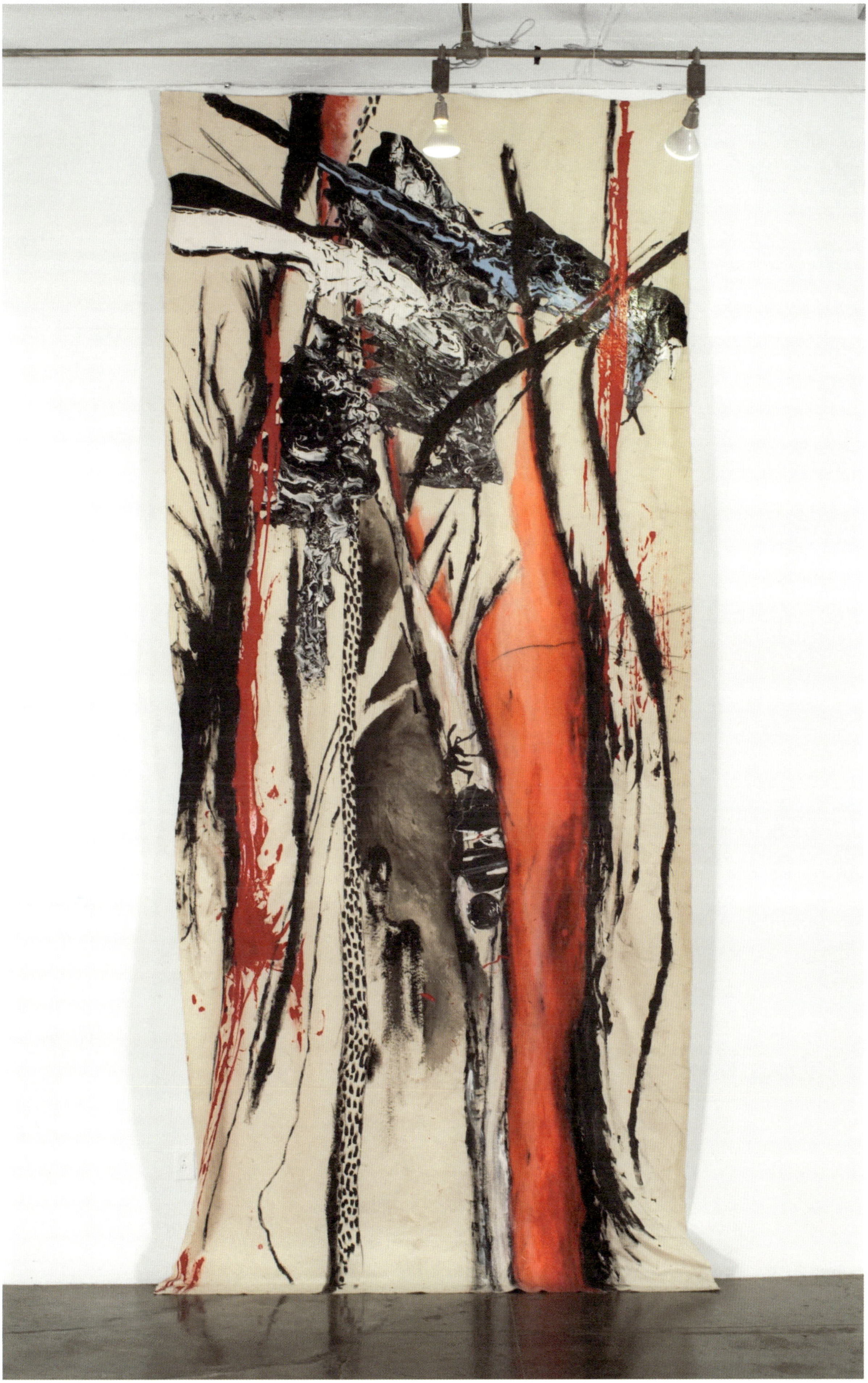

Above and following spread:
Untitled, 2008

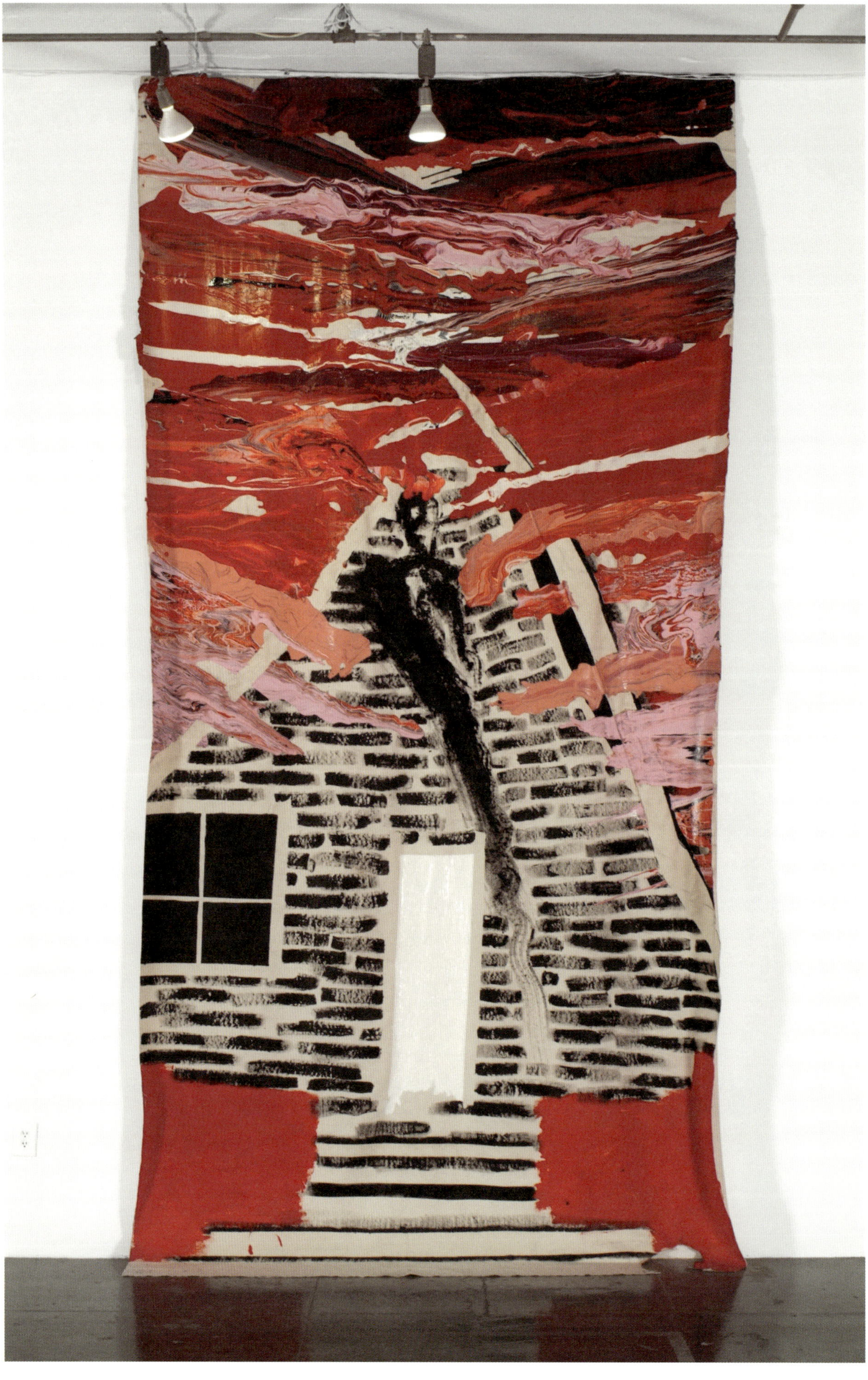

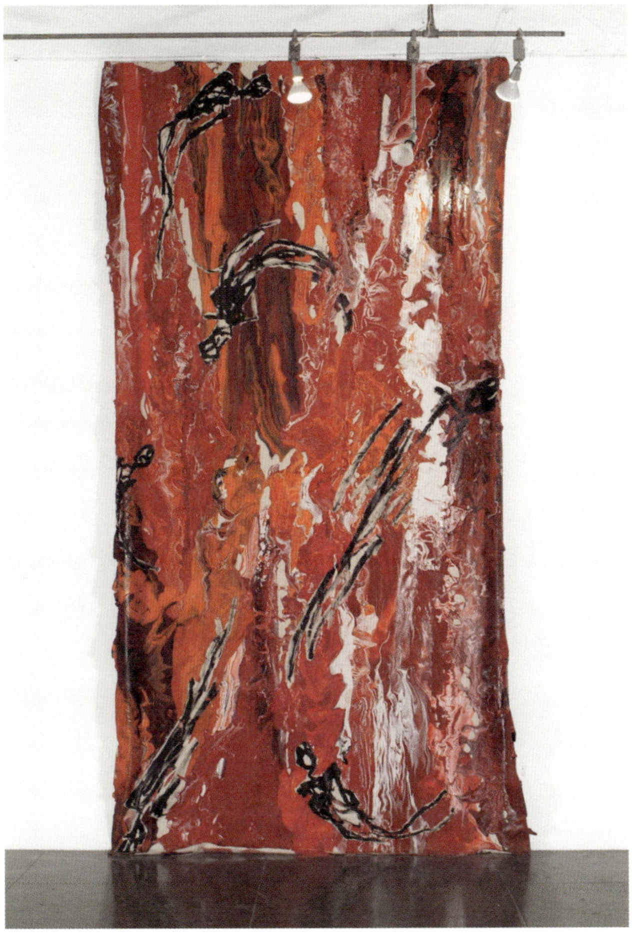

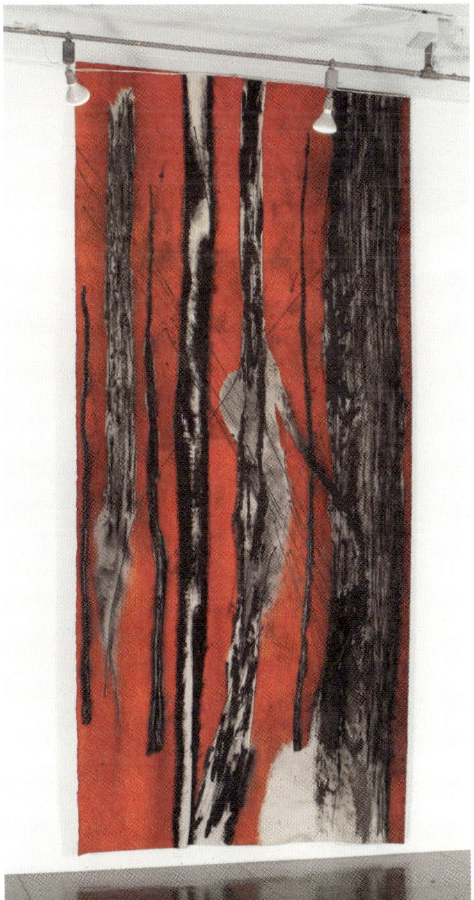

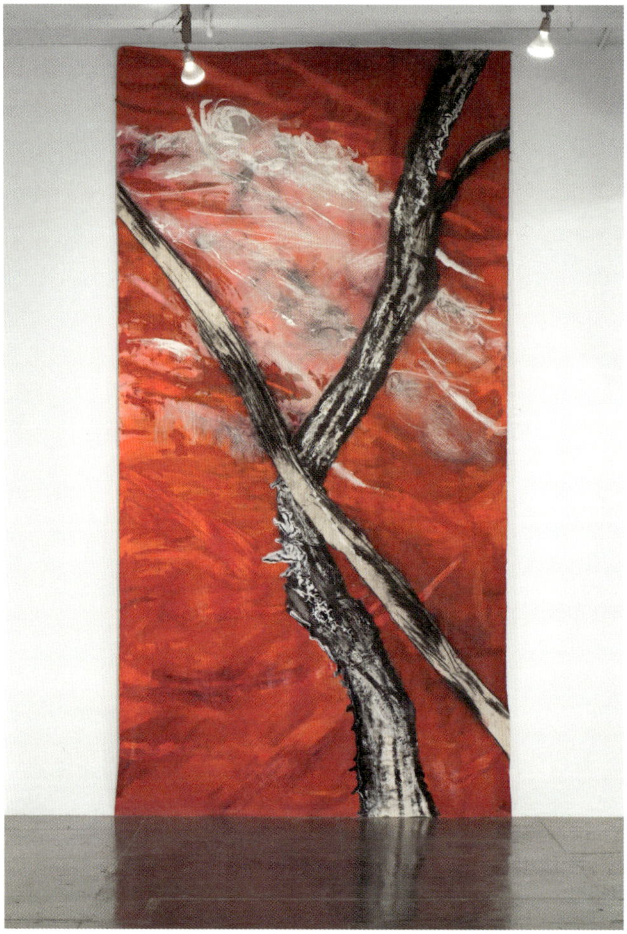

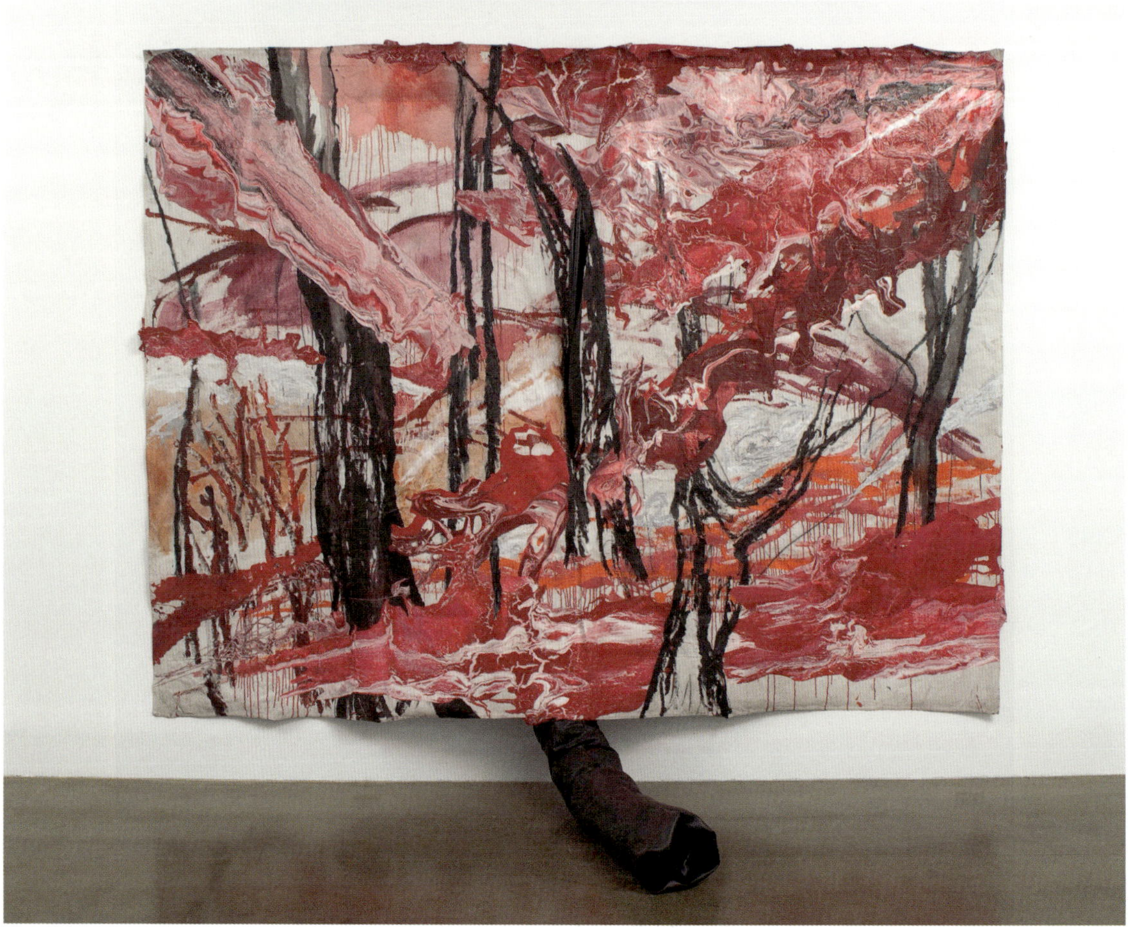

Untitled, 2008
Untitled, 2006–08

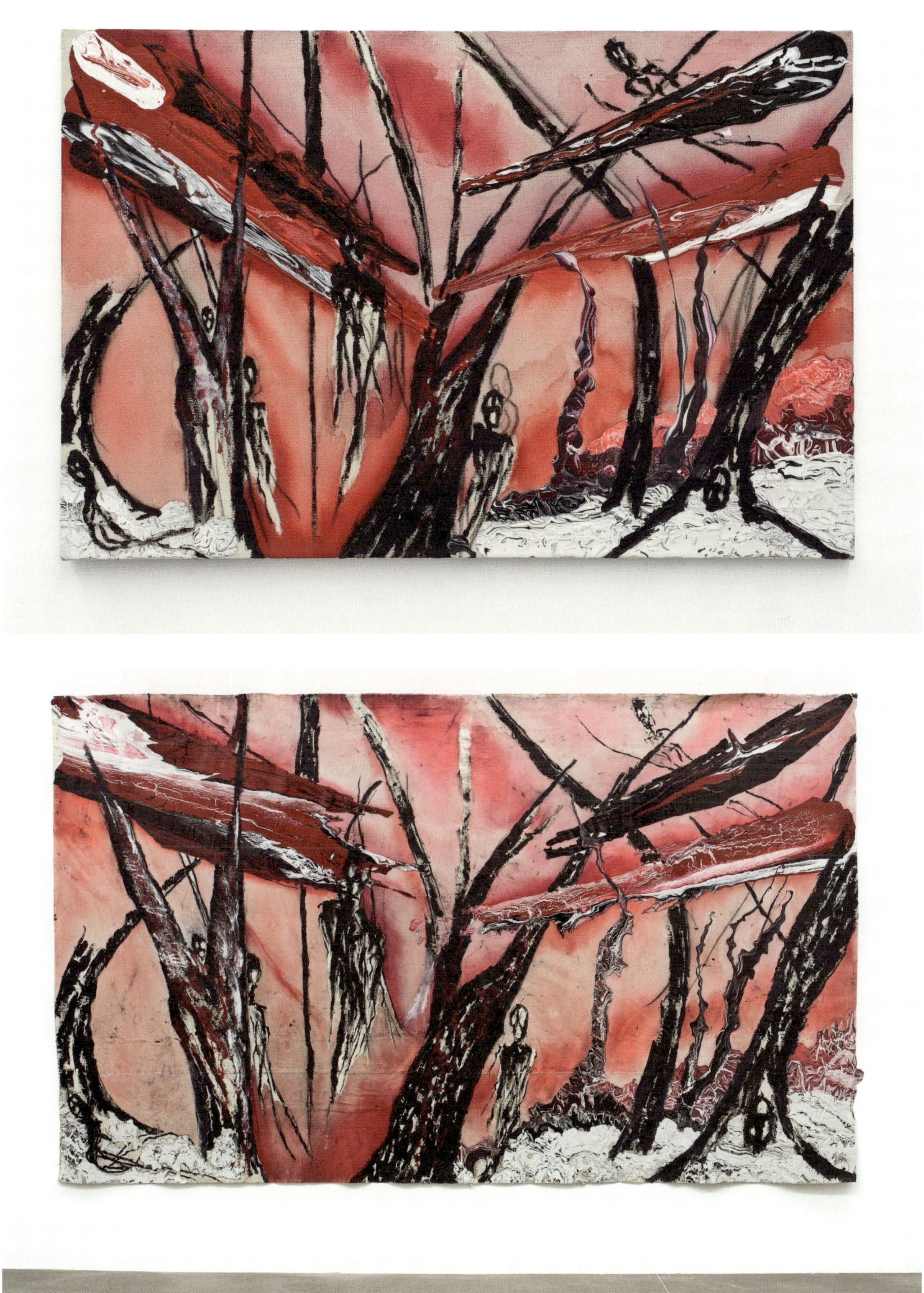

Untitled, 2007

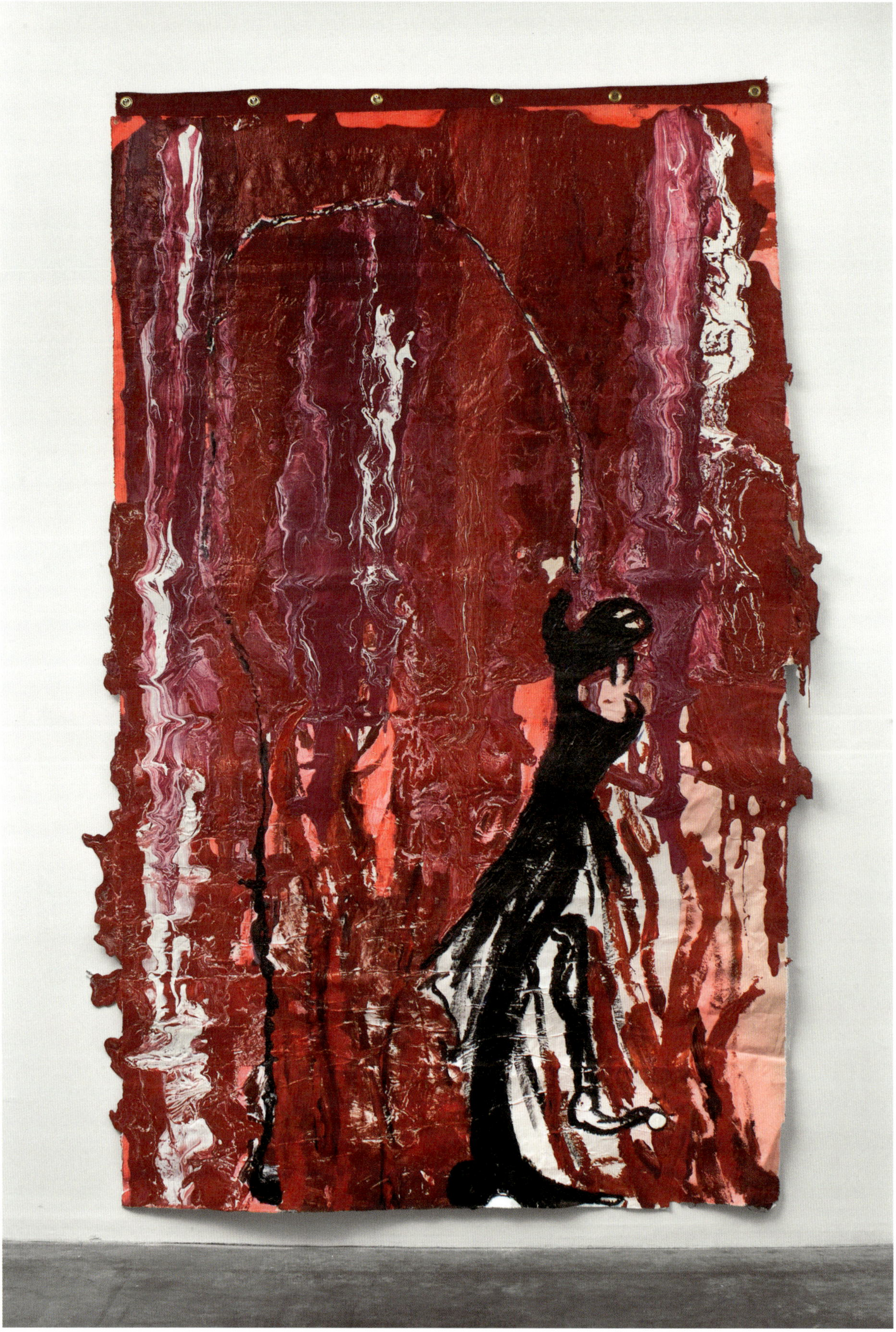

Untitled, 2009

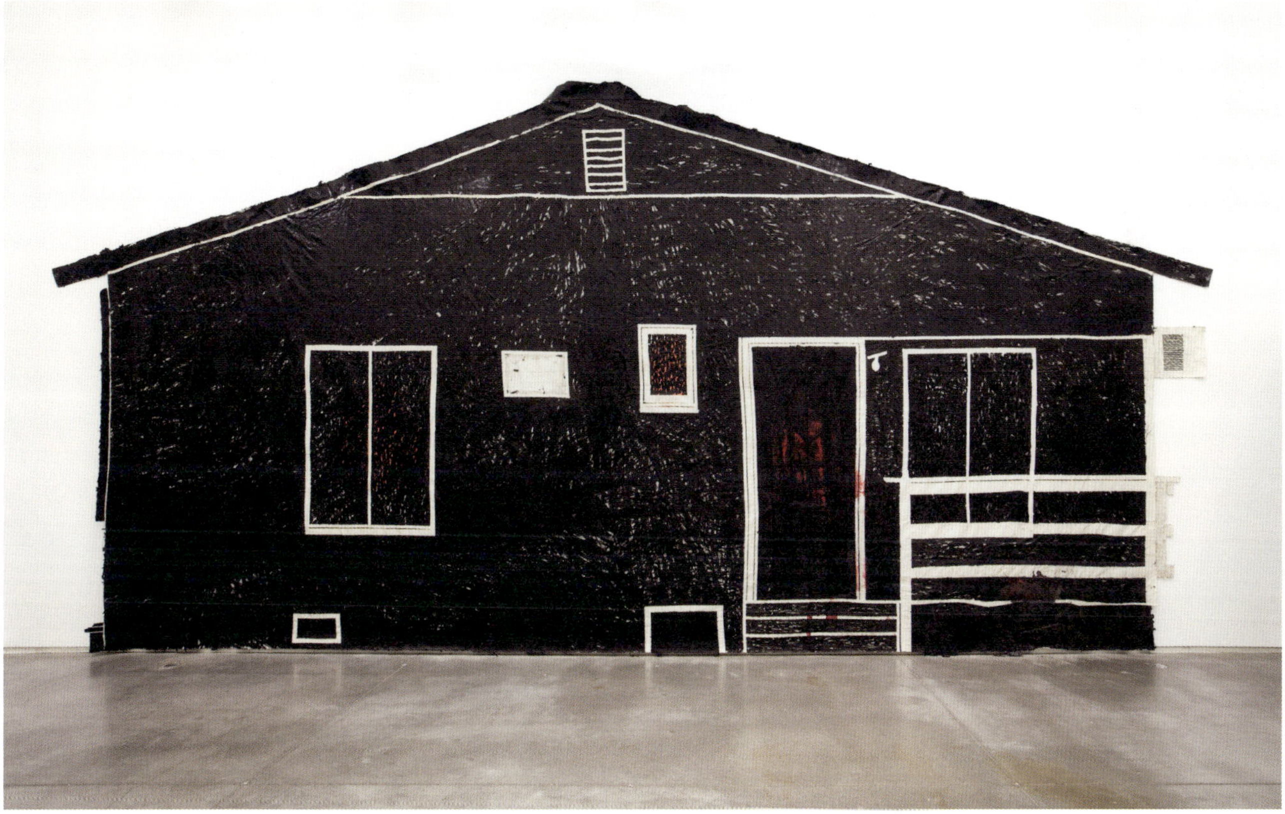

Untitled (4443 Prospect Ave.), 2009

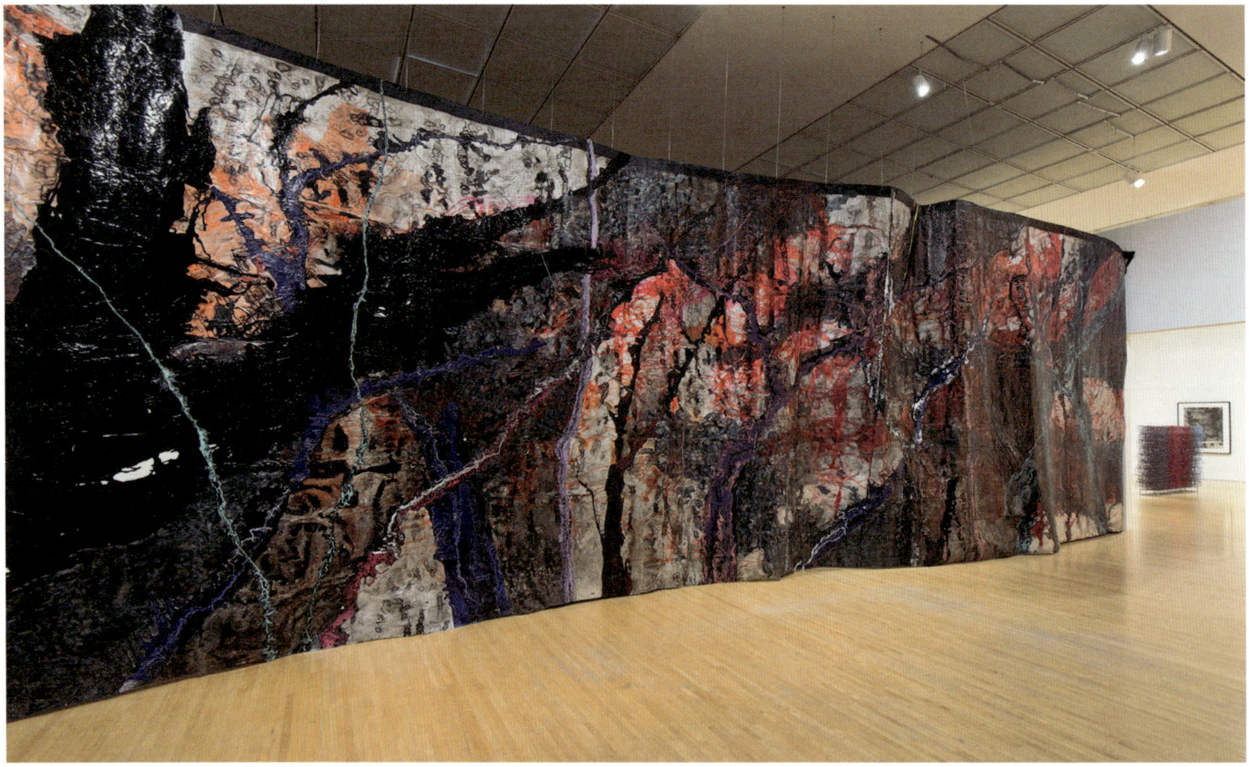

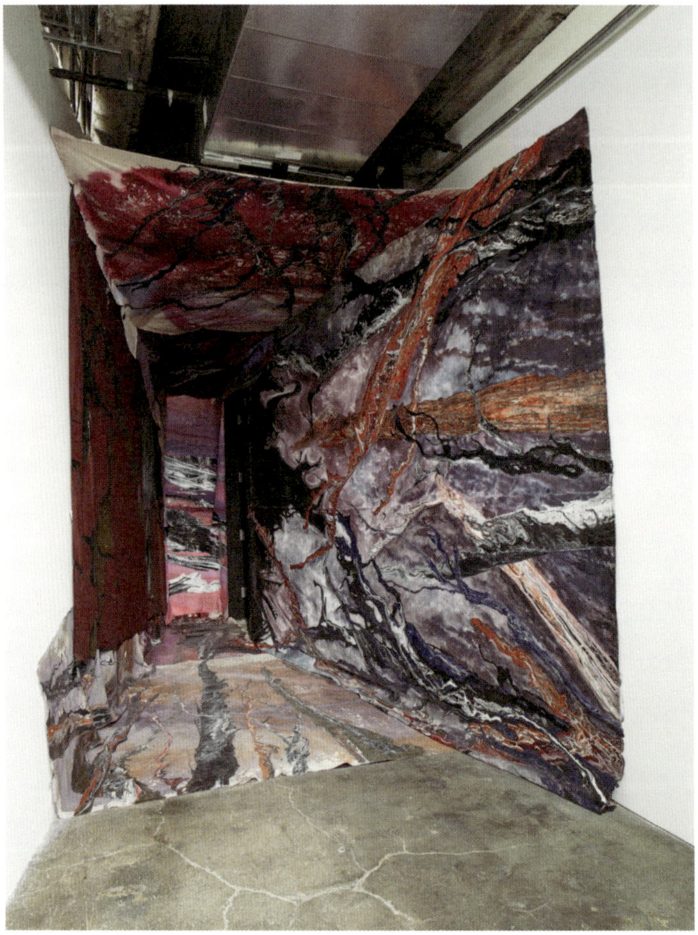

Representation of a Landscape as a Wall, 2012
Installation view: *Prospect Ave*, 2012. Maccarone, New York

Rodney McMillian: Beside Himself

Thomas J. Lax

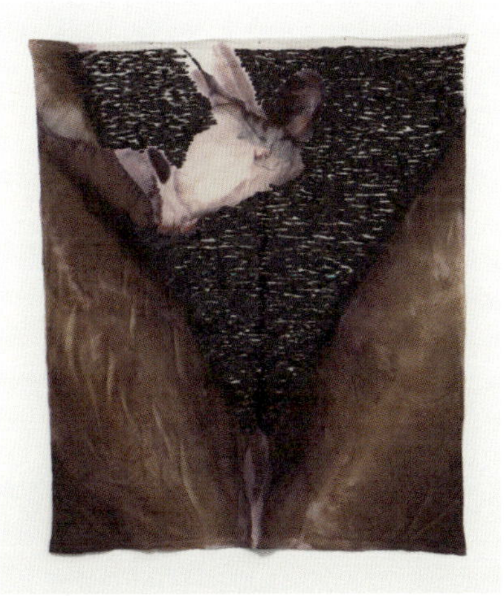

Fig. 1
Untitled (for B. Traylor), I, 2008

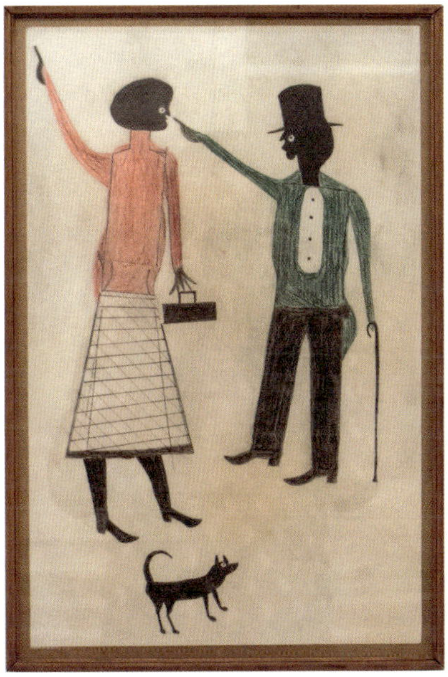

Fig. 2
James Benning, *Woman Pointing,* 2009

...[T]he black American male embodies the only American community of males which has had the specific occasion to learn who the female is within itself...

—Hortense J. Spillers, "Mama's Baby, Papa's Maybe: An American Grammar Book," *Diacritics* (1987)

Genealogy

Rodney McMillian's *Untitled (for B. Traylor), I* (2008; fig. 1) is an anomalous picture in a nearly eighty-year history of image-making inspired by the work of Bill Traylor.[1] Consider at one end of this genealogy, Charles Shannon's photographs and no longer extant murals, both made in the late 1930s. Shannon commemorates Traylor in a large-scale, social-realist mural depicting him above copies of his drawings, sitting with paper and pencil in hand as he would have worked in the streets of segregated Montgomery.[2] At the other end of this genealogy, consider *Woman Pointing* (2009; fig. 2) by James Benning, which renders Traylor's work mimetically—at the same scale, the two are nearly indistinguishable.[3] While Shannon's and Benning's homages both resemble their originals and memorialize Traylor with exactitude, McMillian's work is wholly unfaithful to Traylor's scale, graphic clarity, or content.

An unlikely pairing of title and image, *B. Traylor* tethers the depiction of a female figure's inner thighs and genitals,

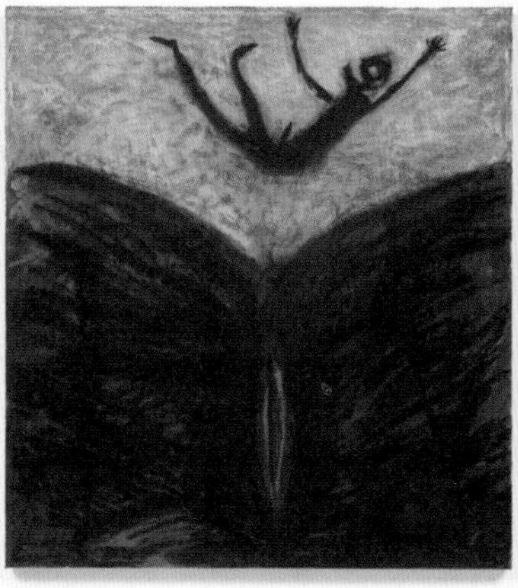

Fig. 3
Untitled (after Bill Traylor) I, 2008

on a bedsheet eighty-four by forty-eight inches wide, with an artist not typically understood for the sexual nature of his images. Inverted, cut off, and displaced from a rendering of her torso or body, the fragmented form appears to represent a typical mode of female eroticization.[4] Yet, the composition is complicated by the figure in its upper third, who at a fraction of the female figure's size, barrels forth either into or from her. Without facial features or fully articulated limbs, the figure lacks the bodily attributes that might depict gender, much like a newborn baby. Indeed, the image's close-up cropping and flatbed vantage point bear less cinematographic resemblance to porno tropes than to the framing of childbirth videos like PBS Nova's *The Miracle of Life* (1983). In addition, the black ground on which the woman lies, rendered in thick lines of black ink applied with varying degrees of density, also resembles a pubis both in its triangular shape and in its broad-stroke illustration of hair. Shifting between these two biomorphologies, the painting does not clearly differentiate between figure and ground, instead entangling the two yonic shapes.[5] Depicted on the surface of a used bedsheet—itself a hyperbolic index for intercourse and the imprints of bodily parts—the painting's materiality further pressures the distinction between pigment and support, surface and base. The mother lode of related, but irreconcilable references—to birth, to mothering, to sexuality—not only makes the image indeterminate, but also provides an unlikely foil for Traylor and his personal history of dispossession and description alike.

B. Traylor is the largest and only sheet painting within a regress of McMillian's smaller-scale "Traylor" canvases. In the first of the series, a silhouetted figure with an erection falls—arms akimbo, mouth agape—toward the vaginal valley of a green mountain (fig. 3). The land is configured as a female body and Traylor is invoked screaming as he tumbles in libidinal terror. While Traylor's graphic style is apparent in the earliest painting, over the course of McMillian's remaking, the resemblance to the earlier artist's work becomes less recognizable. Instead, the black impasto and gestural brushstrokes of McMillian's subsequent canvases express and translate the conditions of Traylor's time and place, and in the process, point to their embeddedness in our own moment. McMillian describes this relationship as the "mining [of] ideas about landscape through [Traylor's] use of the figure and the negative space he employed in his work. Some of it is interpreting his figures to get an understanding of his context and that of the work—thus, the bulging eyes stretched to absorb/absolve a land drenched in blood and bone."[6] He eschews a compositional, iconographic, or stylistic likeness; instead, he reanimates the stakes of Traylor's work, implicating the viewer (much like his falling figure) within the social conditions that produced and are articulated within Traylor's body of work.[7] Unlike strategies of appropriation or amalgamation associated with postmodernist practices in photography and painting, McMillian's critical operation does not mimic or re-present a preceding artwork or event by making visual reference to its antecedent. Instead, he interprets the feeling of Traylor and his context in order to seek redress, creating a relationship of intimacy and risk in which our time is made contiguous with Traylor's.[8]

Similarly, recent scholarship by art historians Helen Molesworth, Mignon Nixon, and Lisa Tickner—informed by feminism and psychoanalysis—has suggested an intergenerational and lateral reading of art history. Their different arguments posit a mode of reception that considers art made in different times and places side by side rather than before or after one another, suggesting that because the history of art made by women has heretofore been structured by omission, women artists are more likely to seek out predecessors than to refute them. Freed from anti-Oedipal drives, artists can encounter and solicit their elected

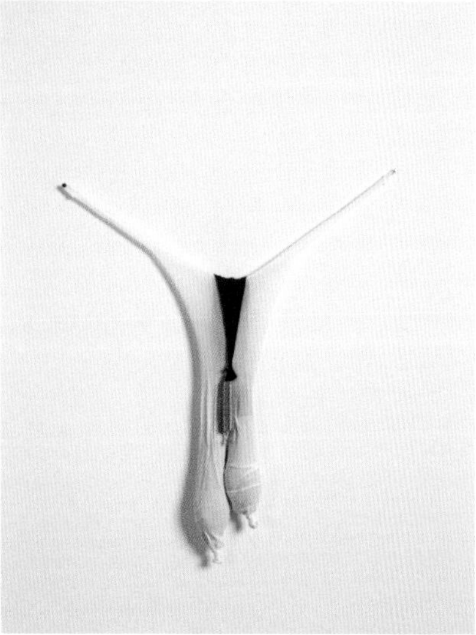

Fig. 4
Senga Nengudi, *Quarante-et-un*, 1977/2014

mothers and fathers as well as their artistic sisters, brothers, and cousins on equal terms.[9] While McMillian's work bears multiple relationships to the history of feminist art and discourse, it is perhaps this model that is most instructive in interpreting his practice.[10] Their psychoanalytic grammar is particularly germane here: *B. Traylor*—brother and sister—is a primal scene of birth, sexuality, and motherhood that pictures and is produced by Traylor's natal alienation. Indeed, Hortense J. Spillers has described "slavery in the United States as one of the richest displays of the psychoanalytic dimensions of culture before the science of European psychoanalysis takes hold."[11] In her attention to the symbolic order she calls the American "Grammar Book," she argues that enslavement is structured by the establishment of a society in which its members are denied kin, who instead are transformed into property; reproduction does not guarantee "birth" in the sense of a parental right or function. Likewise, captivity precludes sexual differentiation, an "ungendering" she attributes to females experiencing external acts of torture and prostration typically inflicted on males. Might the orphaning Spillers describes proliferate the stakes of naming kin across generation, race, and nation, and extend the possibilities for the articulation of sexual difference that Nixon and Tickner proffer? More pertinent to McMillian, to whom might we lay claim as his artistic sisters, mothers, and lovers—as the support system for his symbolic order?

Across his sculptures, paintings, videos, live performances, and immersive installations, McMillian makes use of a range of stylistic approaches. There are what I call his "Eva Hesse" pieces, in which a serialized structure constructs an internally differentiated composition; or his "Senga Nengudi" installations, in which the body (often female, often sexualized) is indexed by its simultaneous absence and literalness (fig. 4).[12] Consider McMillian's untitled work from the Whitney

Biennial (2008; fig. 5) or another untitled piece from *Succulent* (2010; fig. 6), in which distinct components make up a monochromatic field and are visibly assembled by the artist's hand with white thread. While the former is ostensibly phallic in its morphology and the latter anal, both at once protrude and envelop. These works are corporeal—visual puns (black dick, black ass) whose excessive scales ironically deny them any representational function. The limp, wrinkled, and oversized vinyl strongly alludes to sexual organs or surrogates without being filled out by a composite body. Rather than depict a figure, the 2008 piece turns viewers into the work's subjects as they navigate the negative space of the rectilinear gallery, as much as it renders the white cube into a body with its internal plumbing and black circuitry sticking out from the wall. At once biomorphic and mechanomorphic, the references of these two pieces thus hyperbolize their relationships to the body, but ultimately deny viewers a figure to look at—save for themselves with their own sags and holes.

Then there are the "Lynda Benglis" canvases (such as an untitled 2008 piece from ArtPace, San Antonio; fig. 7), with multiple colors deriving from commercially available latex paint poured so that they appear to blur or bleed into one another. Another untitled 2008 work forms a backdrop and environment in which skeletal figures are eerily suspended within the dis-equilibrating flux of the paint's shifting orientation, produced by changes in direction and the pull of gravity while the viscous materials cohered. There are also the "Audrey Flack" pictures (such as *in progress* [2003][13])—photorealist still lifes and vanitas paintings that, like the *trompe l'oeils* from which they derive, remind us of the ever-attenuated transience of life (and progress) and the inevitability of death. Consider also McMillian's "Robert Gober" sculptures and landscapes, whose handmade bodily piping index the fragility of the body's communicative capacity. Or the "Rosemarie Trockel" furniture casts, which like

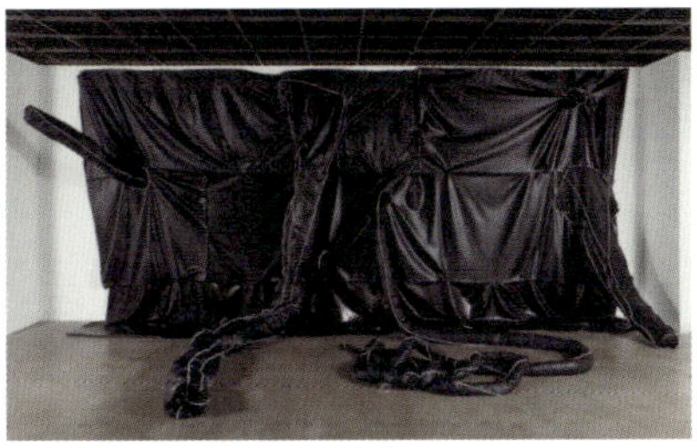

Fig. 5
Untitled, 2008

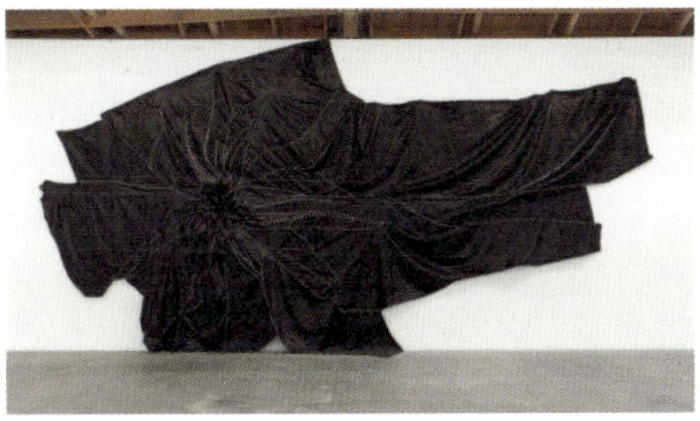

Fig. 6
Untitled, 2010

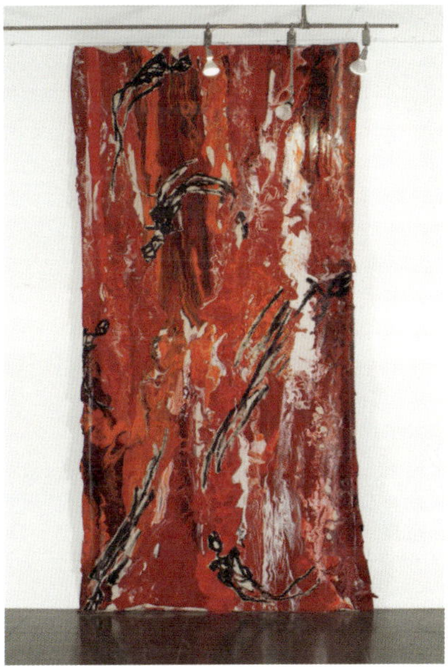

Fig. 7
Untitled, 2008

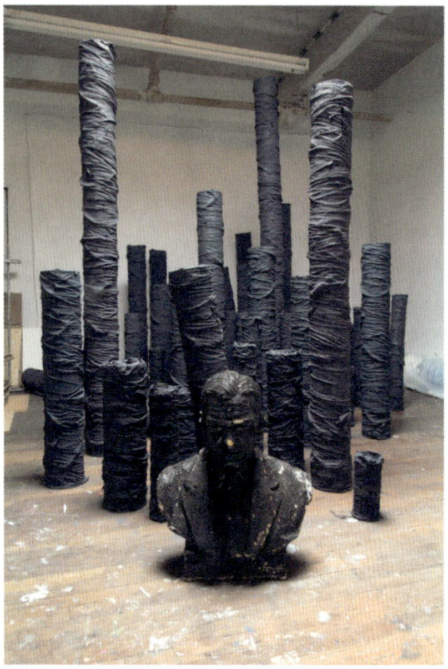

Fig. 8
Untitled (Unknown), 2006

Trockel's *Copy Me* (2013) or *Replace Me* (2011) render sculpture and domestic furniture fungible, much like the emblems of McMillian's home, which can be sold or foreclosed. And of course, the irony of the "Kara Walker" nineteenth-century genres—the silhouette, early narrative film, and landscape painting—rhymes with McMillian's use of historical genres against their original manipulations.

Ultimately, this intergenerational gang of bad feminists far outnumbers McMillian's possible claims to foremothers, pointing to a multitude of invented kin. They echo the pigments of McMillian's Los Angeles peers: teachers like Charles Gaines, as well as his contemporaries and collaborators, including Edgar Arceneaux, Jutta Koether, and Olga Koumoundouros, among others. Indeed, while his colors and materials—the lustrous black of vinyl or the sanguine red of latex—suggest a signature authorship, they are, in fact, chosen from a readily available palette. What's more, the materials recall a range of objects from the domestic sphere: PVC piping, home siding, sex toys—markers of everyday activity and play, which in his hands, intone cycles of desire and desperation.[14]

Genre/Monuments and Memorials

If McMillian's stylistic fluidity and fugitivity attach him to the work of other artists, it is his use and misuse of historic stylistic criteria that likewise allow him to adhere to categories of genre by subverting their conventions. Much of his work mimes the scale, trappings, and spirit of monuments and memorials, but actualizes their goals in counterintuitive ways, reorienting their meaning with reverence and irreverence alike. Consider *Untitled (Unknown)* (2006; fig. 8), an installation made up of approximately sixty columns wrapped in slate-gray canvas cloth installed beside the plaster bust of a man in a suit and tie that

McMillian found in an antique store and then adorned with acrylic paint.[15] As implied by the parentheses in the title, the man memorialized is anonymous, a fact belied by the reality that someone, at some point, deemed him important enough to make a likeness of his image in a semi-durable material. The columns likewise render an object associated with acclaim haphazardly: constructed at uneven lengths ranging from one to eleven feet, they lean at various degrees off-kilter. Unlike pillars that have historically stood alone as monuments, provided structural support for a temple, or functioned as monumental graves, McMillian's columns invert the sense of finish and order associated with their elegiac design.

McMillian's *Untitled (the Great Society) I* (2006; fig. 9) is a live performance and a single-channel video in which the artist recites Lyndon B. Johnson's 1964 "Great Society" speech. (Geometric abstractionist painter Stephen Westfall has also recorded a version for McMillian.) In the original address delivered at the University of Michigan commencement ceremony, the former President expressed his desire to give "every citizen the full equality…whatever his belief, or race, or the color of his skin," as well as "an escape from the crushing weight of poverty." In McMillian's reenactment, performed on multiple occasions as if to caption and contextualize much of the work he was making at that time, the artist positions himself behind a microphone and podium, costumed in a suit and tie.[16] Like in *Untitled (Unknown)*, the artist's live performance of an influential political event is reproduced with a purposefully underwhelming delivery: his lines seem half-memorized, his tone only partially believable. Creating an ambivalent relationship to the promises of the original, the commemorative performance mimics the failures of the sculptural installation, this time vetted by the reactions of a real-time audience.

McMillian's video *A Song for Nat* (2012; fig. 10) is a similar *détournement* of the memorial genre, here through his

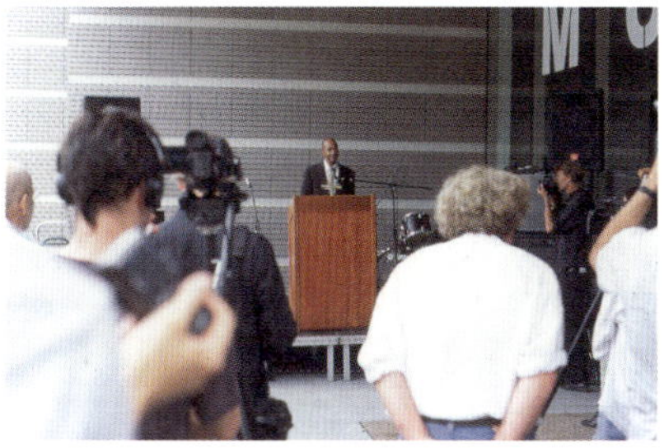

Fig. 9
Untitled (the Great Society) I, 2006 (still)

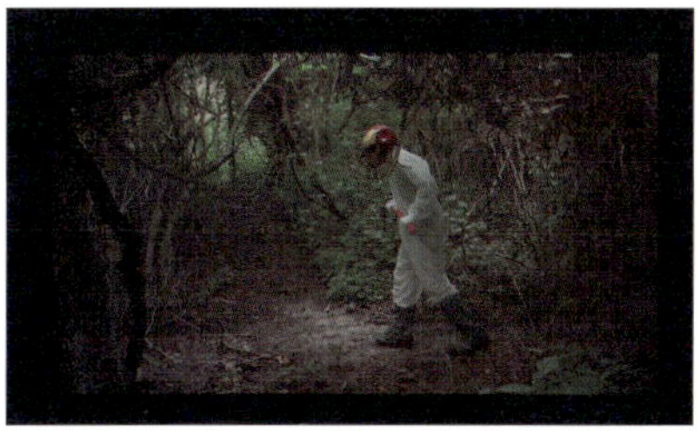

Fig. 10
A Song for Nat, 2012 (still)

speculative and interpretive reenactment of the 1831 antislavery rebellion led by Nat Turner, an enslaved man from Virginia. A deeply religious person who received messages from God via visions and signs in nature, Turner witnessed a solar eclipse, which he interpreted as a sign to begin his insurrection. McMillian's ode is shot against the noisy backdrop of the Mississippi Delta's cicadas while the artist was traveling with curator Bennett Simpson. The artist appears wearing a hazmat suit and an Iron Man mask as he wields an axe, the weapon Turner used to kill his master. McMillian proceeds to encircle a white Southern Manor—a stand-in for the Big House. As it begins to rain and lightning flashes, the intrigue mounts, although no dramatic dénouement is ever achieved. Part pastoral *dérive,* part improvisation, the video moves between the genres of horror, satire, and homage—and expands Situationist strategies from an urban to a rural landscape to not only critique advanced capitalism, but also racial capitalism. Filmed in a different time, location, and affective disposition from Turner's, the piece remains reverential perhaps only to the antislavery ethos of the original act that the artist memorializes.[17]

McMillian's columns and bust to an anonymous figure, his Johnson speech, and his song for Turner are marked by amateur, unconvincing, and improvisatory modes of production whose agonism aligns with the normative stakes of contemporary art. Yet, their earnestness nevertheless allows them to perform the essential tasks of an artistic genre that we associate with memorial sculptures and statues typically sponsored and/or administered by city, state, or national government agencies, merging belief, reverence, and remembrance of something lost.[18] In the artist's irreverent hand and mouth, all three projects ask their viewers to believe in them.

Genre/Landscapes and Romance

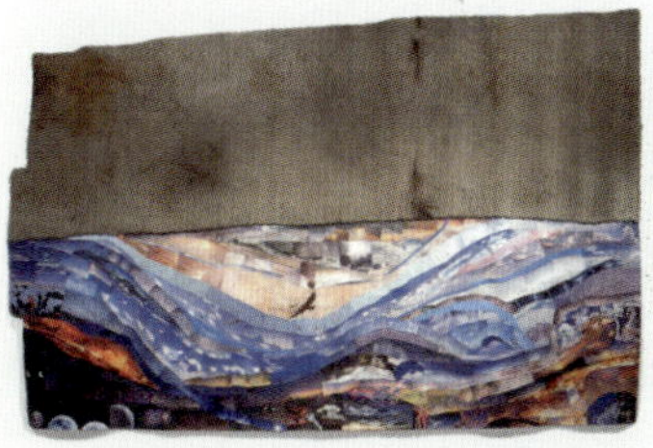

Fig. 11
Untitled, 2003

Several of the strategies McMillian used in his first exhibition at Susanne Vielmetter in 2003 recur in his recent work. An untitled 2003 work, for example, is a landscape divided vertically in two (fig. 11). In the upper half of the composition, a stained brown carpet (left untouched) conjures an image of solid earth, while in the lower half, magazine images are collaged in successive strata, but arranged in a typically inverse order—from bottom up, the cutouts depict the cosmos, the sky, and finally earth. Constructed in undulating layers, the composition mirrors the stacked, interlocking bands of color that characterize the artist's pour paintings. Like those process-oriented plays with gravity's effect on material, this landscape challenges our sense of bodily orientation, addressing a viewer whose standards of perception invert those of gravity-bound humans.[19]

As a genre, landscape painting in the United States is historically bound up with narratives of expropriation. Influenced by English painters including John Constable and J. M. W. Turner, nineteenth-century Hudson River School painters in the United States anticipated—and as some scholars have argued, effected—the accelerated colonization of the American West, the emergence of the national park preservation movement, and the establishment of green city parks.[20] Compositionally, large-scale panoramic views were organized so as to immerse viewers into their scenes, often giving them the impression of beholding a far-reaching vista at precise moments of contact with native communities or pristine, uninhabited pastoral expanses. In this way, the paintings constructed an analogous or continuous relationship between perception and possession. Simultaneous to their use by the Hudson River School, panoramas—hybrids of landscape art and theater culture that depicted scenes on a single cloth harnessed at each end of the stage—were also used by African American abolitionists such as Wells Brown in forms of educational entertainment.

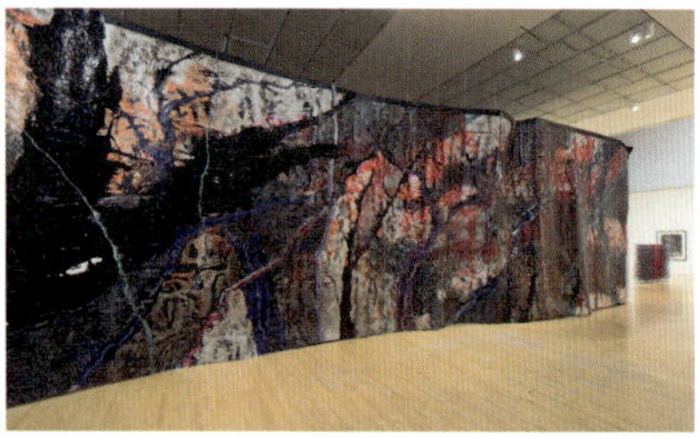

Fig. 12
Representation of a Landscape as a Wall, 2012

Rendered kinetic in 1819, these new "peristrephic" apparatuses revolved and rotated, creating proto–motion pictures whose radical unframing from existing genres and movement offered a physical analog to narratives of escape.[21]

McMillian's landscape painting invokes many of the historic trappings of its genre: the syncretization of painting and theater, the violent intrigue of a historical encounter sublimated through a subjective lens, and the emancipatory possibilities of storytelling. Yet, it reroutes the romance of contact toward more vexed ends. Consider *Representation of a Landscape as a Wall* (2012; fig. 12), a forty-eight-by-fourteen-foot work on paper that bisects the gallery. Expressive and moody washes of orange and red acrylic and intervening blue ink are applied against a black ground of latex house paint. The architectonic work hangs from the ceiling on wire, its support comprised of three layers of acid-free paper connecting one roll to the next through gel mediums, which give its surface a sheen. It bends, undulates, and folds, behaving like a skin that accumulates paint in parts and gathers a density much like a pus or a pore, pouring out or filled in.

Representation cuts off the gallery space, preventing viewers from seeing it as a vista and forcing them to engage with it materially, abstractly, intimately. Indeed, the work's drips and spills seem to speak in the psychologically driven tones of Abstract Expressionism. But as one begins to follow the red and orange veins and glimpse its blue streaks, the pictorial space begins to resemble earth and sky, disoriented and rendered as a postapocalyptic morass in which the ground is indistinguishable from the figural trees or the great beyond. While the picture avoids providing distinct referents that would reveal its location or a figure to act as its protagonist, it does cast its viewers in a freighted spectatorial position. Confronting a vestibular space—at once a corridor and a dead end—they are denied the universal, transparent position afforded the viewer of Romantic landscape painting or of the theatrical panorama.

Enmeshed within this invented, fantastical landscape, they can only access it via direct contact with the picture's skin, entering into the image's uncertain orientation and their precarious position within it.

Genre/Theaters of Speculative Realism

Extending from the wall, floor, and ceiling, McMillian's three-dimensional structures frequently envelop their viewers. Producing beholders and setting the stage for real things to occur, his architectural spaces are at once illusionistic and hyperreal: they are theaters. McMillian's sense of theatricality often appears to lack artifice, instead insisting upon his materials being exactly what they are: a corridor made entirely of black vinyl, a house made entirely of red vinyl. Their handmade, slipshod fabrication guarantees their distancing effect, so that the beholder never believes there is a fourth wall between herself and the work. Yet, they produce associations of fantastical fabrications—invocations of spaces not depicted—of vastly different scales and orders: the blacks and reds of human orifices (the mouth, anus, or wound) or those of the ends of the earth (a black hole or the epicenter of the sun). Stitched together, one piece after another, the vinyl is lustrous and absorptive to behold face to face, and in the sum total of the parts is a house or a church—a passageway from one stage to another.

McMillian first made the house-sized installation *portal: (a state of kemmering in the Council-era of corrosion)* (2010; fig. 13) at Project Row Houses (PRH) in Houston's Third Ward, and later reconstructed it at Maccarone gallery in New York in 2012. The first installation was part of a four-month-long artist "Round," in which PRH's curator invited artists to make a work on-site in a shotgun house. During Round 33, LA–based artists Andrea Bowers, Gaines, and Koumoundouros joined McMillian, each responding to the prompt to make the immaterial material.[22]

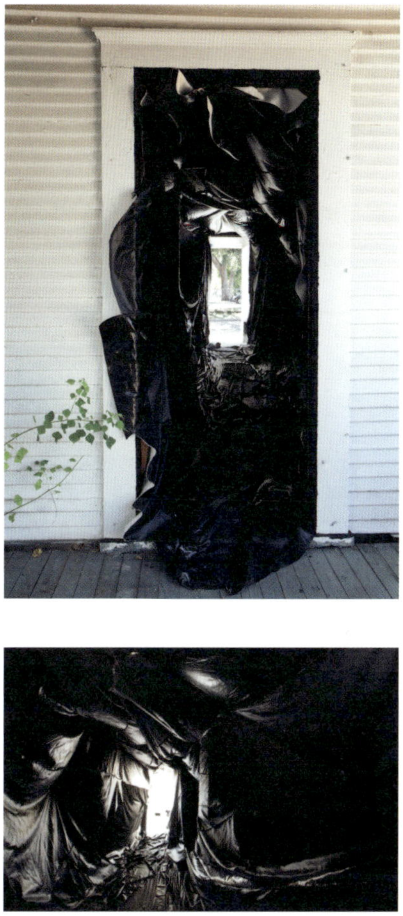

Fig. 13
portal: (a state of kemmering in the Council-era of corrosion), 2010

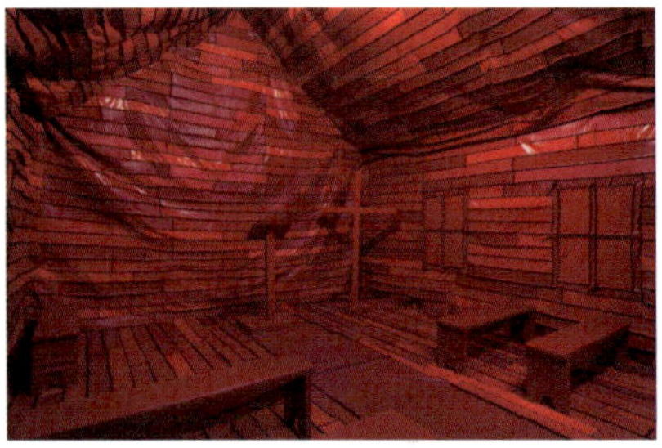

Fig. 14
From Asterisks in Dockery, 2012

In *portal*, McMillian's black vinyl connects the front and back doors of one house, creating a tunnel that hyperbolizes the shotgun nature of the vernacular architecture. While the space structurally requires the building's insides—floor, ceiling, and walls—it is, in effect, turned inside out so that interiority produces a public space by rendering private rooms into a passageway. The neologism "kemmering" in the work's title makes reference to Ursula K. Le Guin's feminist science-fiction novel *The Left Hand of Darkness* (1969), whose protagonist Genly Ai is a black-skinned interloper in the country Karhide on the planet Gethen, which is populated exclusively by brown-skinned inhabitants. When Gethenian's inhabitants are sexually inactive, they lack sexual characteristics; yet, when they enter the "kemmer" state (government-sanctioned leisure time for procreation), they develop the secondary sexual characteristics of males or females and are driven to mate. Gethenians are not predisposed to having sex, nor do they choose their gender; in fact, most adult Gethenians function as fathers and mothers to different offspring. McMillian also draws on expansive depictions of gender, sexual, and racial categories from other speculative fiction writers including Octavia Butler and Samuel Delany who, like Le Guin, often allude to religious texts or the emancipatory potential of radical sexual practices in their own writing. In *portal*, he constructs a tubing system in the name of Le Guin's sexual stage, and in his choice of shape and color, constructs an anal orifice. In McMillian's hands, the space of sanctioned possibility is a two-sided opening and an emphatic declaration of capacity.

McMillian's installation *From Asterisks in Dockery* (2012; fig. 14) constructs a corollary to this immersive space. The artist made the room-sized church, complete with pews, windows, a cross, and a preacher's podium, for the traveling exhibition *Blues for Smoke* (2012–13) organized by the Los Angeles Museum of Contemporary Art. Dockery Plantation, to which the work refers, was a ten thousand–acre cotton plantation and sawmill located on the Sunflower River in Mississippi. Widely regarded as the place where the Delta blues was born after the end of slavery, some of its most noteworthy residents included Charlie Patton, Robert Johnson, and Howlin' Wolf.[23]

The thread that stitches red vinyl to red vinyl in McMillian's *Dockery* gives the entire structure a graphic, theatrical sensibility. It acts in contradictory ways, exaggerating the edges of the fake two-by-fours and windowpanes of the windows, while also guaranteeing their recognizability and verisimilitude. Similarly, the church's usable scale makes it uncomfortably like the real thing—audiences can walk in, sit down on the pews, and stand or even sing at the podium. Yet, its deep red interior declaratively marks it as a copy (and a copy without a recognizable original). Indeed, a look out of the window reminds us that we are bound within and covered by the red vinyl casing.

At one end of McMillian's cosmology is the fabled birthplace of the blues, depicted as a giant red orifice or womb; at the other end of his large-scale monochromatic spectrum is an enterable anus, the place from which life begins in an alternate universe on planet Gethen. What the blues genre shares with science fiction is the rawness of realism conveyed through the ache of articulating a possible future.[24] As Clyde Woods has argued, "The blues became the channel through which the Reconstruction generation grasped reality in the midst of disbelief, critiqued the plantation regime, and organized against it."[25] Both *portal* and *Dockery* are theatrical, vestibular spaces—stages through which this century-plus dream of transformation or descent might come to an end. A locus of fantasy and possibility, these houses of worship and abandon are pass-throughs for their inhabitants' performances of criticism and yearning.

Way Out

What to call the thing that happened to me and all who look like me? Should I call it history? And if so, what should history mean to someone who looks like me? Should it be an idea; should it be an open wound?

—Jamaica Kincaid, *My Garden (Book)* (1999)

Genres, and the gender and racial formations to which they point—memorial sculpture, landscape painting, and speculative fiction—are historically contingent: they cohere and fall apart as aesthetic norms are both formalized and discontinued. McMillian recontextualizes historic genres with a sense of irreverent reverence, putting contemporary conventions into relief with bygone styles that feel like they are of our time precisely because they are out of lockstep with it. Likewise, he draws our attention to the persistence of their social and cultural beliefs, be they prohibitive or liberatory; or, like nineteenth-century American landscape painting and the blues, some ongoing combination of the two.

For McMillian, history is an open wound: it is a location at once real and fabulated to enter into and to be entered by. It holds the names of our symbolic order—not only the names those artists who came before gave themselves, and not only the terms by which their contexts were built, which will only be knowable through the interpretative acts of our historic recovery. It is the wound's unknowability, its multiple cells and panels that constitute it—that hold us within it—which not only keeps its doors open, but might also be our way out.

Notes

1 Traylor (1854–1949), an iconic self-taught artist born into slavery, is known for his pictographic sensibility and use of cobalt blue that predominates in hand-painted signs throughout the South. He used these formal strategies to depict and narrate life in Montgomery, Alabama, where he moved from Benton, Alabama, at the age of eighty-two, leaving his family behind and beginning his cardboard drawings that drew on his experiences making work near a blacksmith's shop.

2 Shannon exhibited Traylor's work at both the New South cultural center in Montgomery (the only exhibition of his work Traylor saw) as well as at the Ethical Culture Fieldston School in Riverdale, New York, where Alfred Barr attempted to acquire it for the Museum of Modern Art. See Josef Helfenstein, "Bill Traylor and Charles Shannon: A Historic Encounter in Montgomery" in *Bill Traylor, 1854-1949. Deep Blues*, ed. Josef Helfenstein and Roman Kurzmeyer, exh. cat. (New York and New Haven: Yale University Press, 1999).

3 In her description of this work on view in the exhibition *Macho Man, Tell It To My Heart* (2013–14) at Artists Space in New York, Roberta Smith writes, "It is so nearly identical to a work by the great outsider Bill Traylor (1854-1949) that I assumed it was, only mislabeled. When told no, I was dumbstruck by Mr. Benning's ego-free yet determined attention and tender accuracy. His drawing is love made visually manifest, and Traylor deserves it—a former slave, he created one of the most significant bodies of American art when he was old, crippled and living on the streets of Montgomery, Ala." Roberta Smith, "Imitation of Life, Outsiders Version: Works by James Benning and Others at Artists Space" in the *New York Times*, February 21, 2014, C5.

4 See Laura Mulvey, "Visual Pleasure and Narrative Cinema" in *Visual and Other Pleasures* (Bloomington: Indiana University, 1989), 19.

5 This is a space Gilles Deleuze might call a "fold"—"the 'teeming,'... perceptual displacement of contours, [which] comes from the projection onto matter of something spiritual..."; or Nathaniel Mackey might name a "sexual cut"—"an insistent previousness evading each and every natal occasion." See Gilles Deleuze, "The Fold" in *Yale French Studies*, No. 80 (1991), 246; and Nathaniel Mackey, *Bedouin Hornbook*, Callaloo Fiction Series, Vol. 2 (Lexington: University Press of Kentucky, 1986), 34–35.

6 Rodney McMillian, email message to author, January 27, 2015.

7 "Reanimation" rings with a return of the Freudian uncanny, the specters of Communism, and the haints of the American South, and has increasingly appeared in discourses around art made now. In "The Year in Re-," Martha Buskirk, Amelia Jones, and Caroline A. Jones define reanimation by invoking R.G. Collingwood and his posthumously assembled *The Idea*

Figures

Fig. 1
Untitled (for B. Traylor), I, 2008. Acrylic, latex, and ink on bedsheet, approx. 84 x 48 in (213.4 x 121.9 cm). Private collection. Courtesy the artist and Susanne Vielmetter Los Angeles Projects. Photo: Robert Wedemeyer

Fig. 2
James Benning, *Woman Pointing*, 2009. Colored pencil on found paper, 18 x 12 in (45.7 x 30.5 cm). Collection of the artist. Courtesy Artists Space, NY

Fig. 3
Untitled (after Bill Traylor) I, 2008. Acrylic, charcoal on canvas, 40 1/4 x 36 1/2 in (102.2 x 92.7 cm). Courtesy the artist and Susanne Vielmetter Los Angeles Projects. Photo: Robert Wedemeyer

Fig. 4
Senga Nengudi, *Quarante-et-un*, 1977/2014. Nylon mesh, sand, and metal spring, 28 x 22 x 2 in (71.1 x 55.9 x 5 cm). © Senga Nengudi. Courtesy White Cube. Photo: George Darrell

Fig. 5
Untitled, 2008. Black vinyl, white thread, stuffing material, approx. 13 1/2 x 22 x 8 ft (4.1 x 6.7 x 2.4 m). Rubell Family Collection. Courtesy the artist and Susanne Vielmetter Los Angeles Projects. Photo: Bill Orcutt

Fig. 6
Untitled, 2010. Vinyl and thread, 14 ft x 27 ft 6 in (4.2 x 8.4 m). Courtesy the artist and Susanne Vielmetter Los Angeles Projects. Photo: Robert Wedemeyer

Fig. 7
Untitled, 2008. Latex paint, canvas; three approx. 15 x 7 ft (4.5 x 2.1 m); two approx. 15 x 8 ft (4.5 x 2.4 m). Originally commissioned and produced by ArtPace San Antonio. Courtesy the artist and Susanne Vielmetter Los Angeles Projects. Photo: Todd Johnson

Fig. 8
Untitled (Unknown), 2006. Mixed media columns, bust (canvas, acrylic paint, empty paint cans, found plaster bust), dimensions variable. Courtesy the artist and Susanne Vielmetter Los Angeles Projects

Fig. 9
Untitled (the Great Society) I, 2006 (still). Single-channel video, color and sound; 15:48 min. Courtesy the artist and Susanne Vielmetter Los Angeles Projects

Fig. 10
A Song for Nat, 2012 (still). Single-channel video, color and sound; 6 min. Courtesy the artist and Susanne Vielmetter Los Angeles Projects

Fig. 11
Untitled, 2003. Carpet and paper on canvas, 160 x 110 in (406.4 x 278.4 cm). Collection of Jeffrey Kerns, Los Angeles. Courtesy the artist and Susanne Vielmetter Los Angeles Projects

Fig. 12
Representation of a Landscape as a Wall, 2012. Acrylic, latex, and ink on paper, 14 x 48.6 ft (4.3 x 14.8 m). MOCA, Los Angeles. Courtesy the artist and Susanne Vielmetter Los Angeles Projects. Photo: Robert Wedemeyer

of History (1946), which proposes an idea of history-writing as requiring "projective interpretations or imaginative reenactments of past thoughts motivating past actions." See Martha Buskirk, Amelia Jones, and Caroline A. Jones, "The Year in Re-" in *Artforum* Vol. 52, No. 4 (December, 2013). Rebecca Schneider has related reanimation to theatricality, describing the theatrical as the "instability of the divide between life and death, or liveness and deadness." See Rebecca Schneider, "It Seems As If. . .I am Dead: Zombie Capitalism and Theatrical Labor" in *TDR: The Drama Review* Vol. 56, No. 4 (Winter 2012), 152–64. In addition to animation, Fred Moten has built on poet John Donne's idea of interanimation, developing the idea of inter(in)animation. For Moten, inter(in)animation both describes an exchange of senses and media—visuality and orality, photography and music—as well as the sound of Emmitt Till's mother's moan in the photograph of Emmitt Till's corpse. Inter(in)animation thus describes an identification of the living with the dead, a bringing to life that requires cocooning death within it. See Fred Moten, "Black Mo'nin' in the Sound of the Photograph" in *In the Break: The Aesthetics of the Black Radical Tradition* (Minneapolis: University of Minnesota Press, 2003), 192–211.

8 Those modernist discourses that have predominated in the United States argued for linearity, causality, and progress; in response, postmodernist artists (as paradigmatic examples, consider Sherrie Levine [b. 1947] and Kerry James Marshall [b. 1955]) made use of appropriation and amalgamation to pressure the notions of medium-specificity, originality, and mastery on which these modernism's values depended. Extending these critiques, McMillian's emphasis on sexual touch, excess, and the horizontality of historical reception has occurred within a culture conditioned by the networks of mass data storage and the global internet.

9 See Helen Molesworth, "How to Install Art as a Feminist" in *Modern Women: Women Artists at the Museum of Modern Art* (New York: Museum of Modern Art, 2010), 498–513; Mignon Nixon, "O + X" in *October 119* (Winter 2007), 6–20; and Lisa Tickner, "Mediating Generation: The Mother-Daughter Plot" in Carol Armstrong and Catherine de Zegher, eds., *Women Artists at the Millennium* (Cambridge, MA: MIT Press, 2006), 85–120.

10 McMillian's wide-ranging feminist influences include depictions of female genitalia and yonic compositions; the release of stringent taboos on representations of sexuality; the significance of quotidian forms of mark-making; the framing of antagonistic relationships as noncontradictory oppositions; and the consideration of spaces often denied influence in the public sphere, which includes the *de rigueur* feminist space of the home, but also the African American church, the juke joint, the natural world, and outer space.

11 Hortense J. Spillers, "Mama's Baby, Papa's Maybe: An American Grammar Book" in *Diacritics*, Vol. 17 No. 2 (Summer, 1987), 64–81. Spillers's essay reads a variety of scenes of first contact including Gomes Eannes de Azurara's mid-fifteenth-century chronicle and Olaudah Equiano's narrative, published in 1789—beginnings that she describes as "a rupture and a radically different kind of cultural continuation." Her objects of study continue through the near-present, including "The Moynihan Report" (1965). She argues, "Even though the captive flesh/body has been 'liberated,' and no one need pretend that even the quotation marks do not *matter*, dominant symbolic activity, the ruling epitome that releases the dynamics of naming and valuation, remains grounded in the originating metaphors of captivity and mutilation (68)." Spillers's acknowledgment that the slave trade dispersed captive persons into horizontally related language groups pinpoints the emergence of "network culture" to a much earlier—and more pernicious—beginning.

12 See Kellie Jones, "Beyond Reverie" in *Senga Nengudi: Alt, Inside the White Cube* (London: White Cube Gallery, 2014), 31–34.

13 The painting depicts a shelf with a dozen books, including nonfiction tell-alls from the heart of American capitalism on the Federal Reserve and the Ford family, as well as novels of various ideological shades about Western expansion (Winston Churchill's *The Crossing* [1904]) and allegories of Chicano farmworkers (Ernest Brawley's *Selena* [1979]). Bringing together a range of American tales, McMillian's *in progress* complicates a narrative of uplift and promise, rendering the *vanitas* at once ironic and thus more haunting than their typical skulls imply.

14 In an artist talk organized on the occasion of the 2014 Whitney Biennial, Amy Sillman discussed McMillian's use of color as "a reduced palette of symbolic reds, browns, blacks, whites, describing a desperate kind of social space with images wrought in desolate reds of desire and despair." Amy Sillman, "Color As Material" (Lecture: Whitney Museum of American Art, New York, NY, May 22, 2014).

15 See Doryun Chong, *Ordinary Cultures*, exh. cat. (Minneapolis: Walker Art Center, 2006), A7.

16 See Trinie Dalton, Whitney Biennial 2008, exh. website, http://whitney.org/www/2008biennial/www/?section=artists&page=artist_mcmillian (accessed January 5, 2015).

17 For more on memorials and counter-memorials in contemporary art, see Thomas J. Lax "From New York, Southward: A Counter-Memorial" in *Mousse* 44 (July 2014), 230–35.

18 For more on the definitions and stakes of public art, see Rosalyn Deutsche, *Evictions: Art and Spatial Politics* (Cambridge: MIT Press, 1998).

19 See Michael Darling, *Painting in Tongues*, exh. cat. (Los Angeles: Museum of Contemporary Art, 2006), 68–70.

20 See Albert Boime, *The Magisterial Gaze: Manifest Destiny and American Landscape Painting c. 1830–1865* (Washington, DC: Smithsonian Institution Press, 1991);

Fig. 13
portal: (a state of kemmering in the Council-era of corrosion), 2010. Vinyl and thread, dimensions variable. Courtesy the artist and Susanne Vielmetter Los Angeles Projects. Photo: Robert Wedemeyer

Fig. 14
From Asterisks in Dockery, 2012. Vinyl, thread, wood, paint, and light bulb, dimensions variable. Installation view: *Blues for Smoke* at the Geffen Contemporary at MOCA, Los Angeles, October 21, 2012–January 7, 2013. Photo: Brian Forrest (and Robert Wedemeyer)

Angela Miller, *Empire of the Eye: Landscape Representation and American Cultural Politics, 1825–1875* (Ithaca: Cornell University Press, 1993); and W.J.T. Mitchell's *Landscape and Power* (Chicago: University of Chicago Press, 1994).

21 See Daphne A. Brooks, *Bodies in Dissent: Spectacular Performances of Race and Freedom, 1850–1910* (Durham, NC, and London: Duke University Press, 2006), 77–84.

22 David A. Feil, "Round 33: The Seventh House," http://www.art-lies.org/article.php?id=2051&issue=68&s=0 (accessed January 5, 2015).

23 Dockery Farms was founded in 1895 by Will Dockery who died in 1936 when the property became part of the National Register of Historic Places in 2006. "Dockery Farms: History," http://www.dockeryfarms.org/history (accessed January 5, 2015).

24 In *Blues Legacies and Black Feminism: Gertrude "Ma" Rainey, Bessie Smith, and Billie Holiday*, Angela Y. Davis describes the "raw realism" of the blues tradition as follows: "The blues women openly challenged the gender politics implicit in traditional cultural representations of marriage and heterosexual love relationships. Refusing, in the blues tradition of raw realism, to romanticize romantic relationships, they instead exposed the stereotypes and explored the contradictions of those relationships." See *Blues Legacies and Black Feminism: Gertrude "Ma" Rainey, Bessie Smith, and Billie Holiday* (New York: Vintage Books, 1998), 41.

25 Clyde Woods, *Development Arrested: Race, Power, and the Blues in the Mississippi Delta* (London and New York: Verso, 1998), 25.

Special thanks to Elizabeth W. Hutchinson, Malik Gaines, Rodney McMillian, Sarah Stephenson, Lanka Tattersall, and Andrew Wallace.

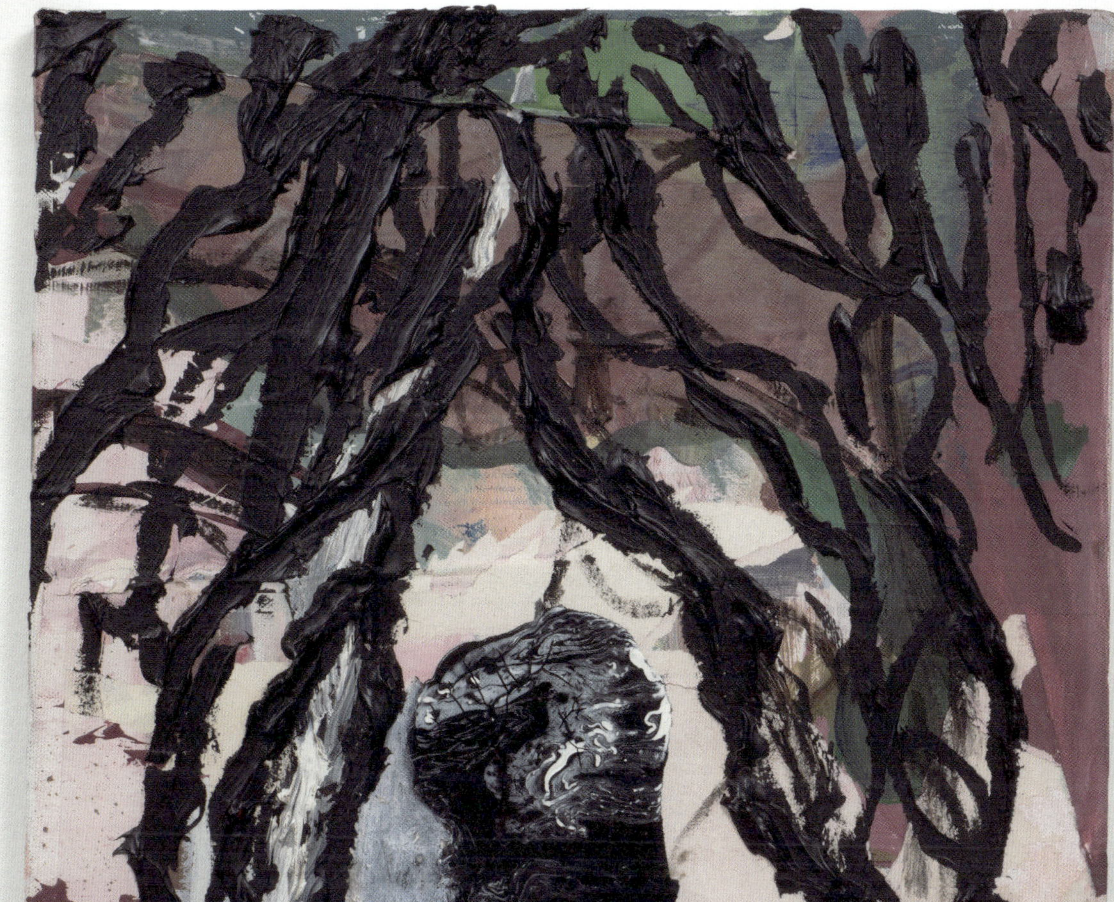

Untitled (after Bill Traylor) III, 2008

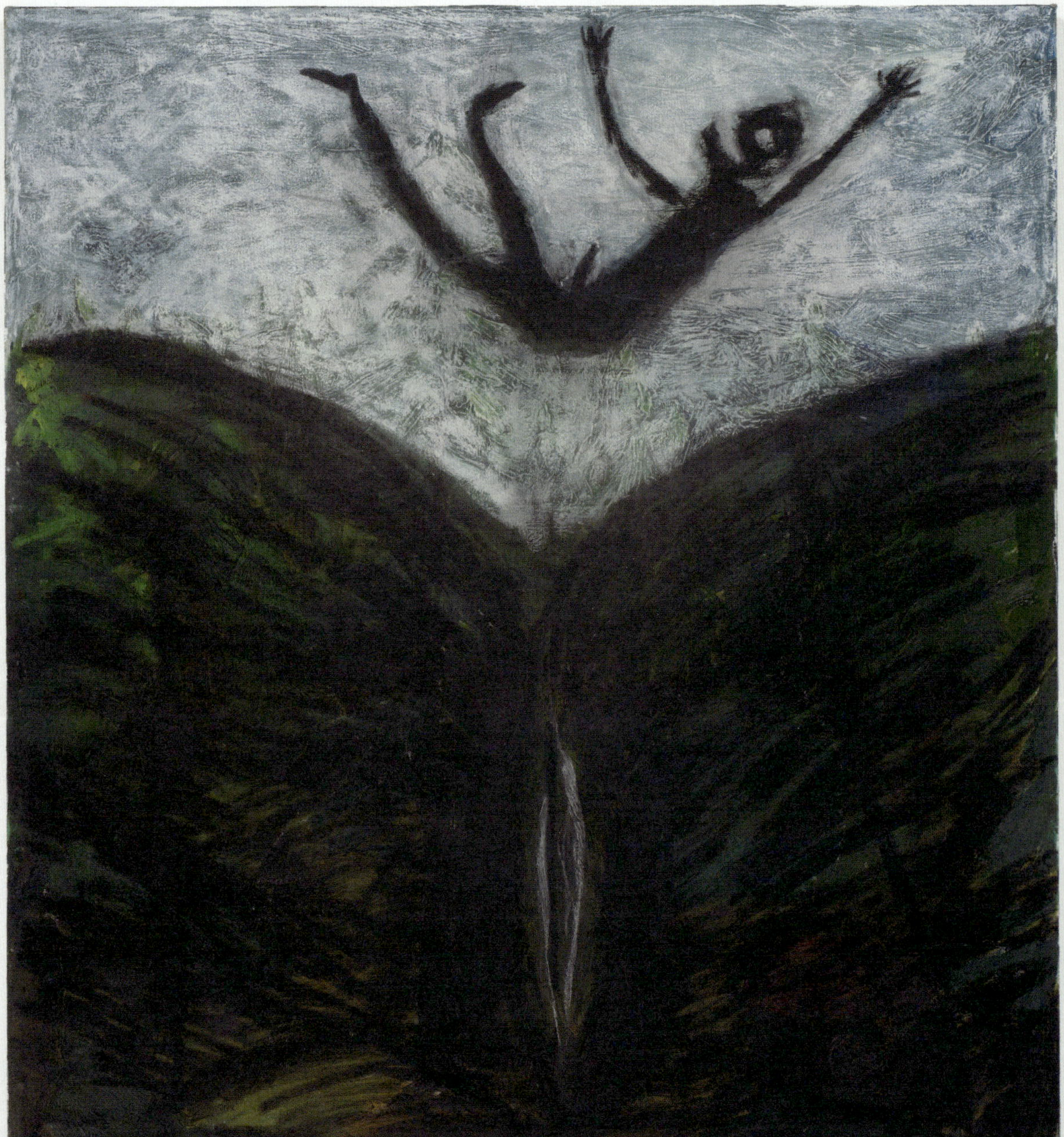

Untitled (after Bill Traylor) I, 2008

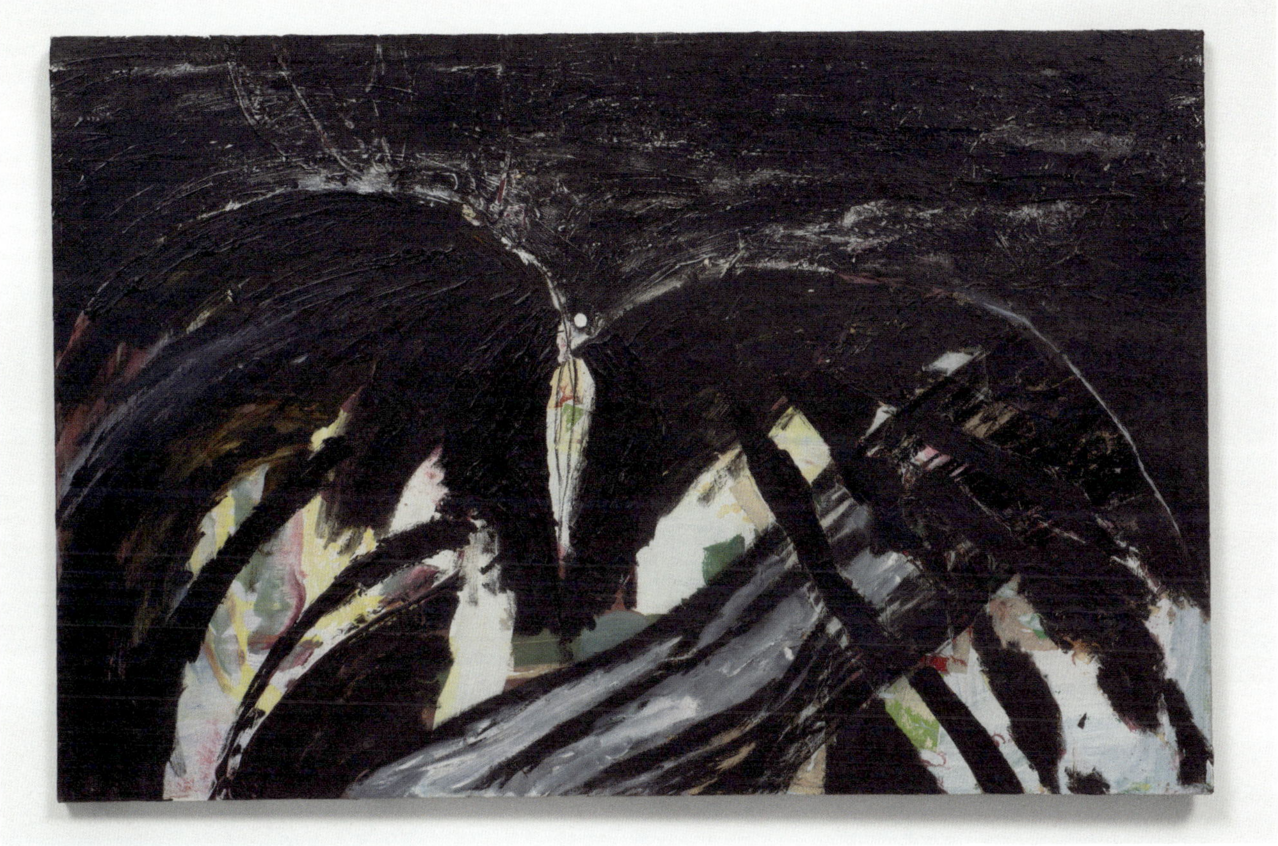

Untitled (after Bill Traylor) II, 2008

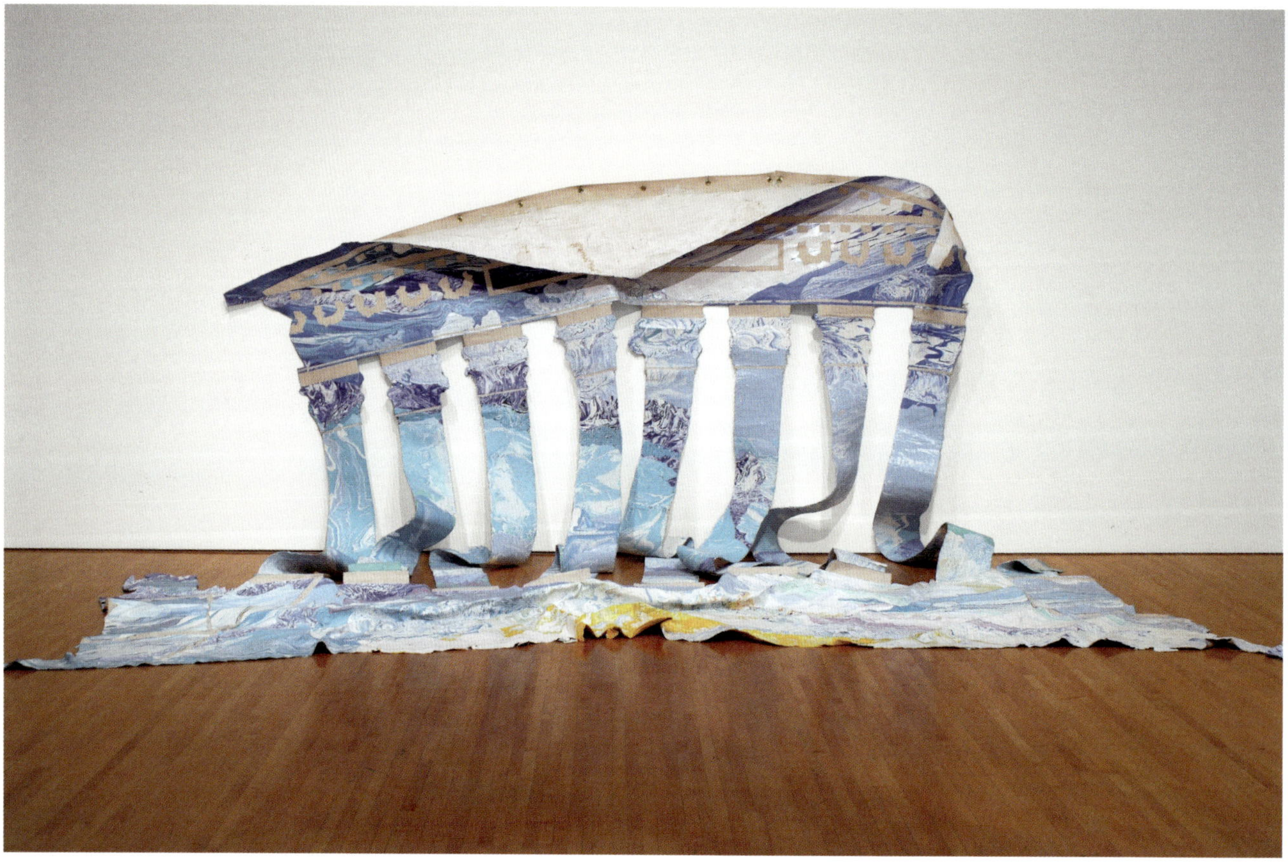

Untitled (The Supreme Court Painting), 2004–06

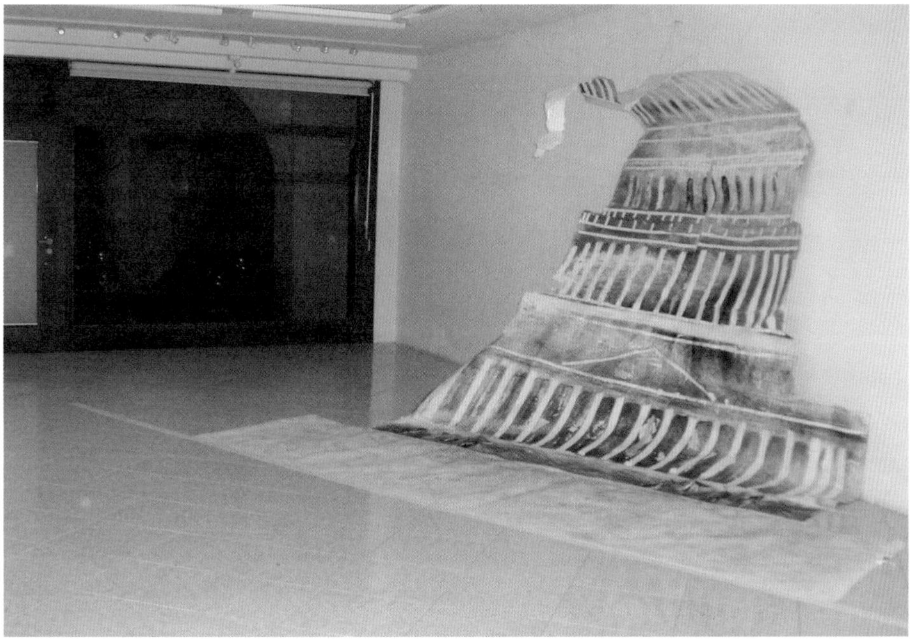

Installation view: *Untitled (The Capital Bldg.)*, 2005. Estro Galleria d'arte, Italy

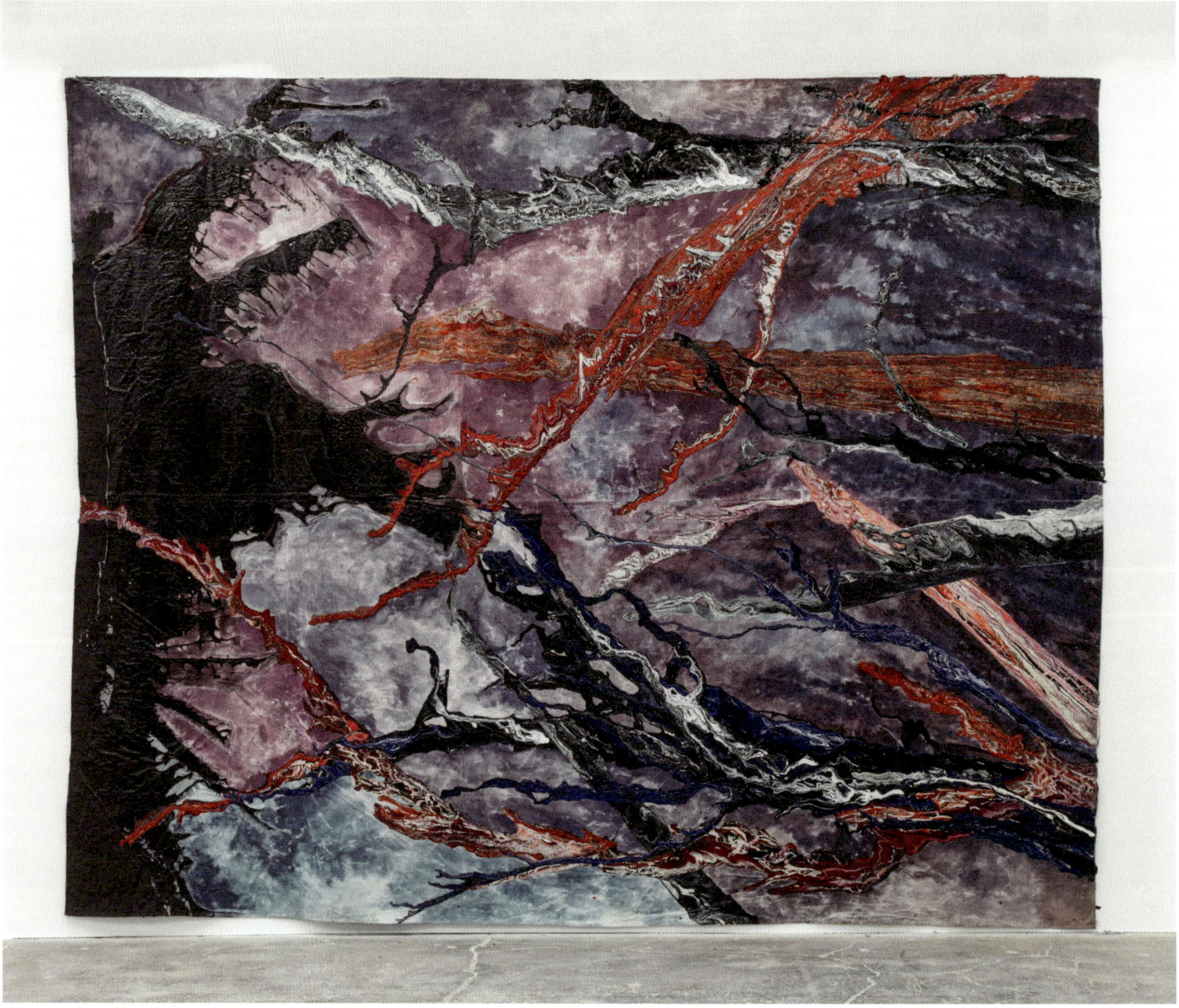

Untitled Landscape #1, 2012

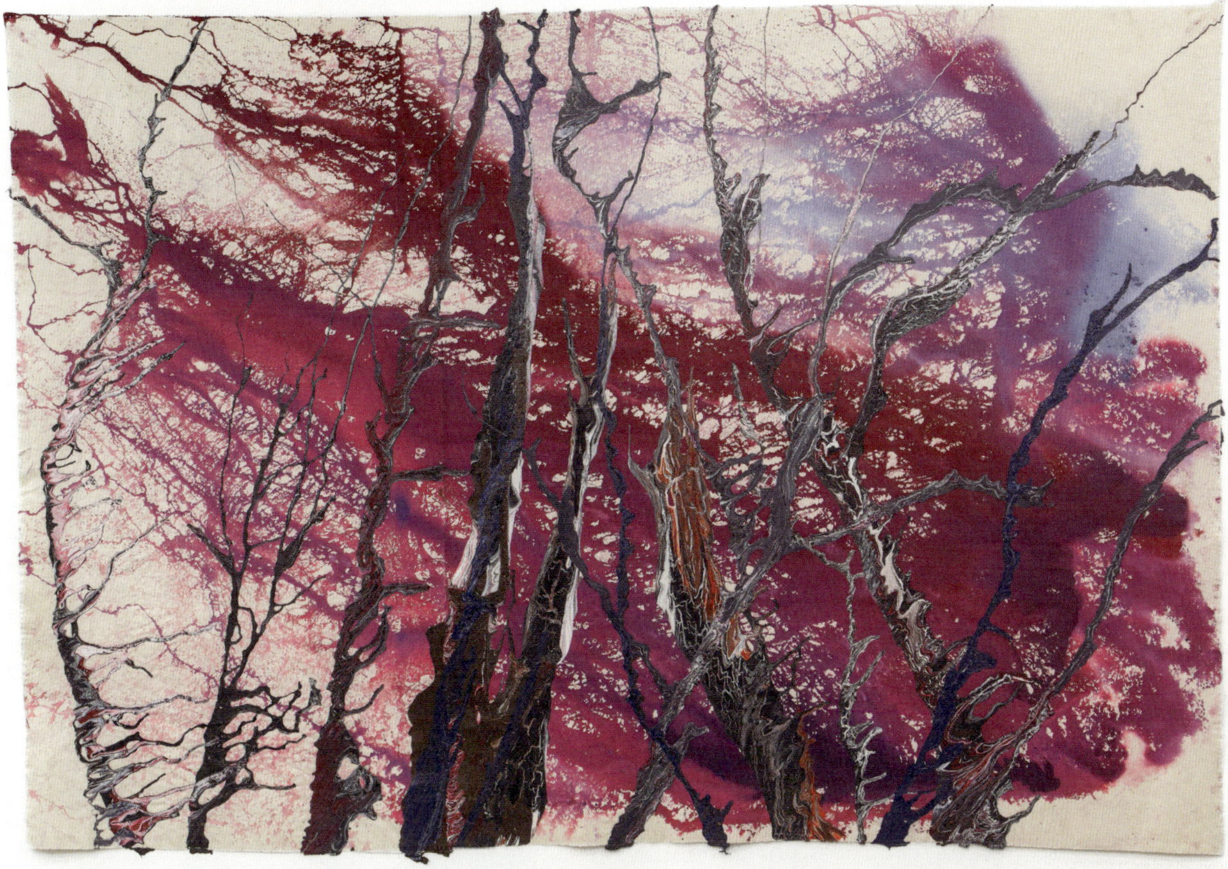

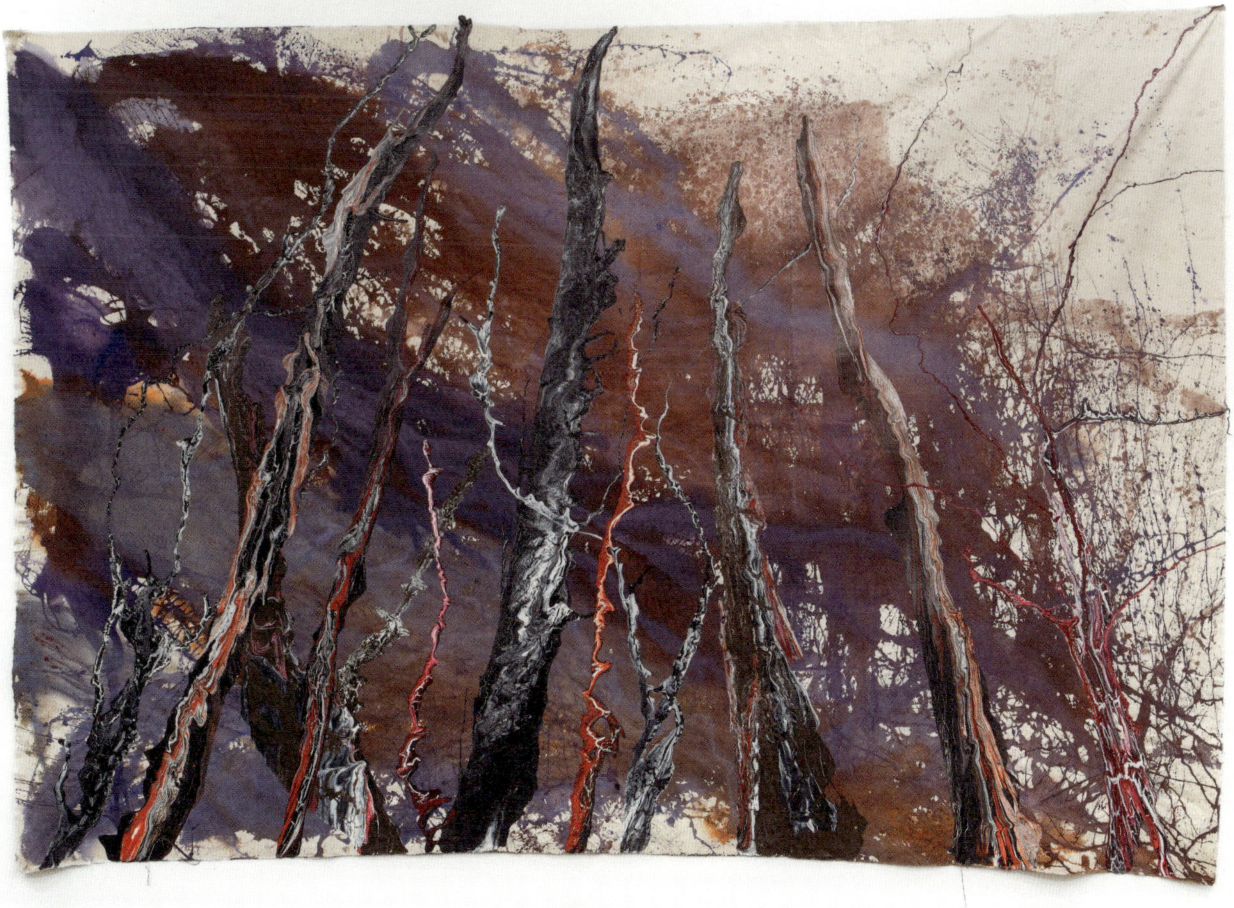

Untitled Landscape #4, 2012
Untitled Landscape #3, 2012

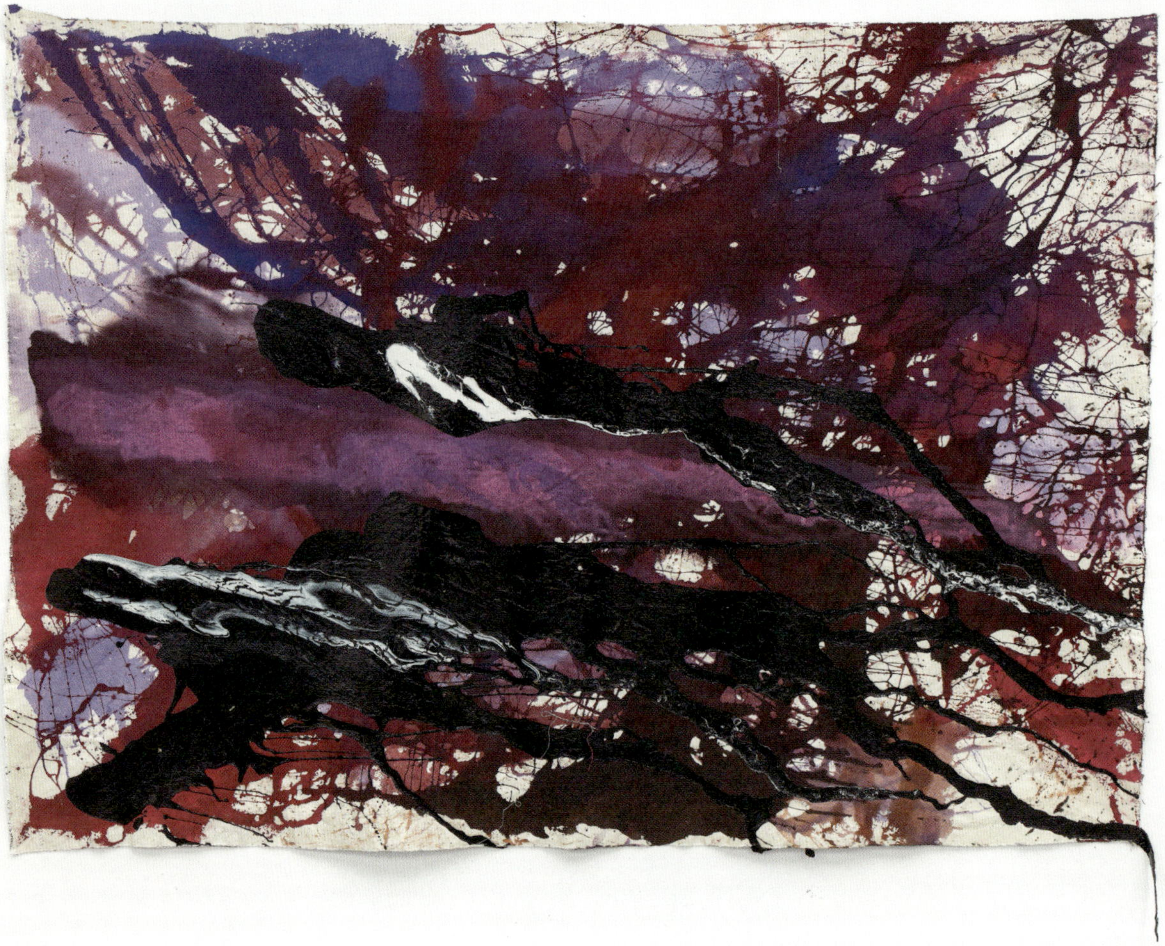

Untitled Cloud #3, 2012

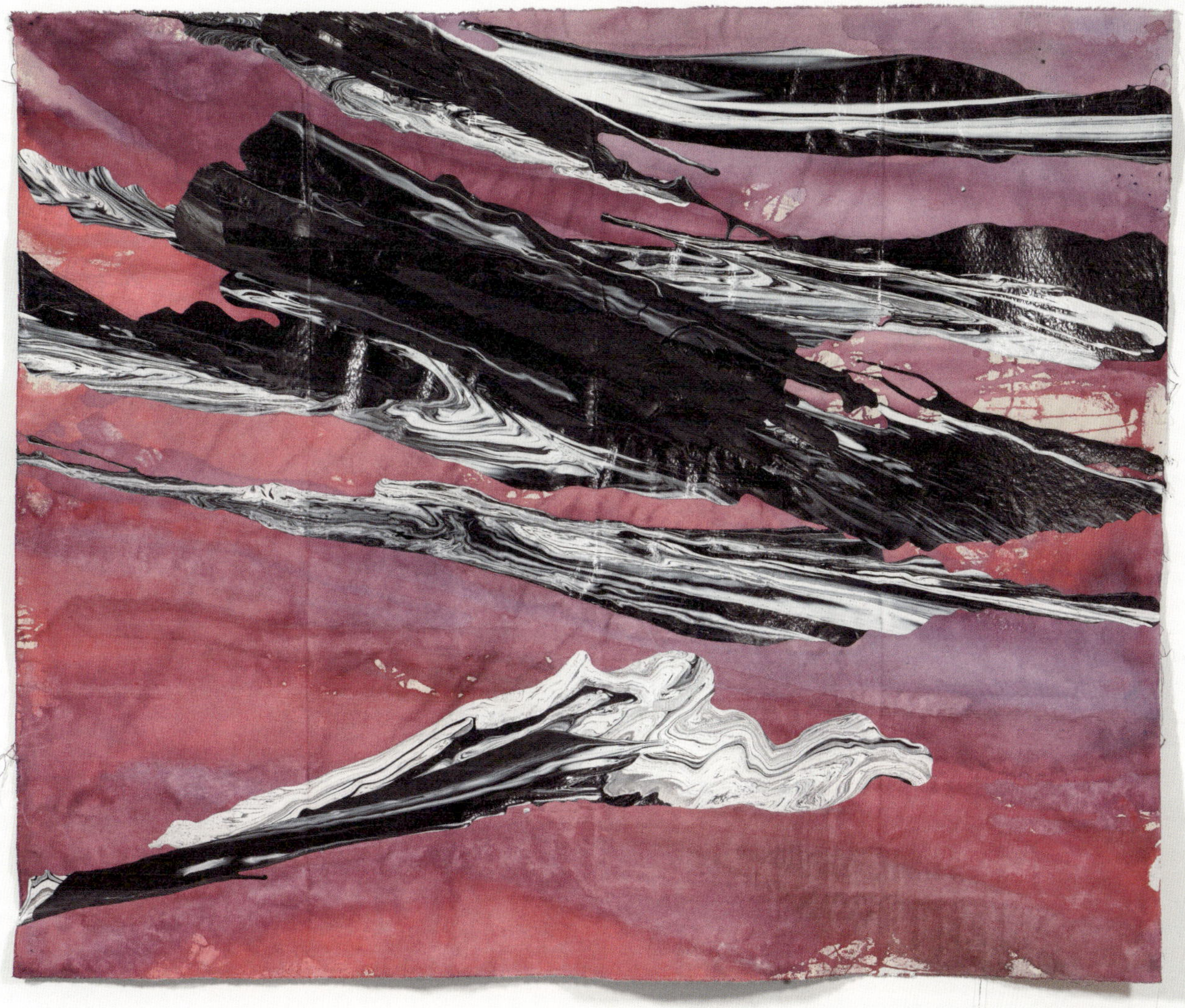

Untitled Cloud #4, 2012

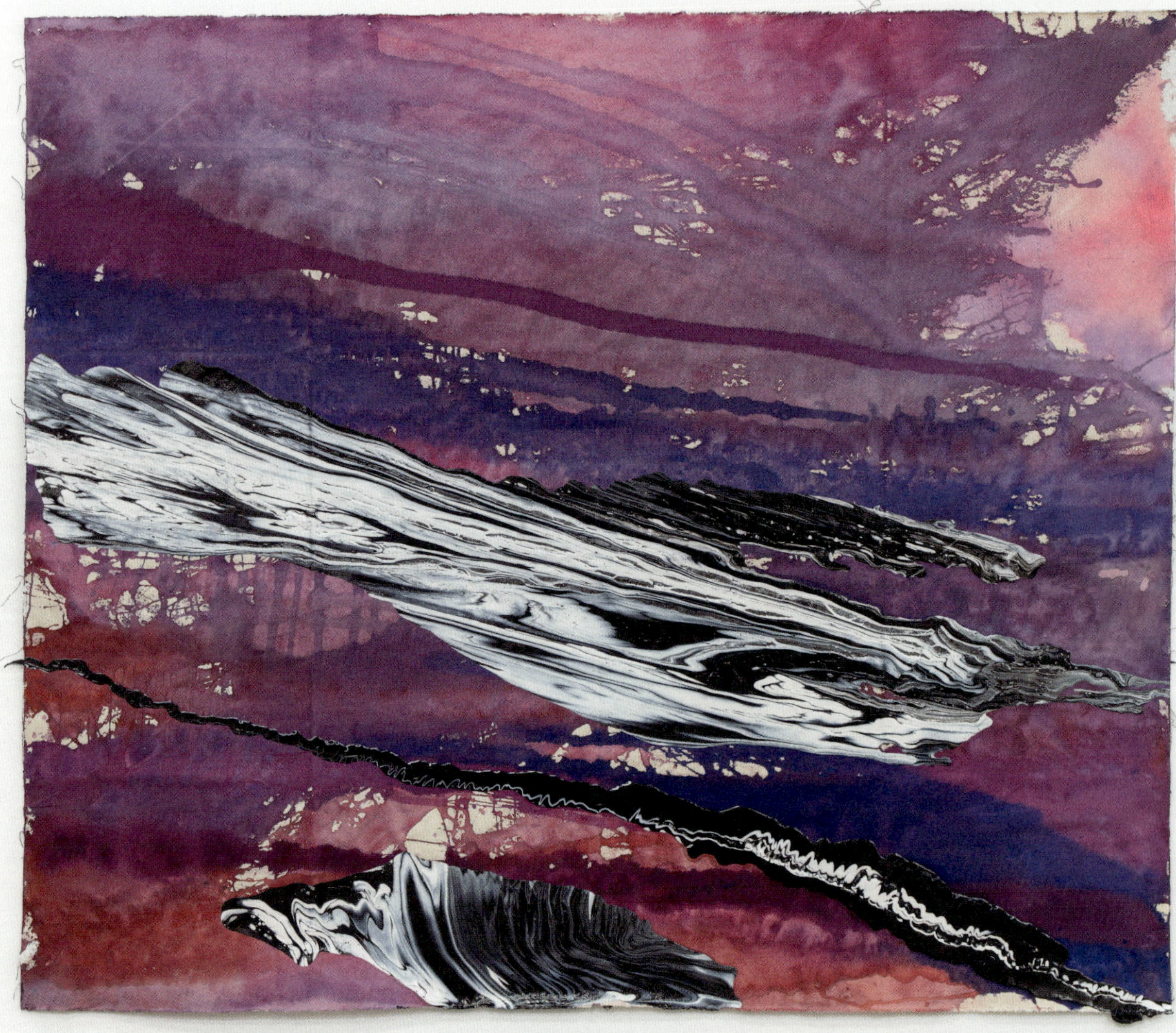

Untitled Cloud #5, 2012

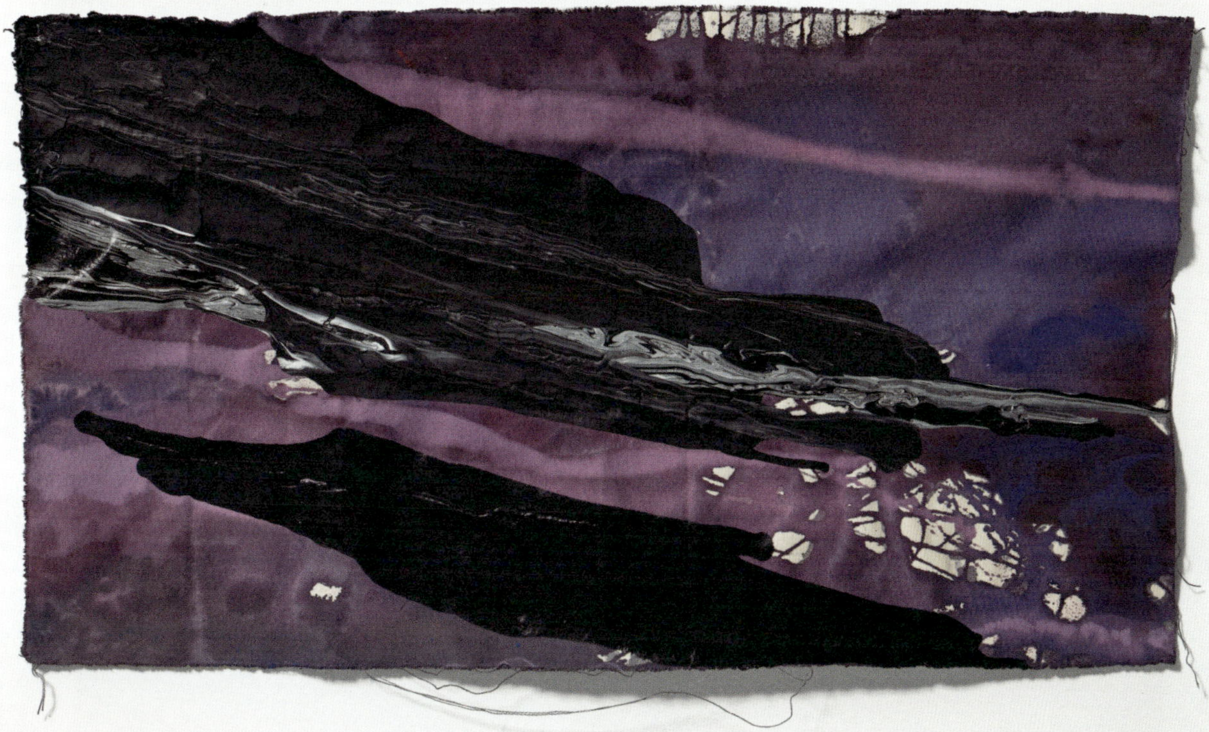

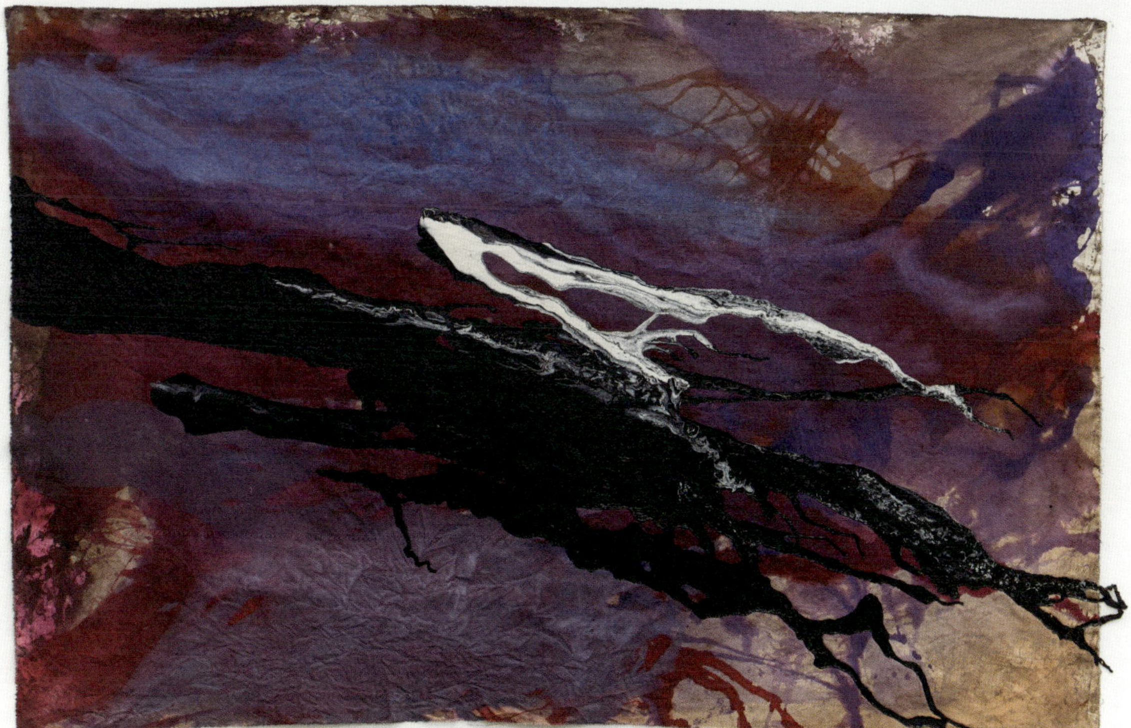

Untitled Cloud #6, 2012
Untitled Cloud #2, 2012

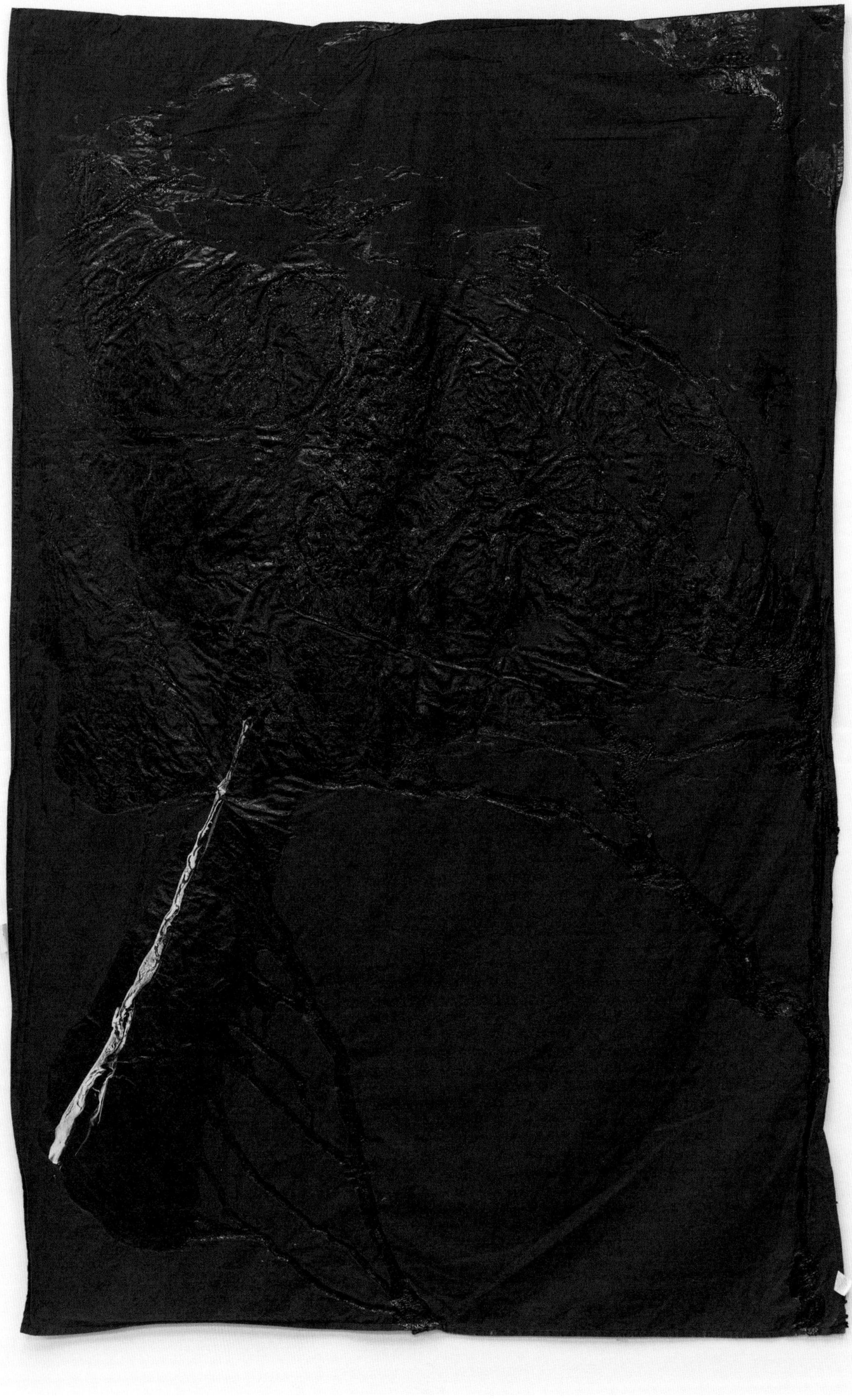

Untitled Cloud #1, 2012

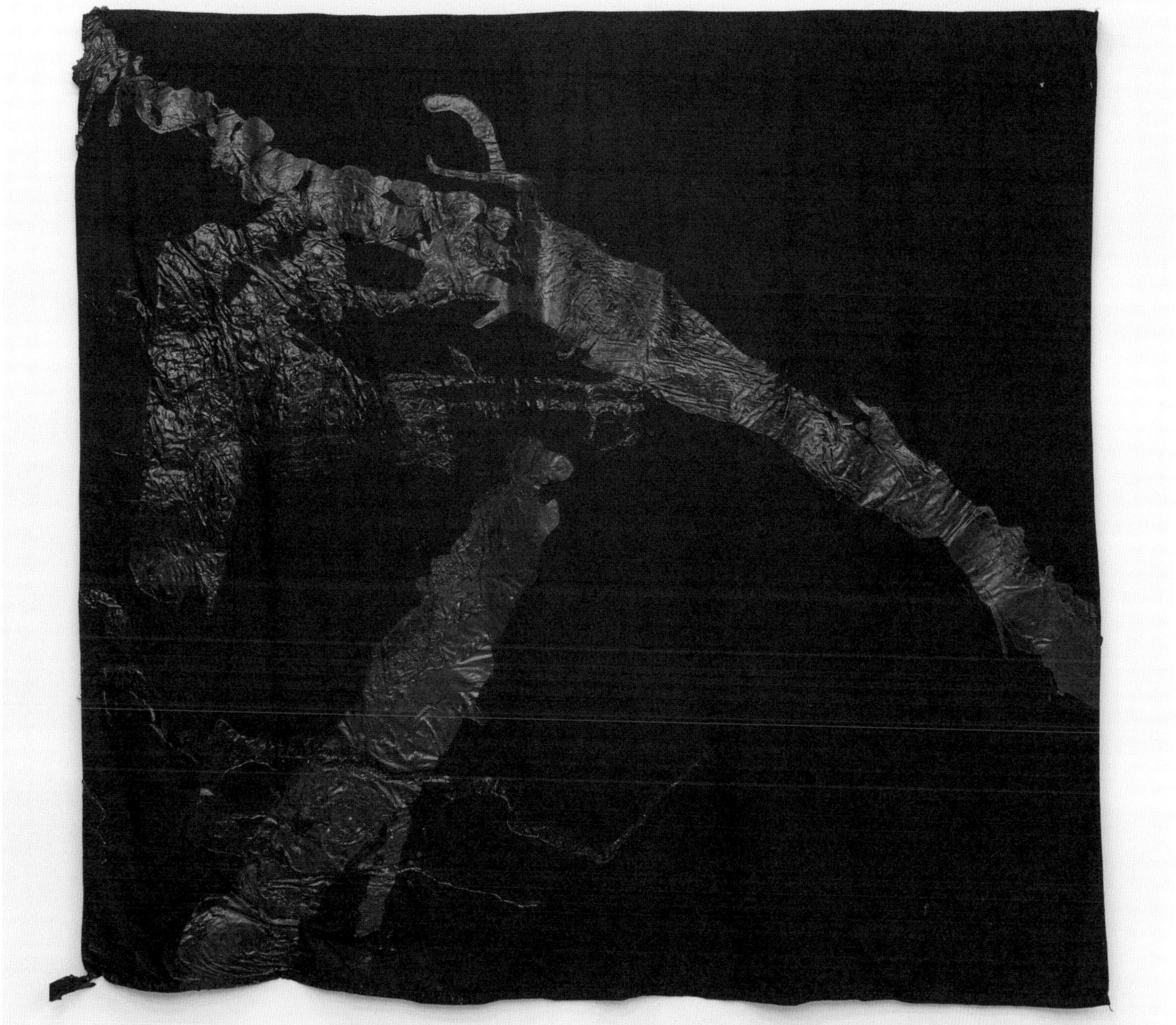

Untitled Landscape #2, 2012

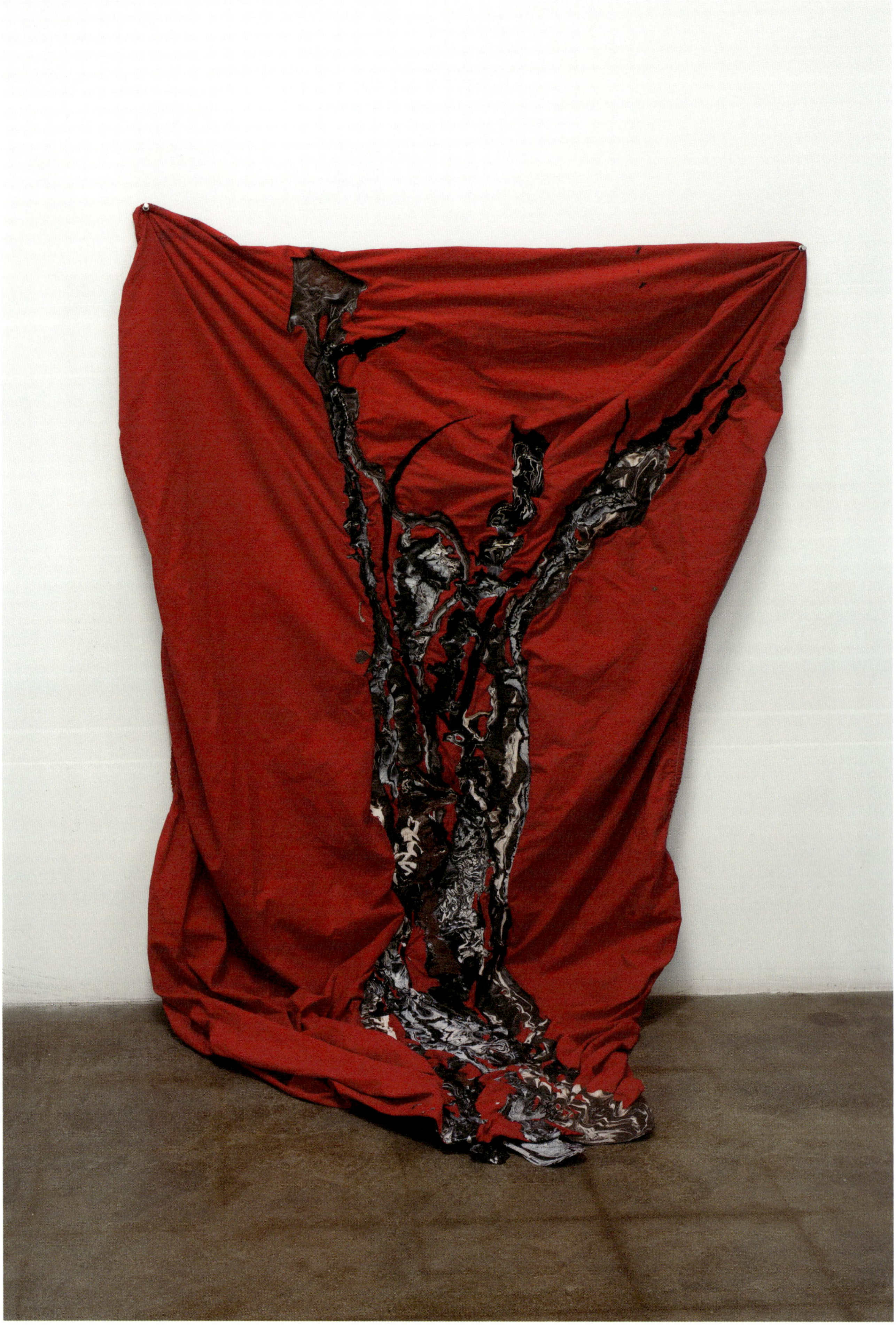

Untitled, 2008–11

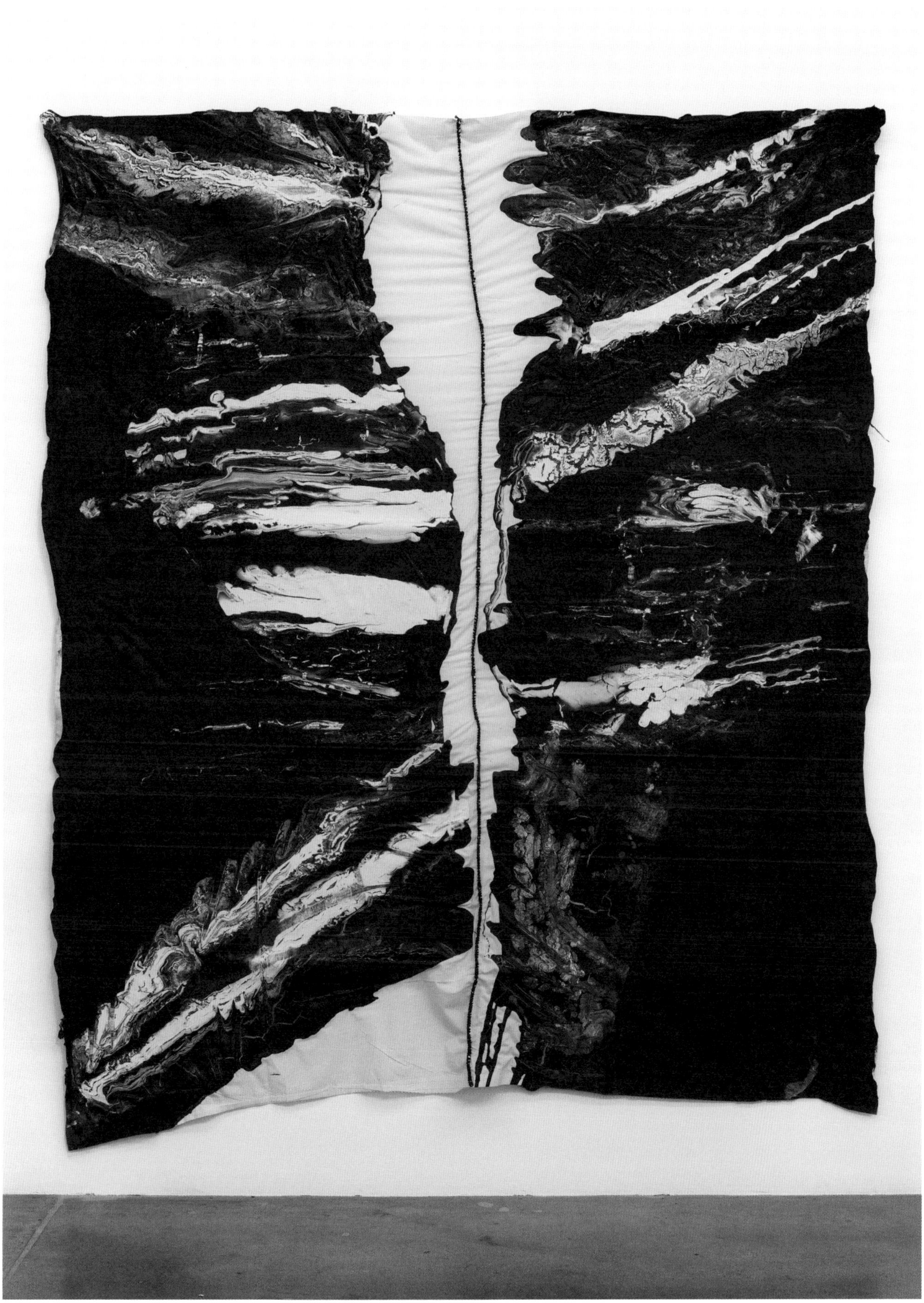

Untitled (zip), 2011

should, I, 2014

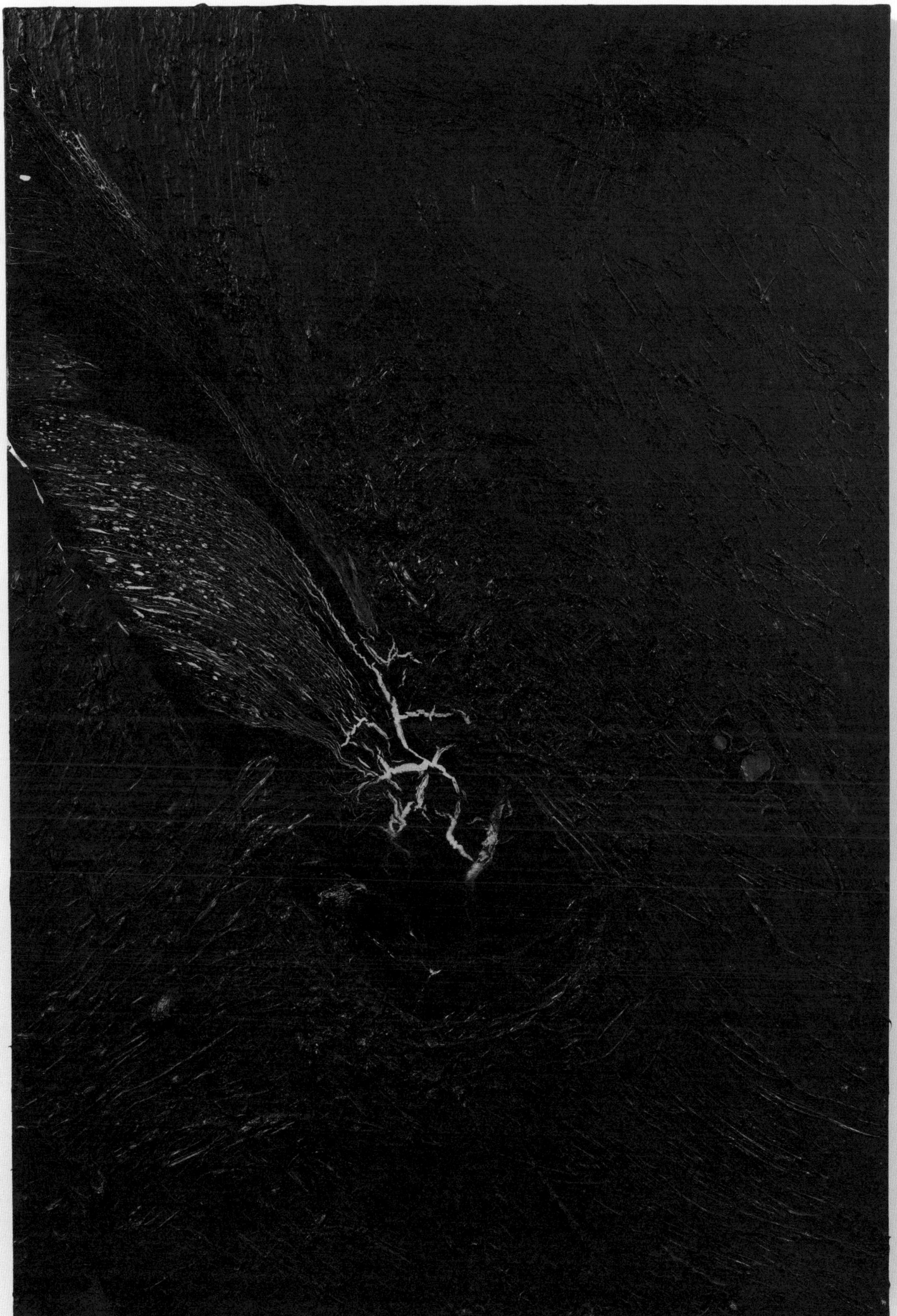

Estuary, 2013

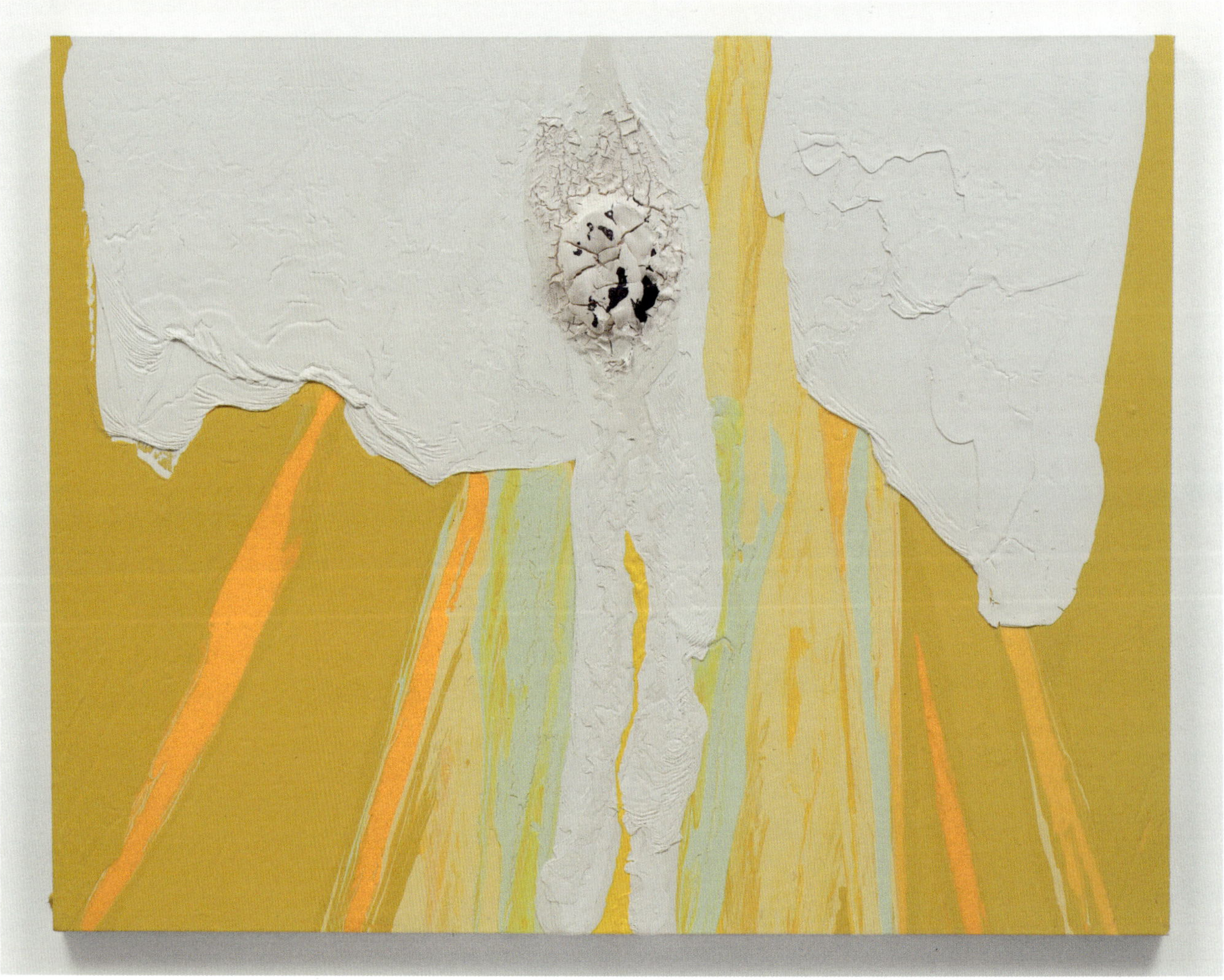

From the Slop: it shines, 2014

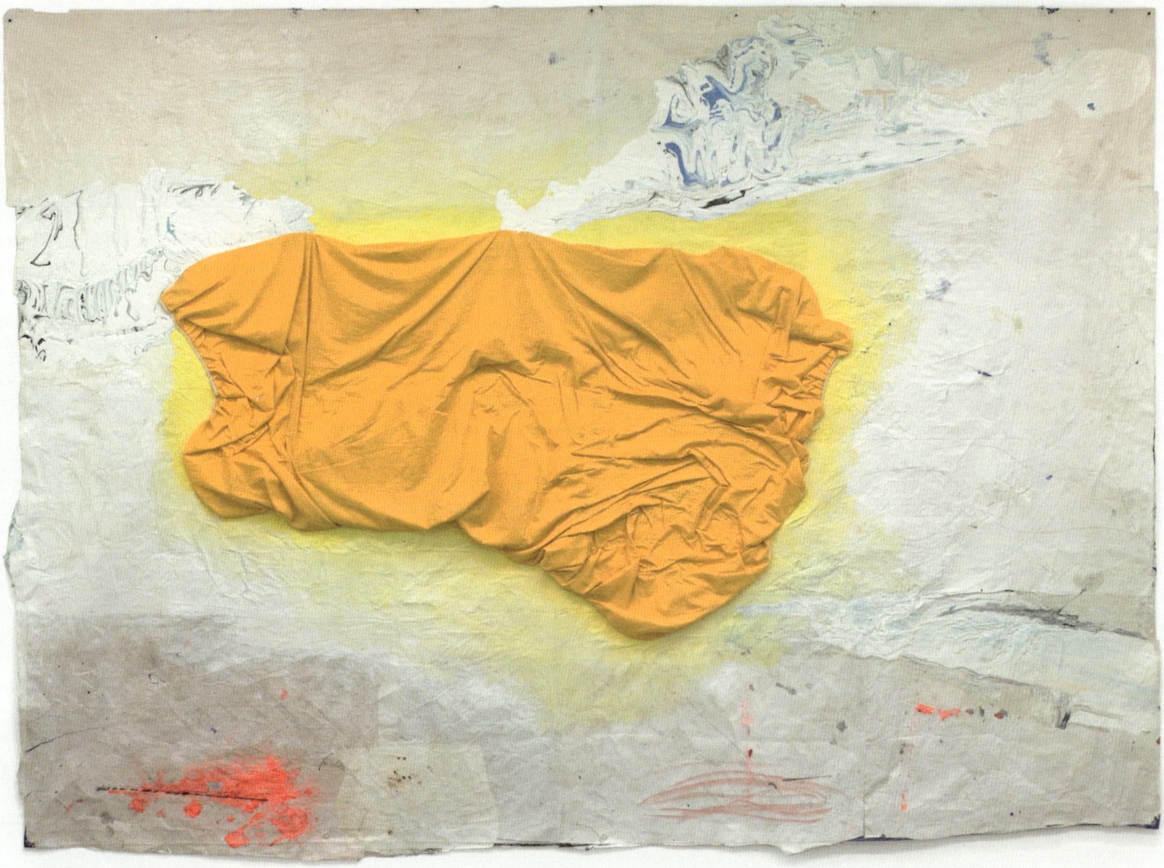

Untitled, 2005/06

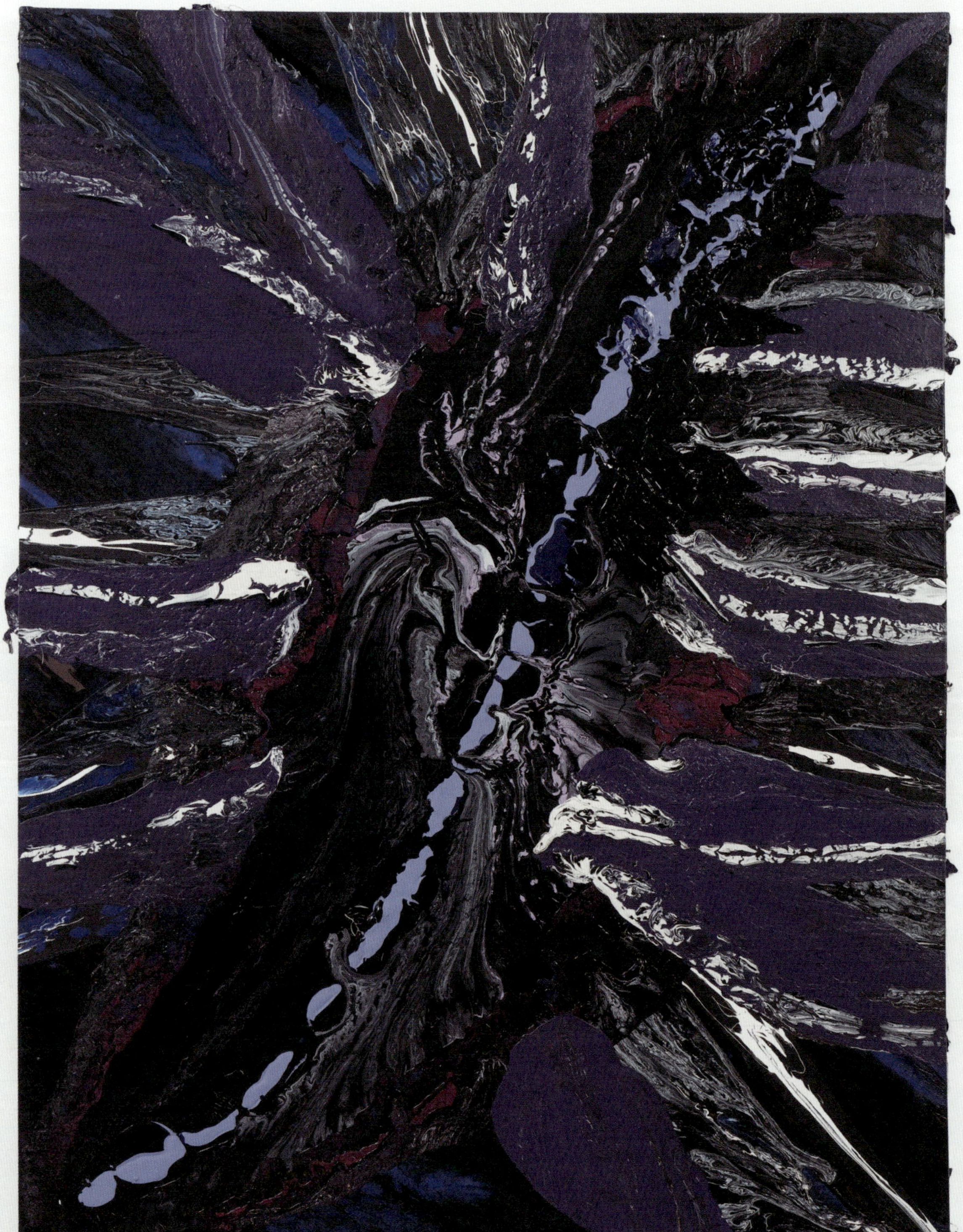

Origins, 2013

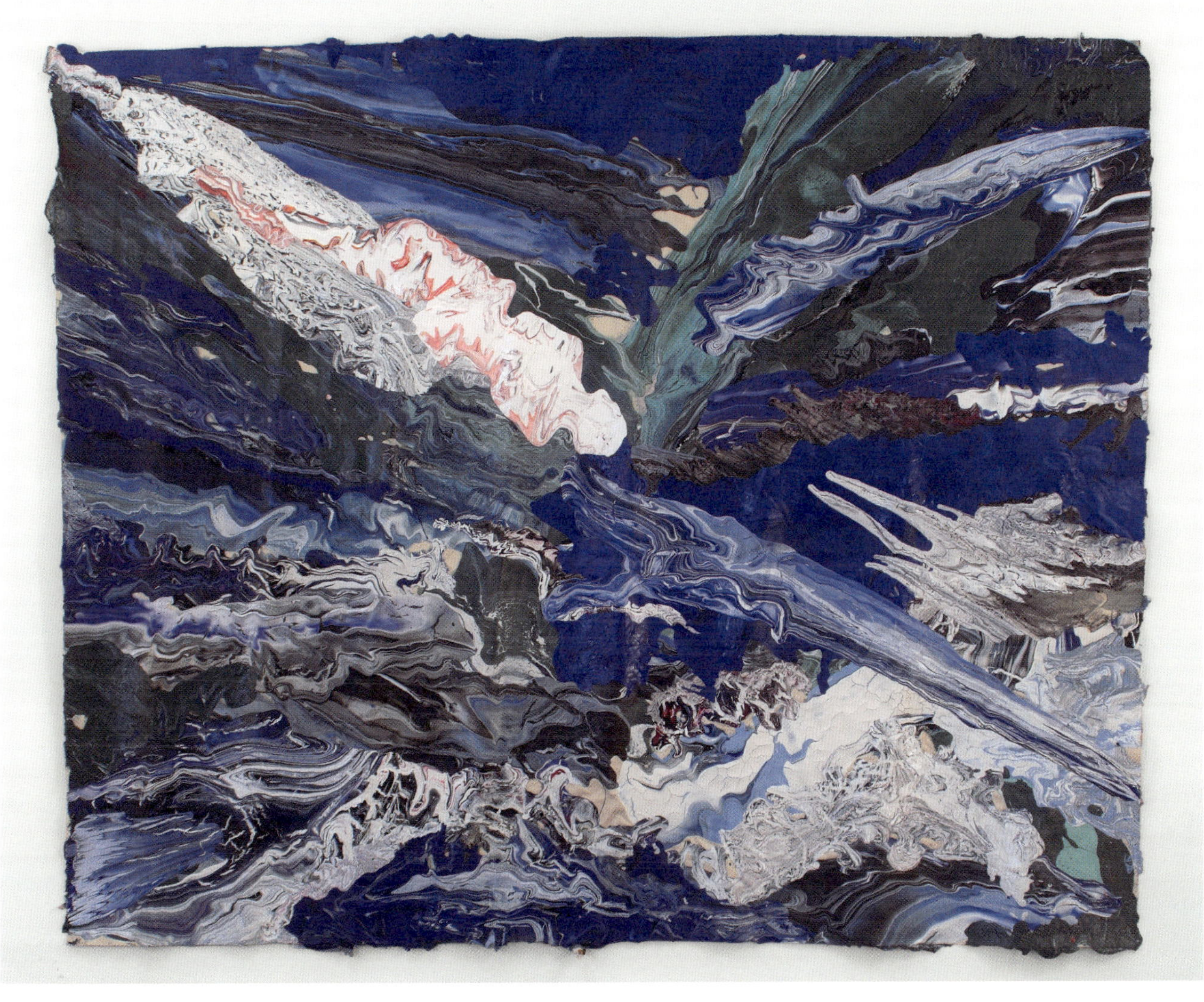

Untitled (sky), 2006

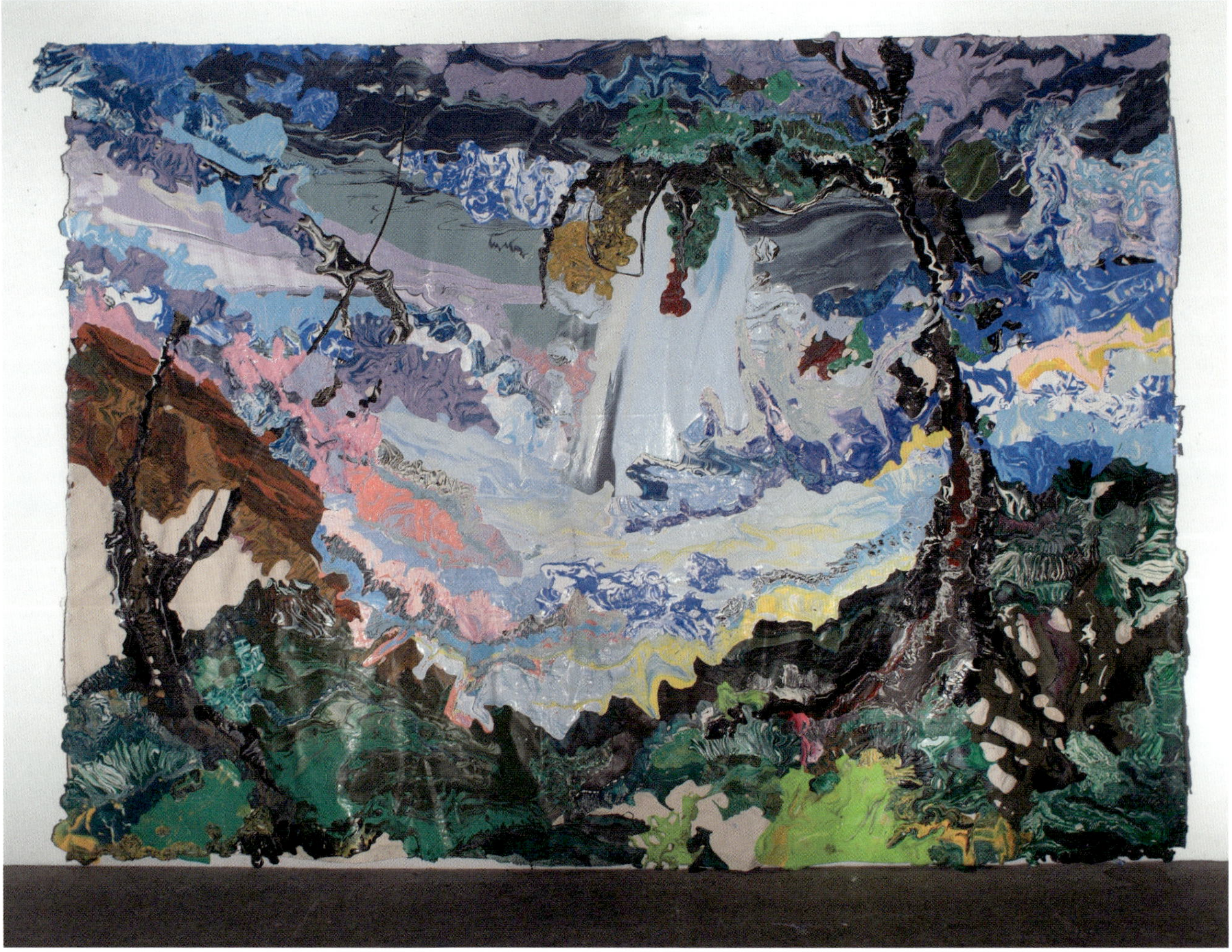

Untitled (Landscape), 2004

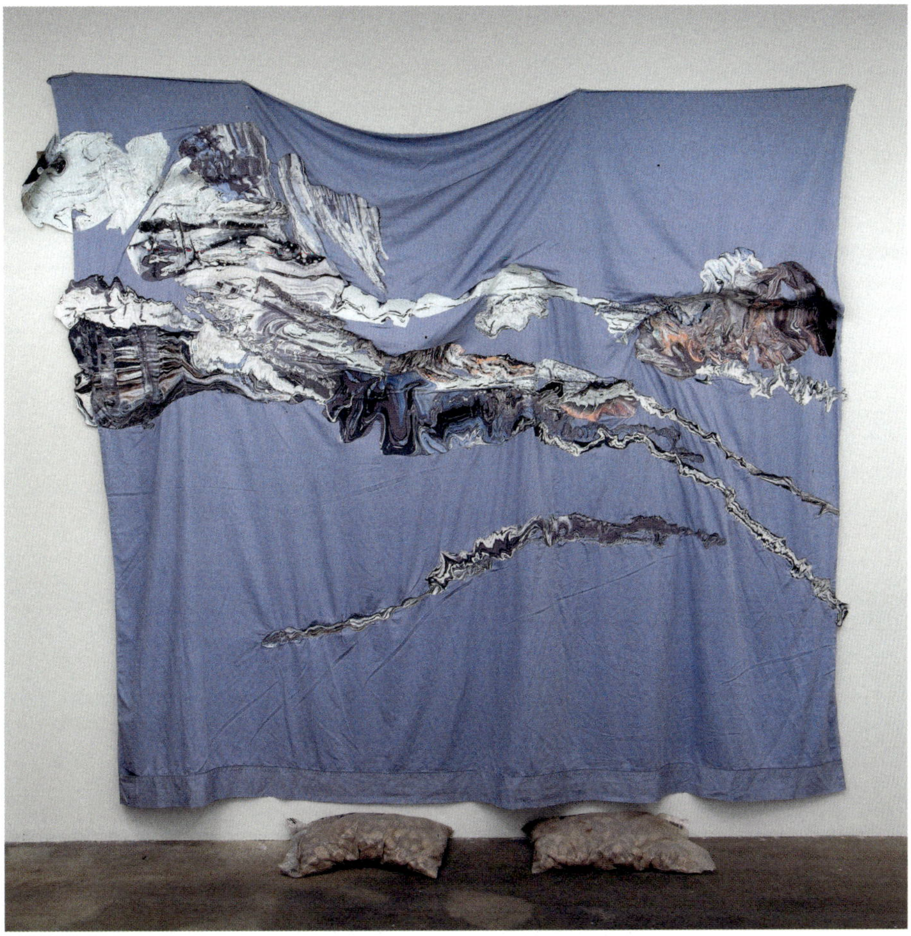

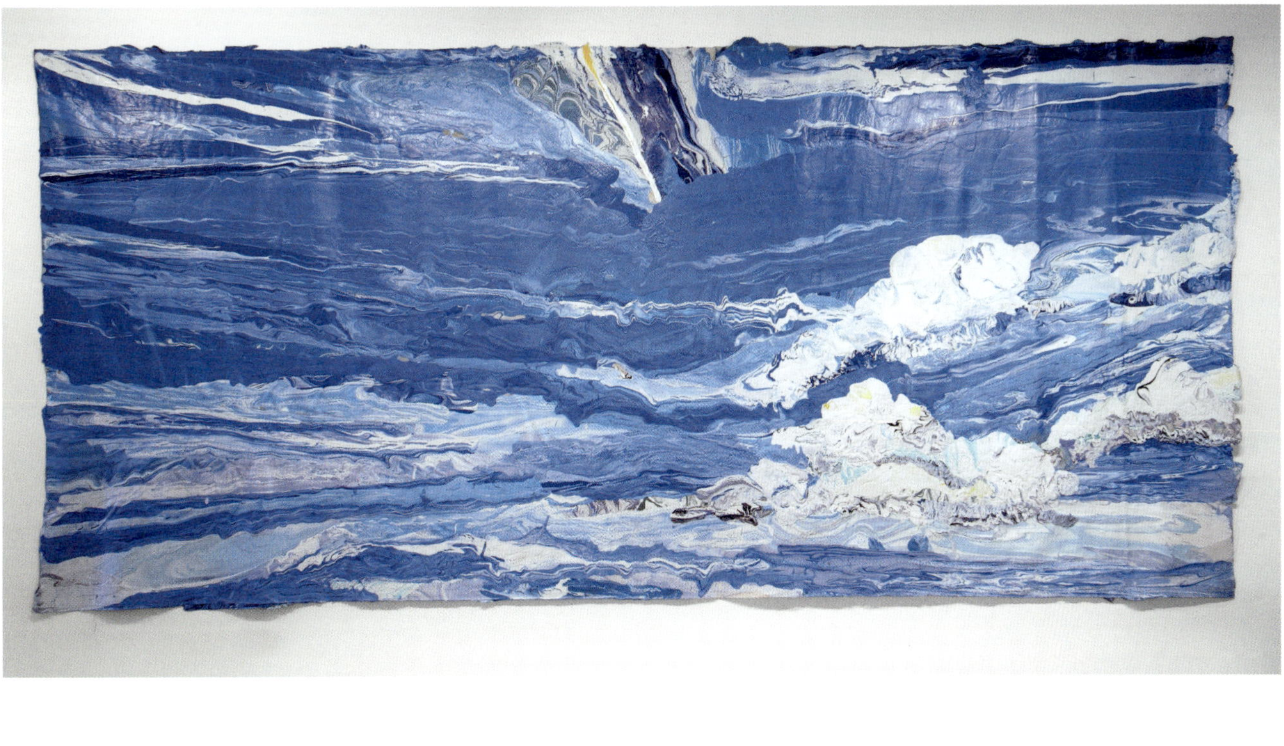

Untitled (for NTAG with love always), 2005
Untitled (Sky), 2006

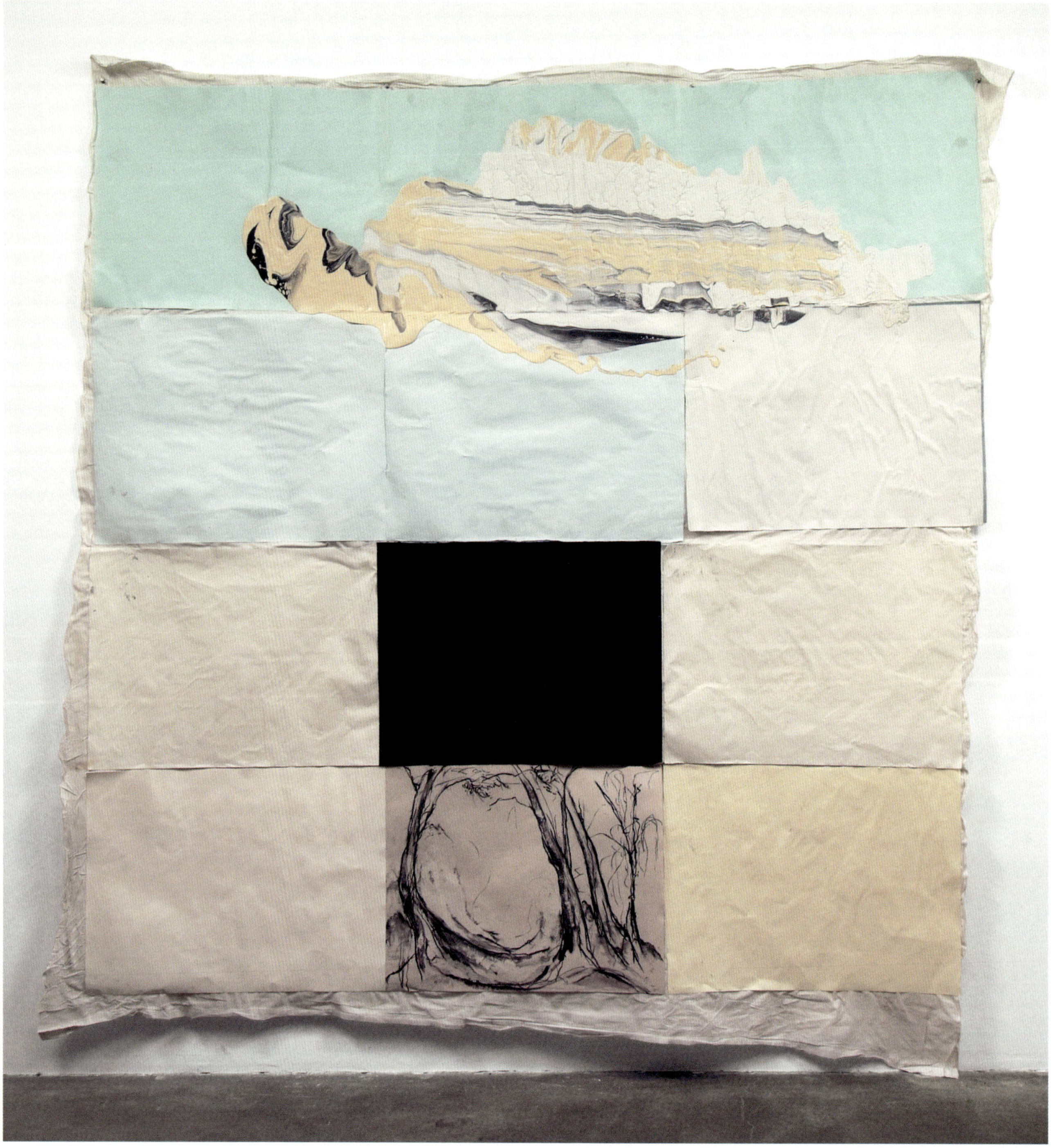

Untitled, 2005

Wildseedling: there are veins in these lands

Rodney McMillian

I

Death is a dream with a beginning, middle, and end.

—Agent Scully, *X Files* (Episode 13, Season 2)

A dream is an answer to a question we don't know how to ask.

—Agent Mulder, *X Files* (Episode 10, Season 4)

FIND A DREAM

2

The paintings are all on bedding materials—bedspreads, blankets, or sheets. The paint is dense in parts, gnarled and hanging and layered. Body parts are suggested as a type of topographical mapping. A mapping that is quite different from American topographical maps detailing the gridding and dividing of land. These works are not about a mythology based on mysticism or an assumption of divined prosperity, they are abstractions, which point to an act of not being able to articulate lived pain. Representing a language of being tongue-tied, emotional, and expressing pathos.

3

I first encountered Bill Traylor's work at the Hirschl & Adler Galleries in New York's Upper East Side in 1997. I would go there and to other galleries in the area on my lunch breaks. I was struck then, as I am now, by the pathos of his work, the bulging eyes (I saw horror and humor in them) of floating figures, human and animal; the blank cardboard, the surface of the paintings; that blankness a stand-in for a landscape that didn't need a description through representation. I saw that representation (the landscape) in the crooked grins, amputated limbs, and the color-blocked shapes that formed his figures.

In the summer of 2008, I began a series of paintings inspired by Traylor. In actuality, there wasn't much of a resemblance to his work, except for one painting of a figure with an erection floating down toward a mountain with a vaginal valley. The mythology of Traylor, the untrained artist, the outsider, was not the allure. I viewed that aspect of his work's reception as a byproduct of the land from which it sprang, a land suffering under the rubric of willful systemic neglect. Plucking this man's art up and inserting it into an art market resembles a land plagued by exploitation, a Columbus-esque discovery, which portends benevolent intentions with oftentimes costly side effects. When viewing his work, I think about the relationship between the land and my body, and bodies. I think about the rate of exchange between his work's insertion into a market and the histories that inspired the images he made. I don't think that rate can be determined. I have often wondered how it could be more properly addressed.

4

Octavia Butler, an African American feminist and writer, and Samuel R. Delaney, both known for their science-fiction literature, have been important touchstones and references for the work I've made over the past seven years. The title for the series of paintings in this exhibition, *Wildseedling,* draws directly from Butler's book *Wild Seed,* from the collection "Seed to Harvest." She and Delaney, as well as other Afrofuturists, offer emancipatory theories that provide escape clauses. They remind me that reality can be a state of mind, an idea of transformation that can be experienced through the body or a site. While reading *Wild Seed,* I was drawn to the transformative abilities of characters such as Anyanwu as well as Doro with his skin-snatching powers. They are able to move through, out of, into, or to a something or a someplace through their bodies and the bodies of others. The orifices, tubular forms, and cavities I've employed in my work are portals, sites of transformation, confounding Euro-ethnic patriarchal stereotyping of Black bodies.

a Mouth: and the galaxy within (2012–15, page 116) is a painting depicting outer space in the interior of an orifice. In outer space, there is no sound or light—it is infinite; and the piece alludes to a primal scream that cannot be heard. This scream is no longer coming out of a man standing on a bridge, as in Munch's *The Scream* (1893–1910). It has been relocated onto an item associated with domestic spaces, a bedsheet. I see in it a relationship to Bataille's "Mouth," which he speaks of as a body part that can become aligned with the spine when frightened, as a defense mechanism. The silence/outer space that is represented in *a Mouth* can be viewed as a machination of defense or one of infinite possibility. Most mouths can create sounds, but then it's also a matter of direction: is that sound projected out or is it vacuumed in?

Gaps: the place where this land's history, individual and collective understandings of political identity, and the powers that shape and inform those formations are lived. I am interested in the material spaces of a bed as well as the imagined/conjured ones of dreams. I'm gleaning, absorbing, piecing together myriad texts, histories, music, and sounds to make representations of this process of synthesis—making sense and making absurd the histories and political circumstances in which I live.

5

I couldn't care less about the modernist tradition of painting. I feel that way about all the possible mediums, forms, or materials I use. I only care about what can be communicated through them. There are some conversations that can only be had through painting...and that's when I decide to paint—to embrace specific processes that denote the ideas needed at that time or for a particular thought.

All of the paintings in *Wildseedling* were born from an evaluation of early American landscape paintings, mainly the Hudson River School paintings. They were tools of propaganda used to expound notions of Manifest Destiny, a belief system propelling early Americans to pioneer and conquer the West. They labored under that Divine Providence to expand our national domain. They carved the land into a grid following the north/south, east/west coordinates of a map regardless of rivers, canyons, mountains, etc.; a schematic for spirituality that not only defined a nation, but also justified through reason that nation's dominance over indigenous people and the land. The art made during that time not only corroborated this story, but was also symbolic of those beliefs. The Hudson River School artists made sweeping landscapes with a westward movement—a religious art devoid of biblical iconography; an art for conquerors without a sign of spilled blood or the abject. Those paintings served as forms of indoctrination, a sublime sun/son landing on the heads of those not warned.

My paintings are the opposite of that colonialist endeavor. They are an attempt to map the endeavor's aftereffects onto ideas of how we perceive and represent a body. The sheets, blankets, or bedspreads are placeholders for a body. But there is no body. There isn't even a ghost. It is an understood absence. There are levels of gestural abstraction that are often confined to a shape that then can spill outside of the frame, but the body has been absorbed, dismembered, or disappeared into the materials and the image and the process.

I'm interested in blood, guts, and gore; and although these works are allegorical, I know full well how problematic the allegorical is, because of the remove, the distance it produces. It's the problem I have not only with most of my work, but also most works in general. The one thing that ebbs this flow away from fatalist thinking is that I remember what art (visual art, literature, music, film, etc.) has offered me. It has created an opening to alternate perspectives, and portals into different ways of constructing the realities and the landscape I inherited. I desperately needed and need those possibilities. I was born in Columbia, South Carolina, the state's capital. The statehouse still bears the marks from Sherman's inland assault during the Civil War. South Carolina was also the first state to vote to secede from the Union, which it did in 1860. The Confederate flag flew over the statehouse from 1962 until 2000, when it was removed and placed onto a flagpole in front of the building. This was the concession to protests for its removal from atop the statehouse. This history is no more or less indicative of the social and racial ills plaguing this great land. It just happens to be where I am from and from where I sought escape. In many ways, I am still in need, even in the perceived paradise that is Los Angeles, California.

That's why I reread and teach Adrian Piper's "The Logic of Modernism" about twice a year. It doesn't provide room for "art for art's sake." It treats that idea as an ideological position. There is no nature, no inherent belief systems, and especially, no inherent desires within this vocation. Art is an act of conscious making. Piper's text offers a perspective that squares painting into a lineage of political and cultural awareness and response. This thinking was clear to me the moment I decided I needed to make a performance for a video. If a painting could have done the job, I would have made one.

The paintings are descriptions of what sleeping in this land can be like for some folks like me—an uncomfortable and sometimes unbearable abstraction. Since the time I could walk and talk, I have been aware that every time I leave my house, I can be misidentified and end up with a State-sanctioned bullet to the head. My paintings are about representation—representing an image, idea, or process. There is no way to represent trauma. I have no interest in trying to. I'm more interested in presenting a representation of a lived state that includes trauma. The *Wildseedling* works are intended as conversations about our shared experiences.

And I'm back to thinking of Bill Traylor. I think about all of the hardship, terror, and brutality any Black man during his time experienced either firsthand or from firsthand knowledge, and yet he made art. Sometimes, I can't make sense of it any more than I can make sense of anything else that's going on in the world or driving my work or the work of others. We all have struggles and yet that is not enough. Like *Wild Seed*'s Anyanwu, I simply understand the desire to transform into a dolphin, earthworm, sea sponge, or panther for play or necessity.

With art, I get to be, when the cells are aligned, like one of Prince's yelps—disembodied and yet from a body, independent, but not without a context and relationship to other notes. It is a precise utterance or is layered onto other sounds to accentuate or declare a point, a perspective—a glorious thing to be.

6

About five or six years ago, I was home visiting childhood friends who had either moved back to or never left Columbia. We went to a large karaoke restaurant and were about seven to nine people deep. When we got there, we entered from the foyer (there is a door that separates the restaurant/singing area from the entrance) and everyone in the place was singing "Dixie." I was ready to get the fuck up out of there. But our table was ready and my friends decided we should be seated—I was a "guest." I later asked them why; how could it be ok to stay there? I remember something said to the effect of, "The song was almost over so it's no big deal. And if we left every time there was something like this going on, there'd be no place to go."

"Fly me to the moon..."

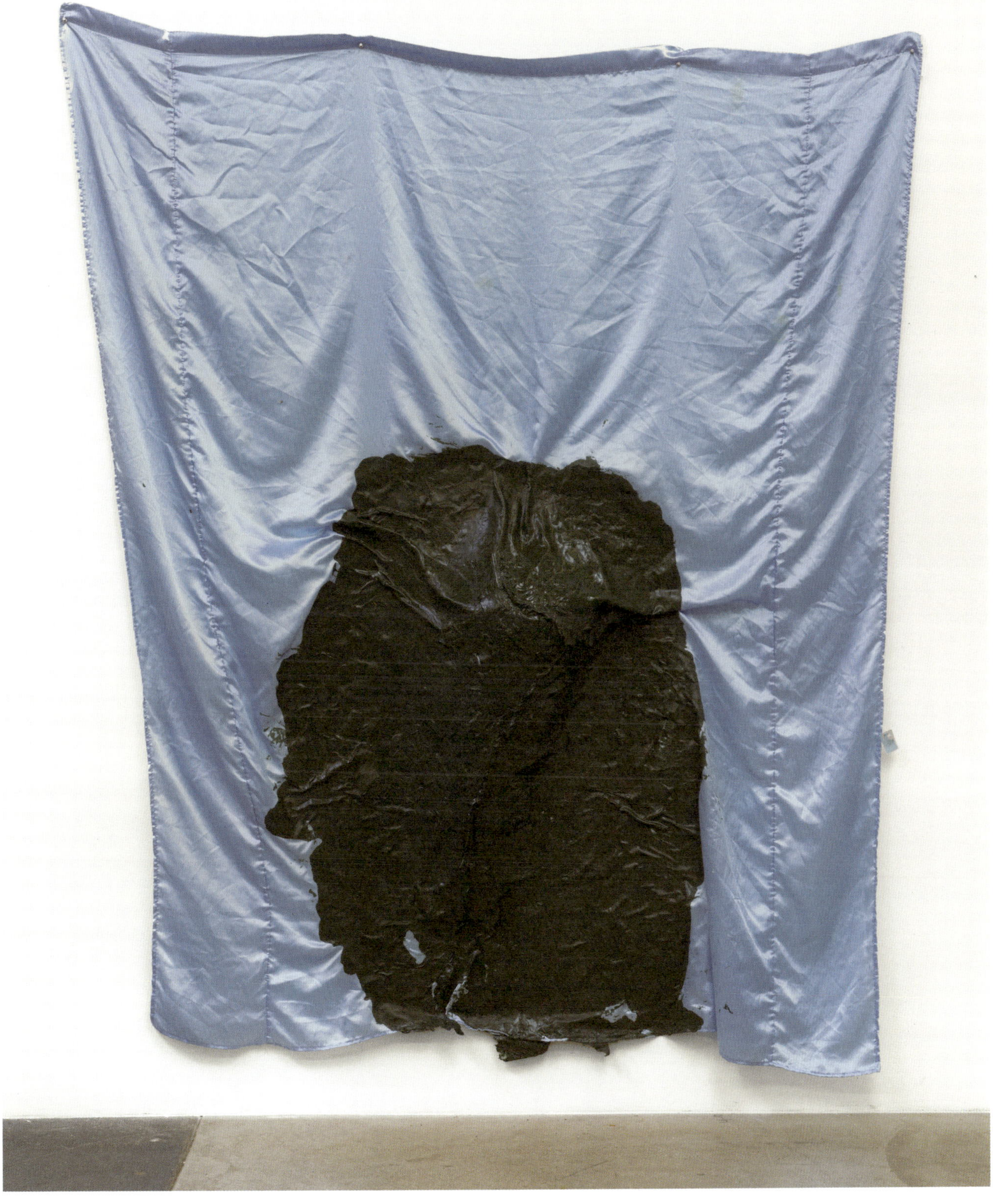

Wildseedling: it was already there, 2014–15

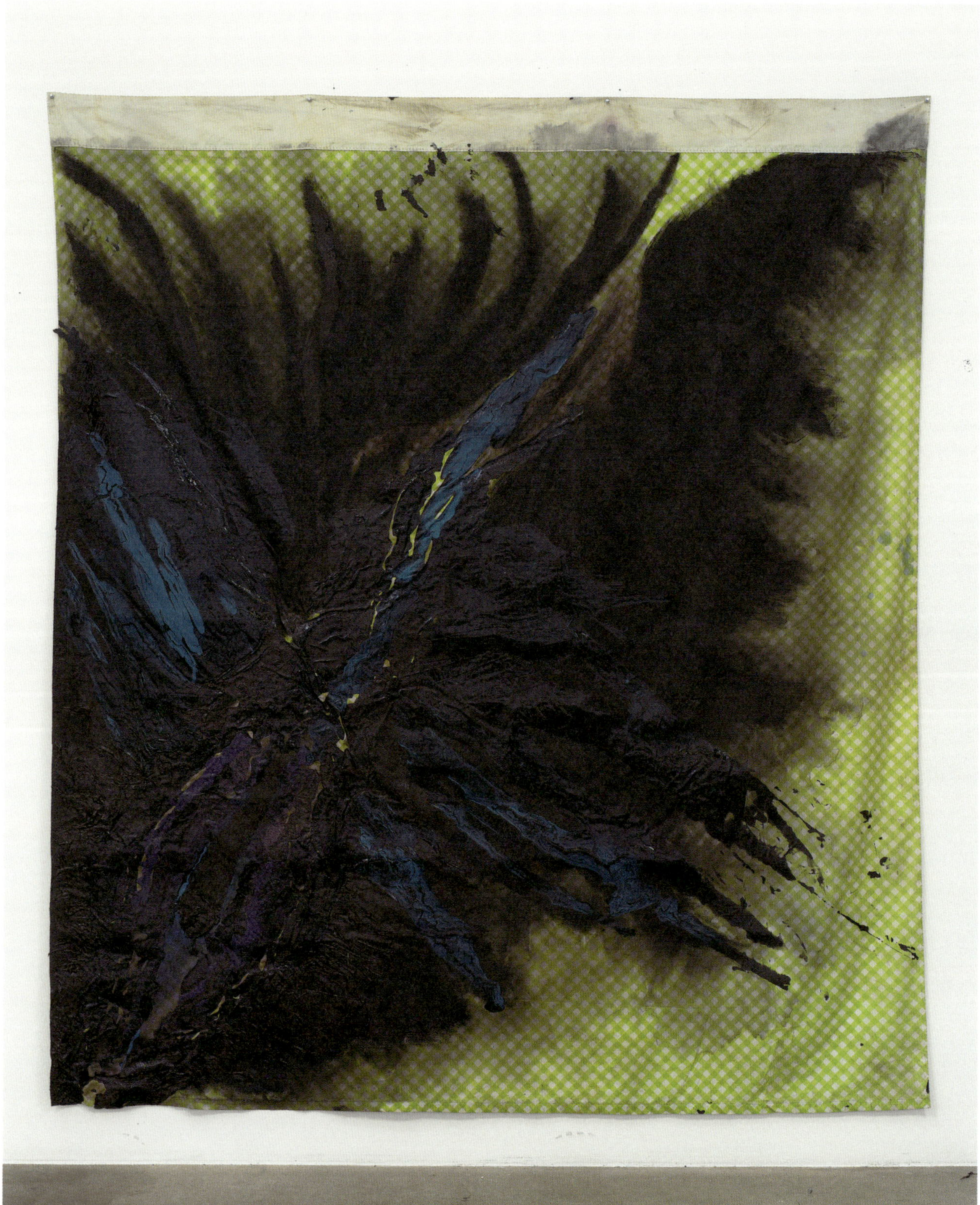

Site #1: an origin narrative, 2008–13

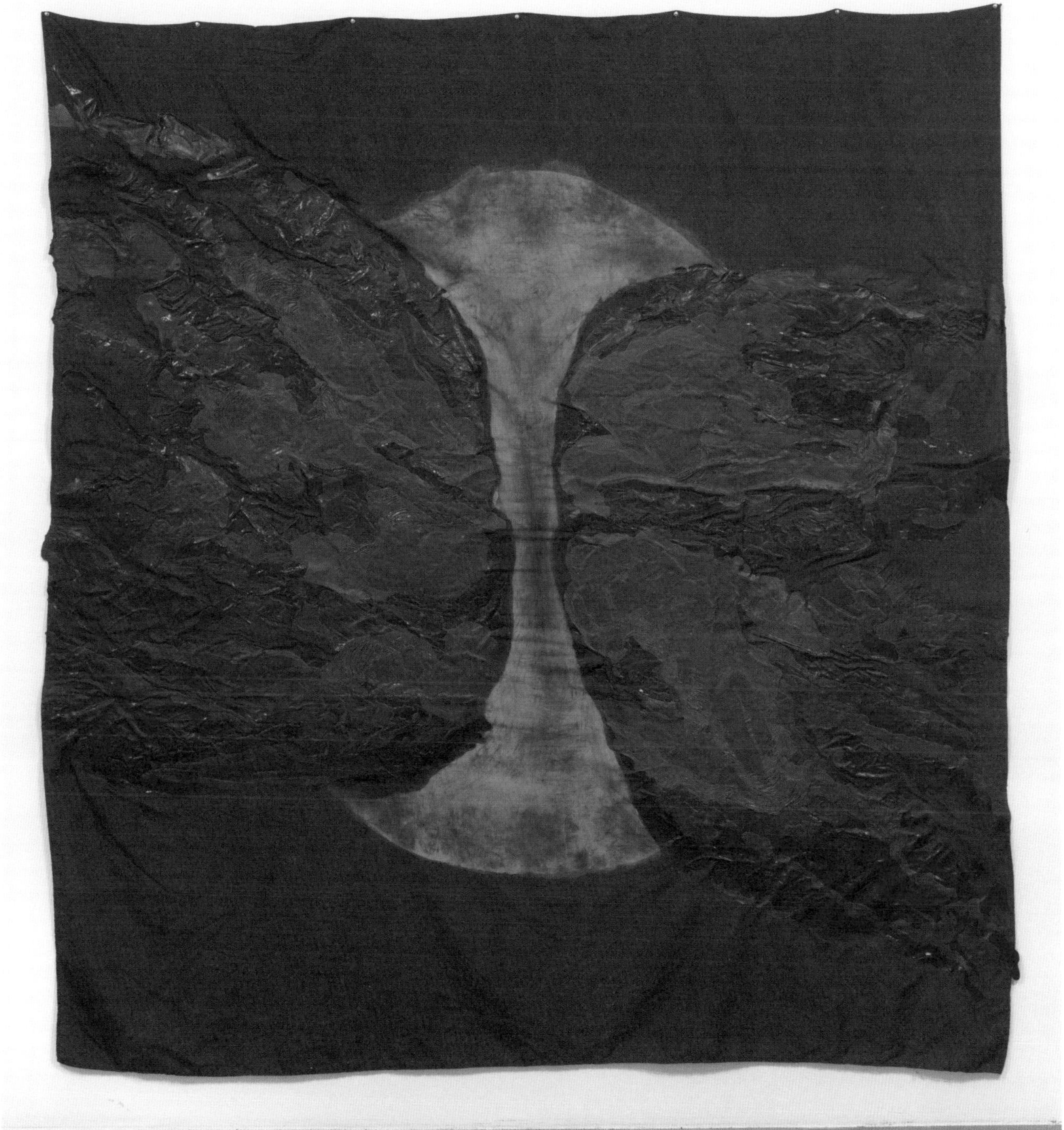

Blue Sun, 2014–15

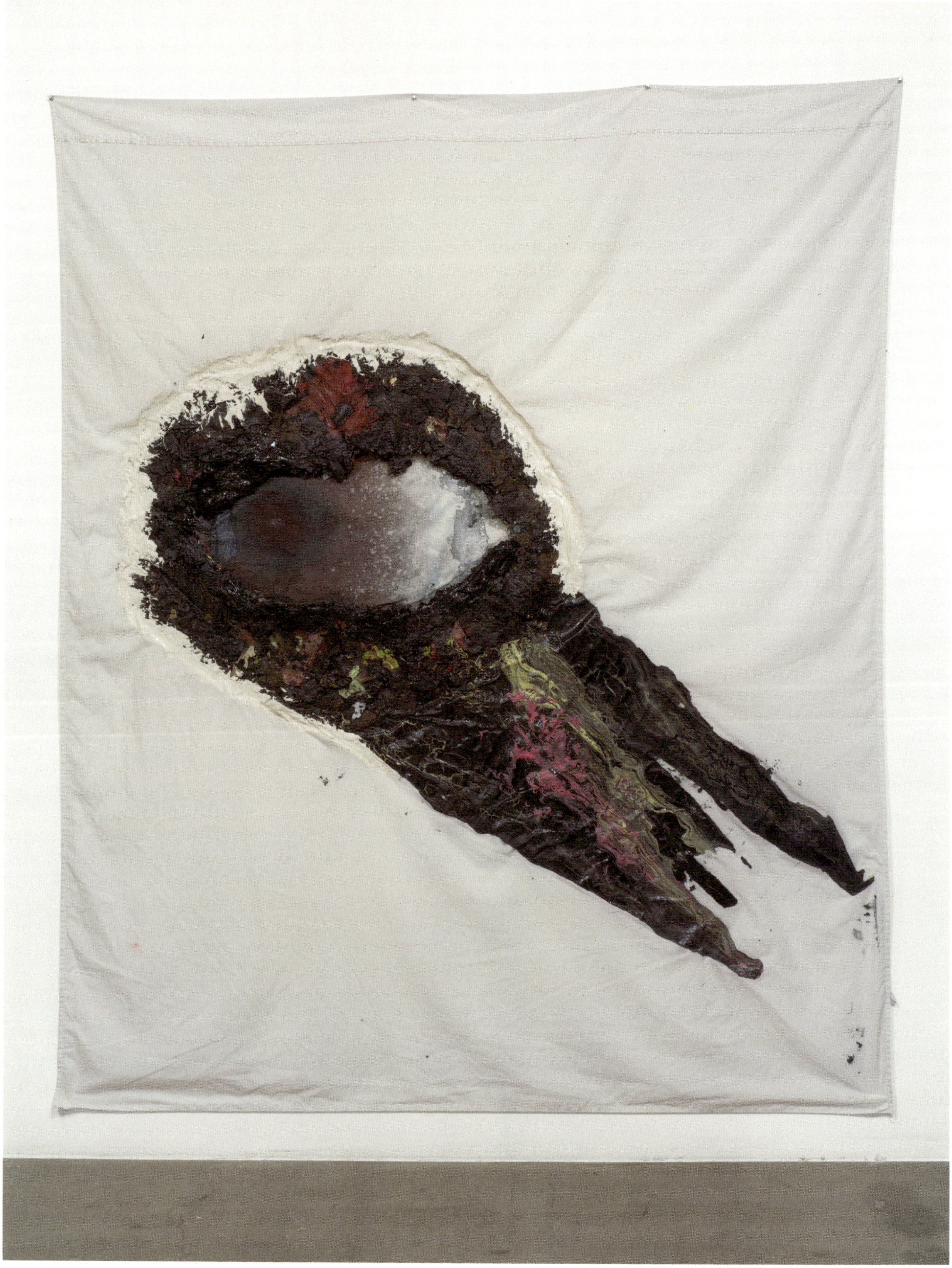

a Mouth: and the galaxy within, 2012–15

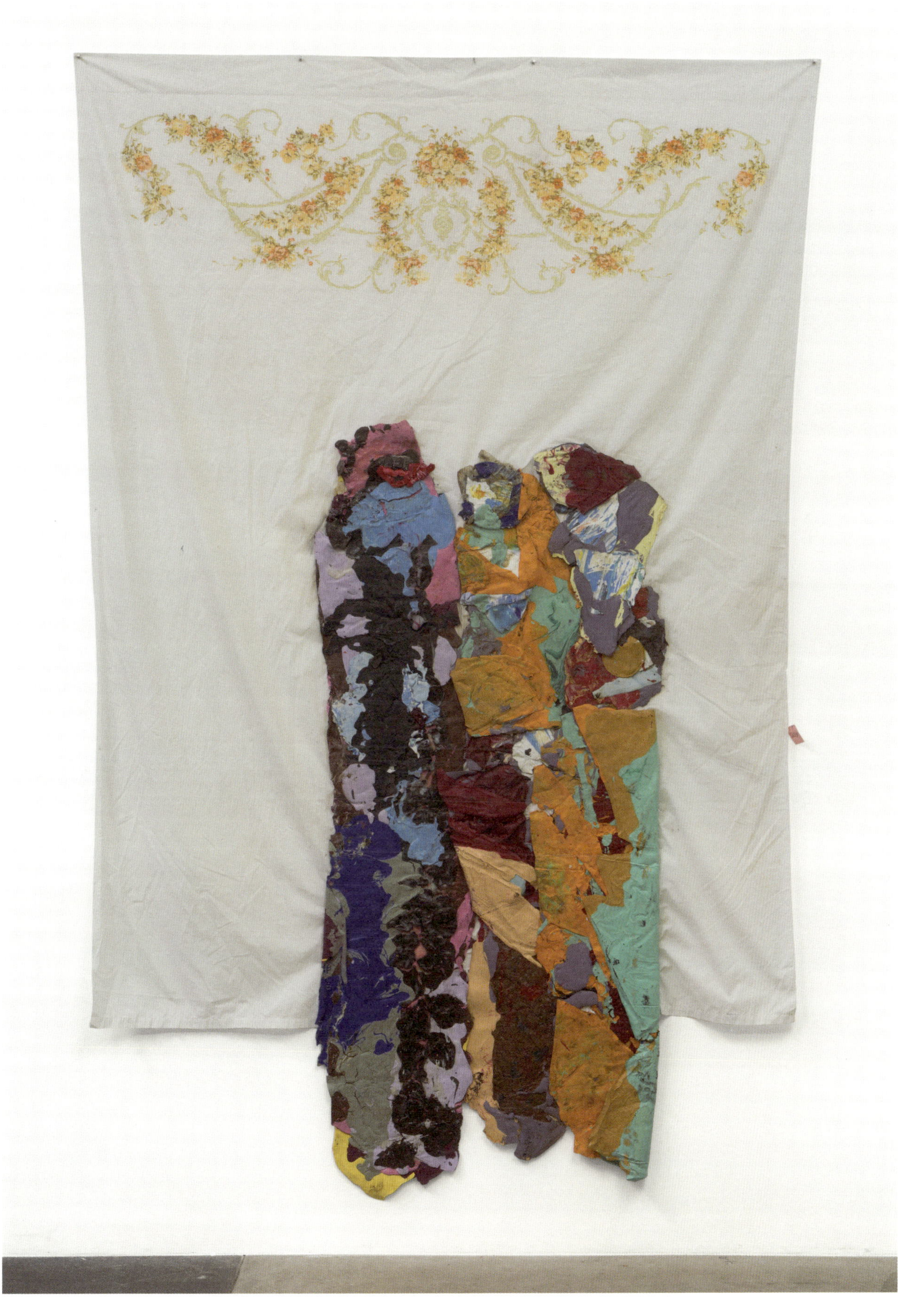

Site #3: stumps in plain sight, 2008–14

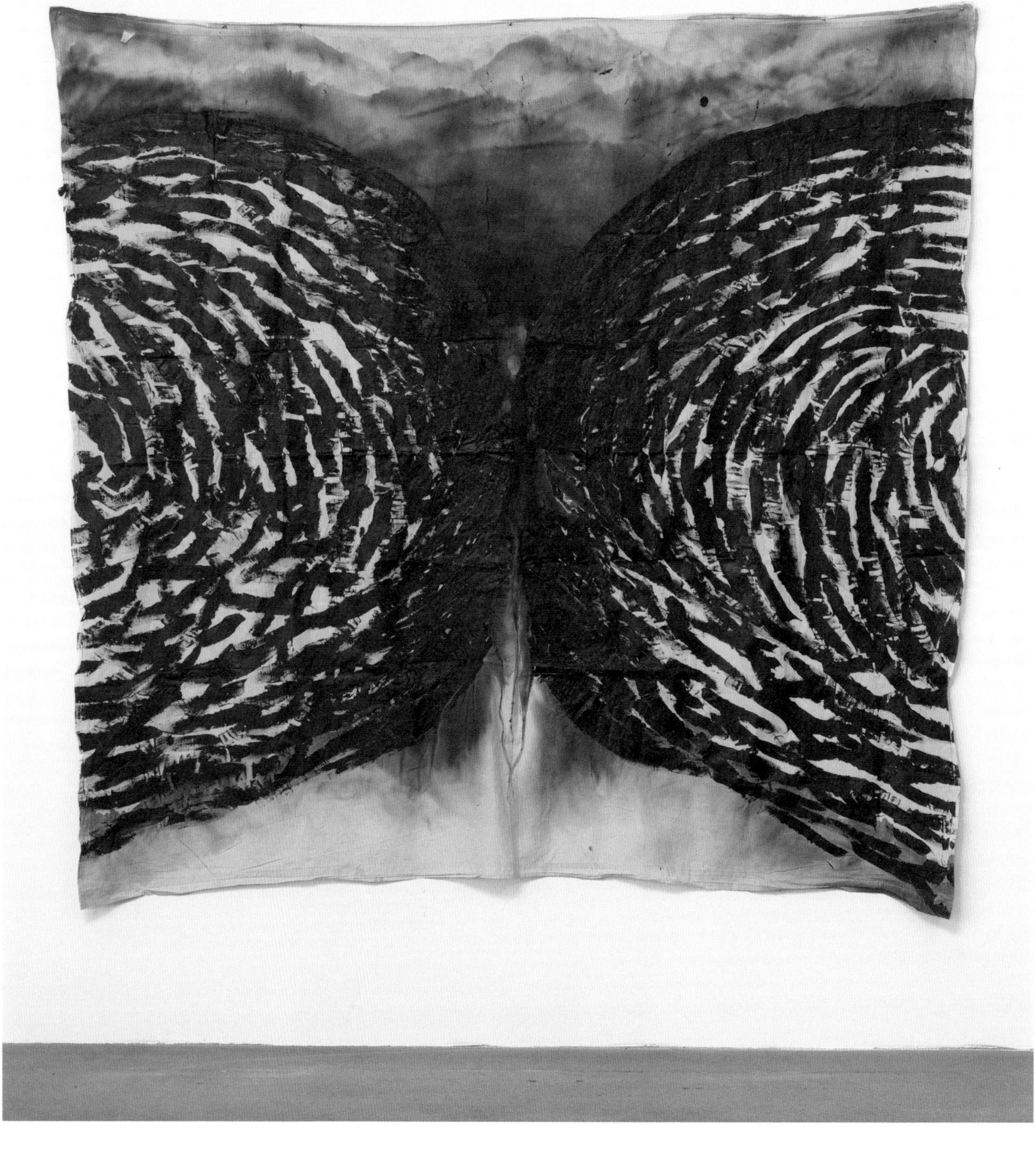

Untitled (for B. Traylor), II, 2008

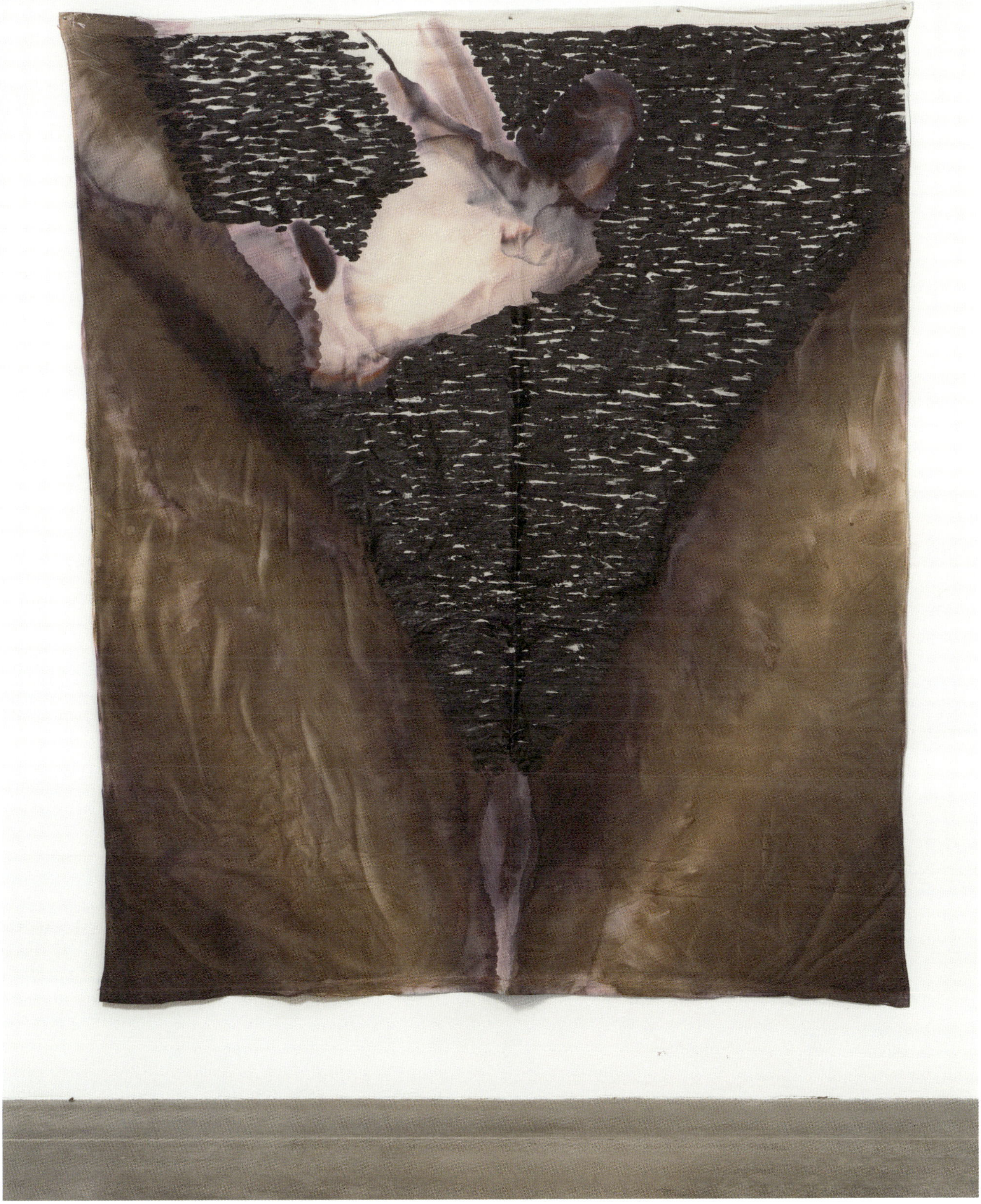

Untitled (for B. Traylor), I, 2008

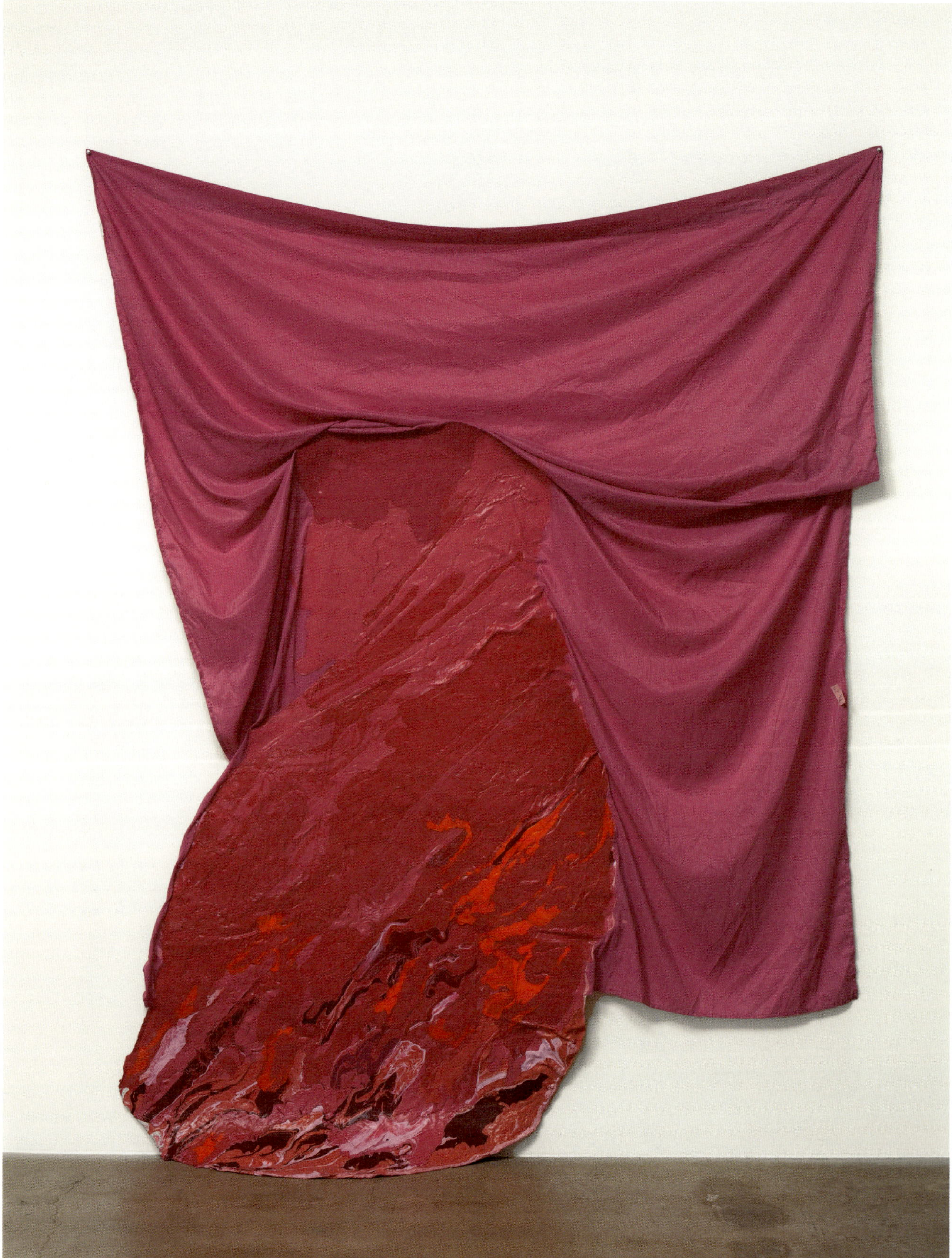

Untitled (tongue), 2014

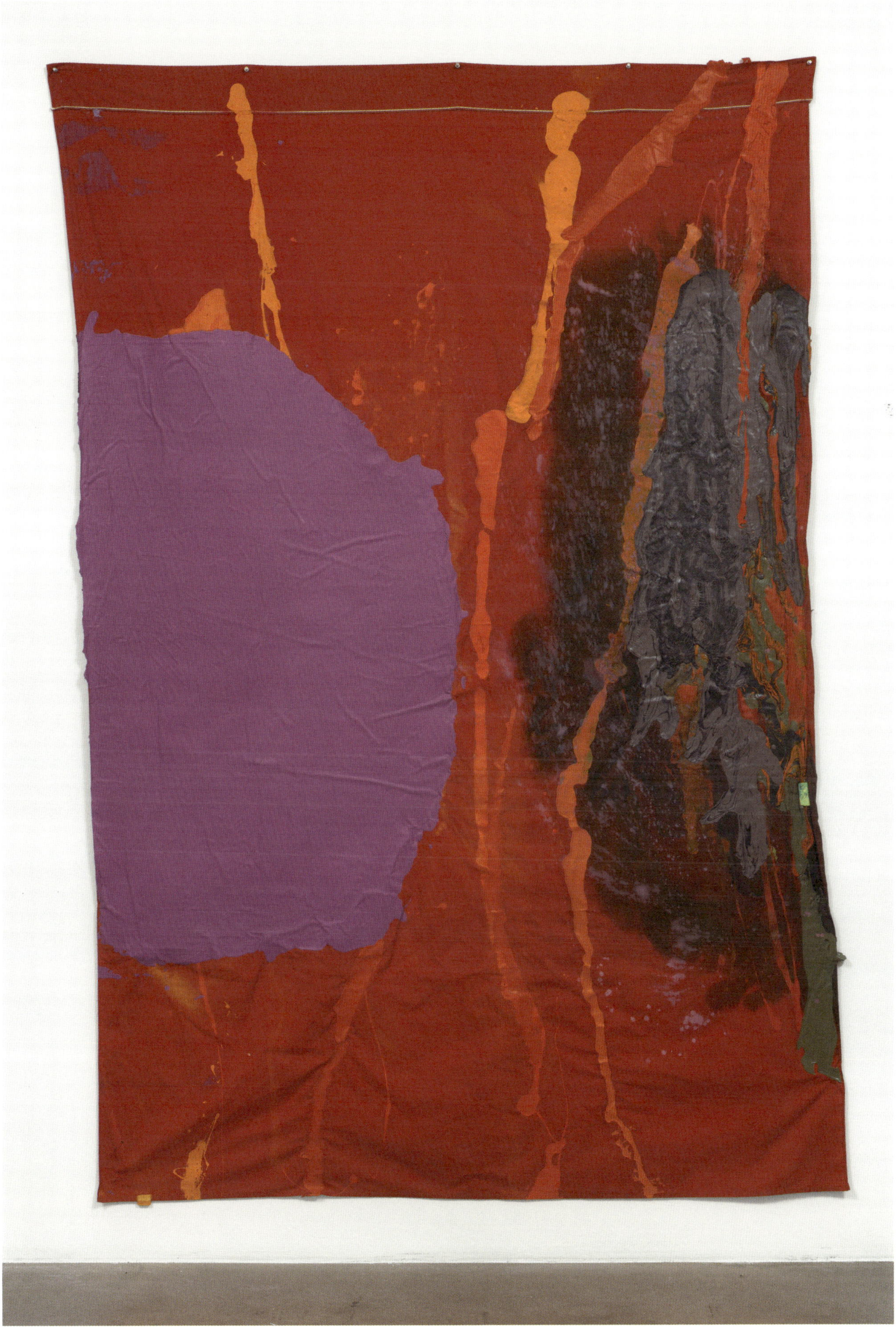

Purple Moon, 2014–15

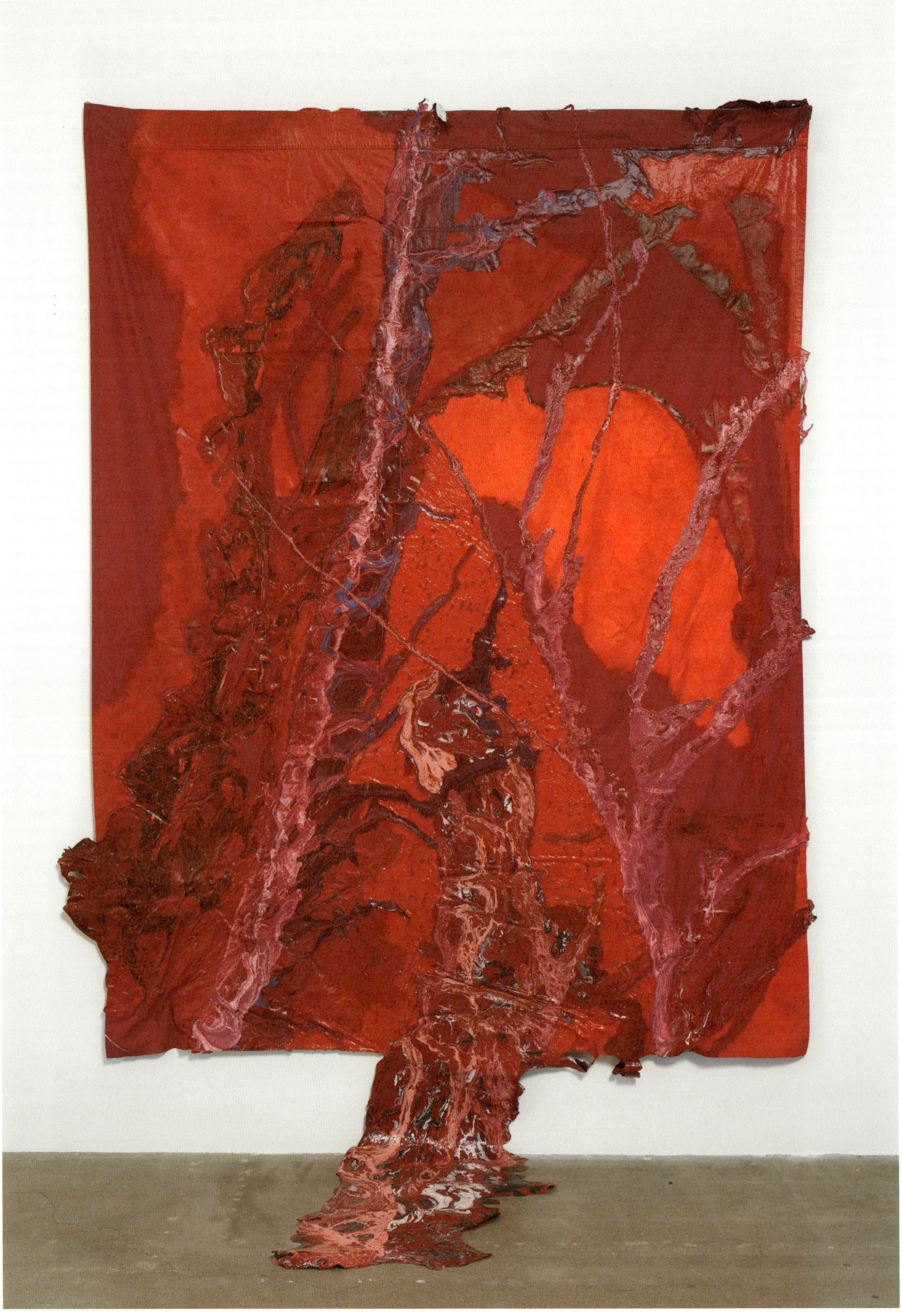

There are veins in these lands, I, 2007–13

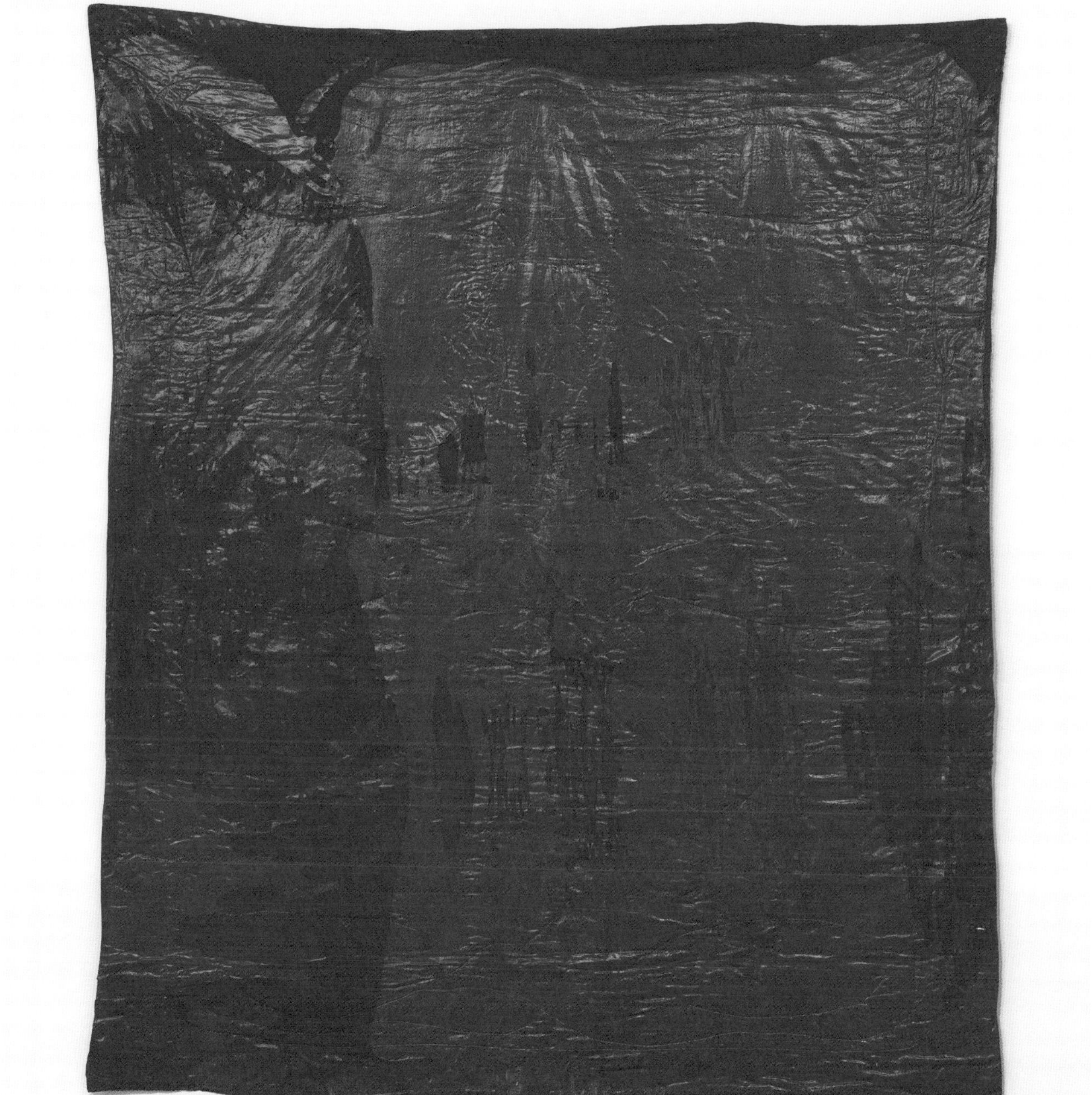

Untitled (for Francine Hughes), 2008–14

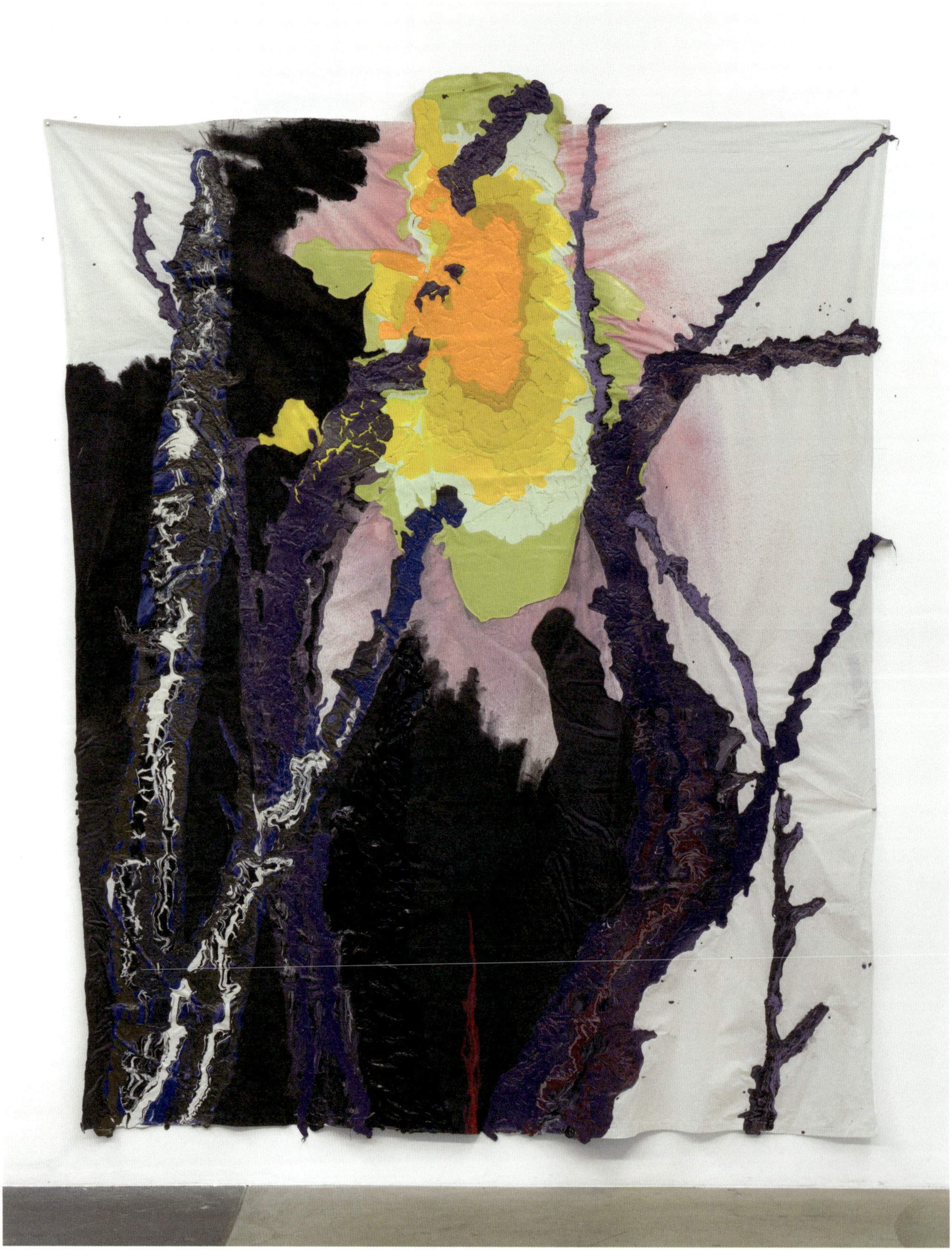

There are veins in these lands, II, 2010–14

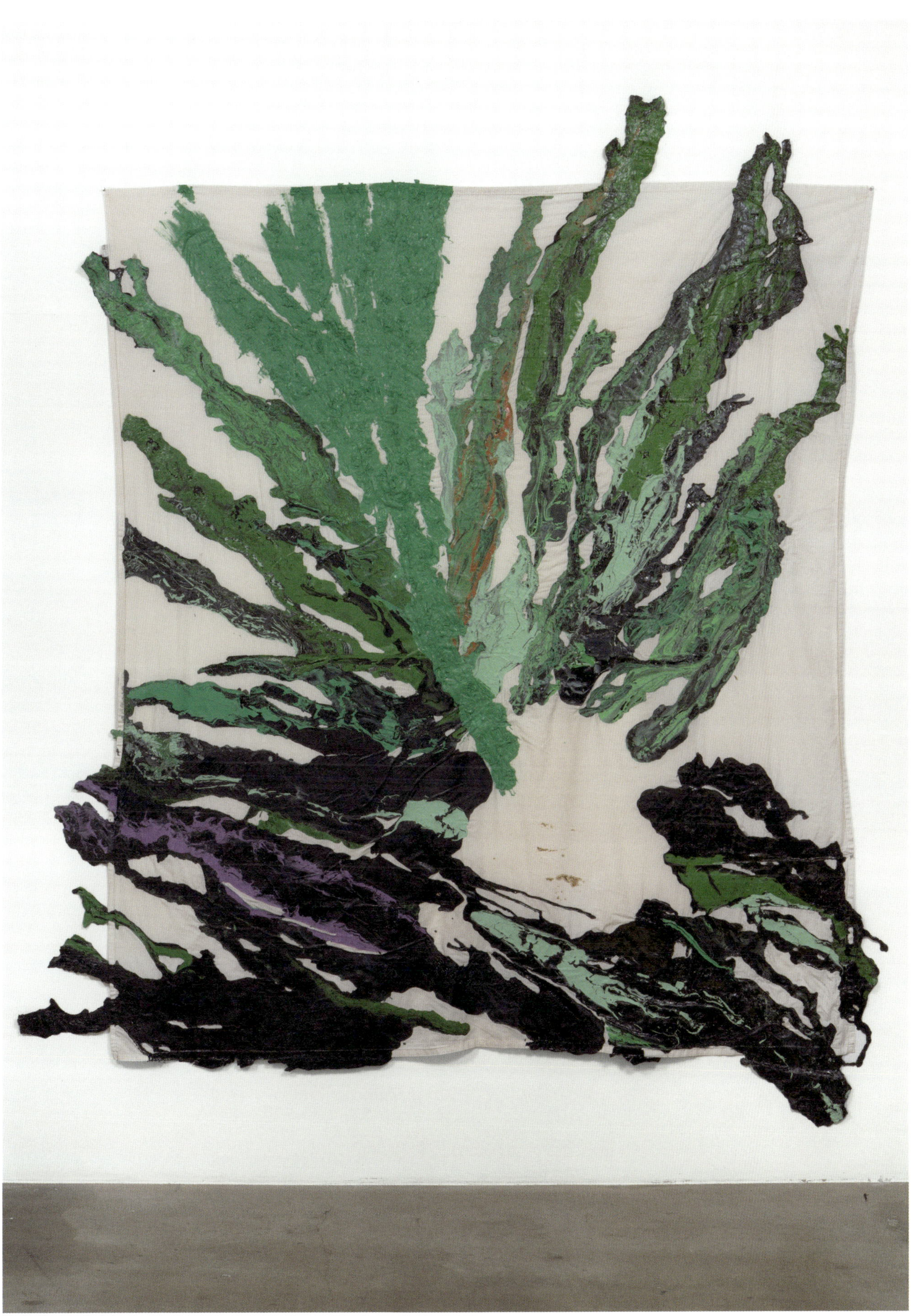

A seed is a star, 2015

Rodney McMillian

1969	Born in Columbia, SC
	Lives and works in Los Angeles, CA

Education

2002	MFA, California Institute of the Arts, CA
2000	Skowhegan School of Painting and Sculpture, ME
	School of the Art Institute of Chicago, IL
2000	Post-Baccalaureate Certificate, Presidential Scholar
	Edward L. Ryerson Fellowship Recipient
1998	BFA, School of the Art Institute of Chicago, IL
1991	BA Foreign Affairs, University of Virginia, Charlottesville, VA

Solo & Two-Person Exhibitions

2015	Studio Museum in Harlem, NY
	Landscape Paintings, Aspen Art Museum, CO
2013	*Against a "Civic Death": an overture*, Susanne Vielmetter Los Angeles Projects, Culver City, CA
2012	*Prospect Ave.*, Maccarone Gallery, New York, NY
2010	*Succulent*, Susanne Vielmetter Los Angeles Projects, Culver City, CA
2009	*Sentimental Disappointment, Momentum 14: Rodney McMillian*, Institute of Contemporary Art, Boston, MA
	Haubrokshows, Berlin, Germany
2008	The Kitchen, New York, NY
2007	*Jutta Koether / Rodney McMillian*, Susanne Vielmetter Berlin Projects, Germany
	Rodney McMillian and Olga Koumoundouros: On A Porch, LAXART, Los Angeles, CA
	Neuer Aachener Kunstverein, Aachen, Germany
	Adamski Galerie, Aachen, Germany
2006	*Odes*, Susanne Vielmetter Los Angeles Projects, Culver City, CA
2005	*Untitled (ellipses) III*, Triple Candie, New York, NY
	Rodney McMillian – Untitled, Estro Galleria d'arte, Padua, Italy

2004 *on comfort,* Adamski Galerie, Aachen, Germany
2003 *Untitled (ellipses) II,* Susanne Vielmetter Los Angeles Projects, CA
2002 *Untitled,* Finesilver Gallery, San Antonio, TX
Untitled (...on love), Gallery A-402, Valencia, CA

Select Group Exhibitions

2015 Sharjah Biennial 12: *The past, the present, the possible,* United Arab Emirates
Misappropriations: Recent Acquisitions, Orange County Museum of Art, Newport Beach, CA
2014 *When the Stars Begin to Fall: Imagination and the American South,* Studio Museum in Harlem, NY; NSU Art Museum, Fort Lauderdale, FL; Institute of Contemporary Art, Boston, MA
Ruffneck Constructivists, Institute of Contemporary Art, University of Pennsylvania, Philadelphia, PA
Outside the Lines: Black in the Abstract, Part 2, Contemporary Arts Museum, Houston, TX
2013 *Room to Live: Recent Acquisitions and Works from the Collection,* Museum of Contemporary Art, Los Angeles, CA
Bald Eagle, Sammlung Haubrok, Berlin, Germany
Homebodies, Museum of Contemporary Art Chicago, IL
Haubrok Collection - No Desaster, Sammlung Falckenberg, Harburg, Germany
Selections from the Grunwald Center and the Hammer Contemporary Collection, UCLA, Hammer Museum, Los Angeles, CA
2012 *Blues for Smoke,* Museum of Contemporary Art, Los Angeles, CA; Whitney Museum of American Art, New York, NY; Wexner Center for the Arts, Columbus, OH
my.LA, Haubrokshows, Sammlung Haubrok, Berlin, Germany
2011 *VideoStudio,* Studio Museum in Harlem, NY
The Bearden Project, Studio Museum in Harlem, NY
Human Nature, Los Angeles County Museum of Art, CA
Shapes, Sammlung Haubrok, Berlin, Germany
Agitated Histories, Contemporary Museum, Baltimore, MD; SITE Santa Fe, NM
2010 *Edgar Arceneaux, Andrea Bowers, Olga Koumoundouros, Rodney McMillian, Charles Gaines, Nery Gabriel Lemus,* Project Row Houses, Houston, TX
The Artist's Museum: Los Angeles Artists 1980–2010, Museum of Contemporary Art, Los Angeles, CA

2010 *New Art for a New Century: Contemporary Acquisitions '00–'10,* Orange County Museum of Art, Newport Beach, CA

2009 *The Moving Image: Scan to Screen, Pixel to Projection II,* Orange County Museum of Art, Newport Beach, CA

MONITAUR, Aspen Art Museum, CO

Out of School, City of Brea Art Gallery, CA

2008 *30 Americans,* Rubell Family Collection, Miami, FL; North Carolina Museum of Art, Raleigh, NC; Corcoran Gallery of Art, Washington, DC; Chrysler Museum of Art, Norfolk, VA; Milwaukee Art Museum, WI; Frist Center for the Visual Arts, Nashville, TN

It's All About Sculpture, Sammlung Haubrok, Berlin, Germany

California Biennial 2008, Orange County Museum of Art, Newport Beach, CA

Index: Conceptualism in California from the Permanent Collection, Geffen Contemporary at the Museum of Contemporary Art, Los Angeles, Newport Beach, CA

Whitney Biennial 2008, Whitney Museum of American Art, New York, NY

BLACK IS, BLACK AIN'T, Renaissance Society, University of Chicago, IL; Museum of Contemporary Art, Detroit, MI; H&R Block Artspace at the Kansas City Art Institute, MO; Temple Gallery at the Tyler School of Art, Philadelphia, PA

International Artist-in-Residence New Works 08.1, Artpace, San Antonio, TX

Männerfantasien II, COMA, Berlin, Germany

Disorderly Conduct: Recent Art in Tumultuous Times, Orange County Museum of Art, Newport Beach, CA

2007 *An Atlas of Events,* Calouste Gulbenkian Foundation, Lisbon, Portugal

Philosophy of Time Travel, Studio Museum in Harlem, NY

Hammer Contemporary Collection, UCLA Hammer Museum, Los Angeles, CA

stop.look.listen: an exhibition of video works, Herbert F. Johnson Museum of Art, Cornell University, Ithaca, NY; Haggerty Museum of Art at Marquette University, Milwaukee, WI; Orlando Museum, FL

USA: American Video Art at the Beginning of the 3rd Millennium, 2nd Moscow Biennial, Russia

Silicone Valley, MoMA P.S.1, Long Island City, NY

2006 *USA Today,* Royal Academy of Art, London, UK

Black Alphabet: conTEXTS of Contemporary African American Art, Zachęta National Gallery of Art, Warsaw, Poland

Ordinary Culture: Heikes/Helms/McMillian, Medtronic Gallery at Walker Art Center, Minneapolis, MN

Painting in Tongues, Museum of Contemporary Art Los Angeles, CA

2005–08 *Uncertain States of America*, Astrup Fearnley Museum of Art, Oslo, Norway; Bard Museum Center for Curatorial Studies, Bard College, Annandale-on-Hudson, NY; Reykjavík Art Museum, Iceland; Herning Kunstmuseum, Copenhagen, Denmark; Centre for Contemporary Art, Warsaw, Poland; Le Musée de Sérignan, France; Galerie Rudolfinum, Prague, Czech Republic

2005 *Frequency*, Studio Museum in Harlem, NY

Menschensgladbach - Neue Ankäufe und Leihgaben, Städtisches Museum Abteiberg, Mönchengladbach, Germany

Thing - New Sculpture from Los Angeles, UCLA Hammer Museum, Los Angeles, CA

2004 *White Noise*, REDCAT, Los Angeles, CA

Currents: African American Video Art Today, Cheekwood Museum of Art, Nashville, TN

Seeds and Roots: Selections from the Permanent Collection, Studio Museum in Harlem, NY

2003–04 *Gibt's mich wirklich: Vier Raeume aus der Sammlung Schuermann*, K21, Düsseldorf, Germany

2003 *aufgeschraubt & abgestaubt II—Die Sammlung im Prozess der Neuprasentation*, Ludwig Forum, Aachen, Germany

Veni Vidi Video, Studio Museum in Harlem, NY

Urban Aesthetics, California African American Museum, Los Angeles, CA

Select Bibliography

2014 Lax, Thomas. "From New York, Southward: A Counter-Memorial." *Mousse*, No. 44, Summer

Oelze, Sabine. "Supersized art takes over Art Basel." *Deutsche Welle*, June 19

Rosenberg, Karen. "The Antidote to Sweet: Kara Walker is curator of 'Ruffneck Constructivists.'" *New York Times*, May 12

McClister, Neil. "Review: 'Ruffneck Constructivists' at the ICA Philadelphia." *Artforum*, May

Bader, Graham. "Review: 'Outside the Lines' at Contemporary Art Museum Houston." *Artforum*, April

Demaree, Joshua Michael. "Ruffneck Constructivists // ICA Philadelphia." *The Seen, Chicago's International Online Journal of Contemporary & Modern Art*, March 3

2013 Petry, Michael. *Nature Morte: Contemporary Artists Reinvigorate the Still Life*. London: Thames & Hudson, October

Ise, Claudine. "There is nothing cozy about MCA's 'Homebodies.'" *Chicago Tribune*, July 17

2013 Soto, Paul. "Rodney McMillian." *Flash Art,* May/June
Kiyoizumi, A.J. "Artist Rodney McMillian Discusses Process: Los Angeles Artist Melds the Political and Artistic with Keen Performances." *Daily Californian,* April 9
Molesworth, Helen. "Blues for Smoke." *Artforum,* March
Friedwald, Will. "The Jazz Scene: Even Uptown Gets the Blues." *Wall Street Journal,* February 7
Cotter, Holland. "Mood Indigo: A Playlist for the Mind. 'Blues for Smoke' at the Whitney Museum." *New York Times,* February 7
Mizota, Sharon. "Rodney McMillian on the puppets of politics." *Los Angeles Times,* January 24
Mosheni, Yasmin. "In the Air." ArtInfo.com, January
2012 Wilson, Michael. "Review: Rodney McMillian at Maccarone." *Artforum,* December
Schultz, Charles Marshall. "Review, New York: Rodney McMillian at Maccarone." *Art in America,* December
Schwarting, Jen. "Rodney McMillian Prospect Ave." *Brooklyn Rail,* November
Knight, Christopher. "Blues Reverberates at MOCA." *Los Angeles Times,* October 29
Johnson, Reed. "MOCA's 'Blues for Smoke' riffs on a wider aesthetic." *Los Angeles Times,* October 27
Wood, Mikael. "MOCA Examines Blues Music." *Los Angeles Confidential,* October
2011 Simpson, Bennett. "And Your Mind Will Follow." *Artforum,* October
Muchnic, Suzanne. "50 years of support—and changing tastes—at the Los Angeles County Museum of Art." *Los Angeles Times,* May 15
2010 Miles, Christopher. "Rodney McMillian at Susanne Vielmetter Los Angeles Projects." *LA Weekly,* February 11
Ollman, Leah. "Around the Galleries." *Los Angeles Times,* February 5
2009 Sholis, Brian. "Rodney McMillian: The Kitchen." *Artforum,* January
2008 Copeland, Huey. "The Blackness of Blackness." *Artforum,* October
Markle, Leslie. "Disorderly Conduct." *artUS,* Summer
O'Connell, Brian. "Ghostly Media: What Would an Invoking Media Look Like?" *Art & Research,* Summer
Menzies, Michelle. "Black Is, Black Ain't." *Flash Art,* July
Grabner, Michelle. "Black Is, Black Ain't." *Time Out Chicago,* May 22
Salsbury, Britany. "Critic's Picks: Black Is, Black Ain't." *Artforum,* May
Volk, Gregory. "Spring In Dystopia." *Art in America,* May
Schjeldahl, Peter. "Lessness: The Whitney Biennial." *New Yorker,* March 17

Schuker, Lauren A.E. "The Fine Art of Less." *Wall Street Journal,* March 7
Cotter, Holland. "Art's Economic Indicator." *New York Times,* March 7
Mizota, Sharon. "World in Upheaval." *Los Angeles Times,* February 10
2007 Vogel, Carol. "Whitney Biennial Stretches to Armory." *New York Times,* November 16
Myers, Holly. "Social issues leave imprint in 'Touched.'" *Los Angeles Times,* August 22
Finkel, Jori. "A Reluctant Fraternity, Thinking Post-Black." *New York Times,* June 10
Firstenberg, Lauri. "Rodney McMillian: Los Angeles." *Art Papers,* January/February
Ellis, Patricia. "Catching up with Charles (Saatchi)." *Flash Art,* January/February
2006 Smith, Roberta. "More Than You Can See: Storm of Art Engulfs Miami." *New York Times,* December 9
Searle, Adrian. "Rebels without a cause." *Guardian,* December 9
Nys Dambrot, Shana. "Rodney McMillian: Odes." *Art Review,* December
Lawson, Thomas. "Best of 2006." *Artforum,* December
Morgan, Jessica. "Best of 2006." *Artforum,* December
Nys Dambrot, Shana. "Rodney McMillian: Odes." *Lifescapes,* November
Knight, Christopher. "Falling short of a Great Society." *Los Angeles Times,* October 6
Brooks, Amra. "Must See Art: Rodney McMillian." *LA Weekly,* October 5
Bedford, Christopher. "Rodney McMillian." Artforum.com, October 5
CG. "Rodney McMillian: Odes." *Artkrush,* October 4
Muchnic, Suzanne. "The Art Explosion." *Los Angeles Times,* October 1
Kenning, Dean. "Uncertain States of America." *Art Monthly,* October
Kent, Sarah. "States of the Art." *Time Out,* September 20
Glover, Michael. "An Orgy of Appropriation." *Independent,* September 13
Abbe, Mary. "'Ordinary' becomes extraordinary." *Star Tribune Minneapolis,* August 17
Smith, Roberta. "Endgame Art? It's Borrow, Sample and Multiply in an Exhibition at Bard College." *New York Times,* July 7
Landi, Ann. "Multiple Personalities." *Artnews,* April
Harvey, Doug. "Glossolalia for Dummies." *LA Weekly,* February 22
Knight, Christopher. "Painting Can Speak In Many Tongues." *Los Angeles Times,* February 3
Campagnola, Sofia. "Focus Los Angeles." *Flash Art,* January/February
Kastner, Jeffrey. "Frequency." *Artforum,* January
2005 Cotter, Holland. "Happenstance." *New York Times,* December 30
Boston, Nicolas. "Give Them the Chair." *New York Observer,* December 5
Smith, Roberta. "Where Issues of Black Identity Meet the Concerns of Every Artist." *New York Times,* November 18

2005	Pagel, David. "Summer sampler has a dark side." *Los Angeles Times,* July 8
	Forgacs, Eva. "Thing." *artUS,* July
	Firstenberg, Lauri. "Thing." *Frieze,* June
	Mack, Joshua. "Thing: New Sculpture from Los Angeles." *Modern Painters,* April
	Ned Holte, Michael. "West Coast Thing." Artforum.com, February 10
	Knight, Christopher. "The next big 'Thing' in L.A." *Los Angeles Times,* February 9
	Cotter, Holland. "Rodney McMillian at Triple Candie." *New York Times,* January 21
	Tumlir, Jan. "THING: New Sculpture from Los Angeles." *Artforum,* January
2004	Myers, Holly. "Disposable Society." *Los Angeles Times,* October 13
	Myers, Julian. "Edgar Arceneaux - Rodney McMillian at Susanne Vielmetter Los Angeles Projects." *Frieze,* May
	Davis, Phillip. "What we saw at Art Basel Miami Beach." *Dwell,* April
	Knight, Christopher. "A chronicle of race, rage, ritual." *Los Angeles Times,* February 17
	Harvey, Doug. "Color Theory - Fade to black." *LA Weekly,* February 13
	Adamski, Stephan. *Kunstforum,* January

Grants/Awards

2008	United States Artists Broad Fellow
	Art Matters, Spring 2008 Grantee
2007	William H. Johnson Prize, winner
2005	William H. Johnson Prize, finalist

Installation Views: *Landscape Paintings*

Aspen Art Museum

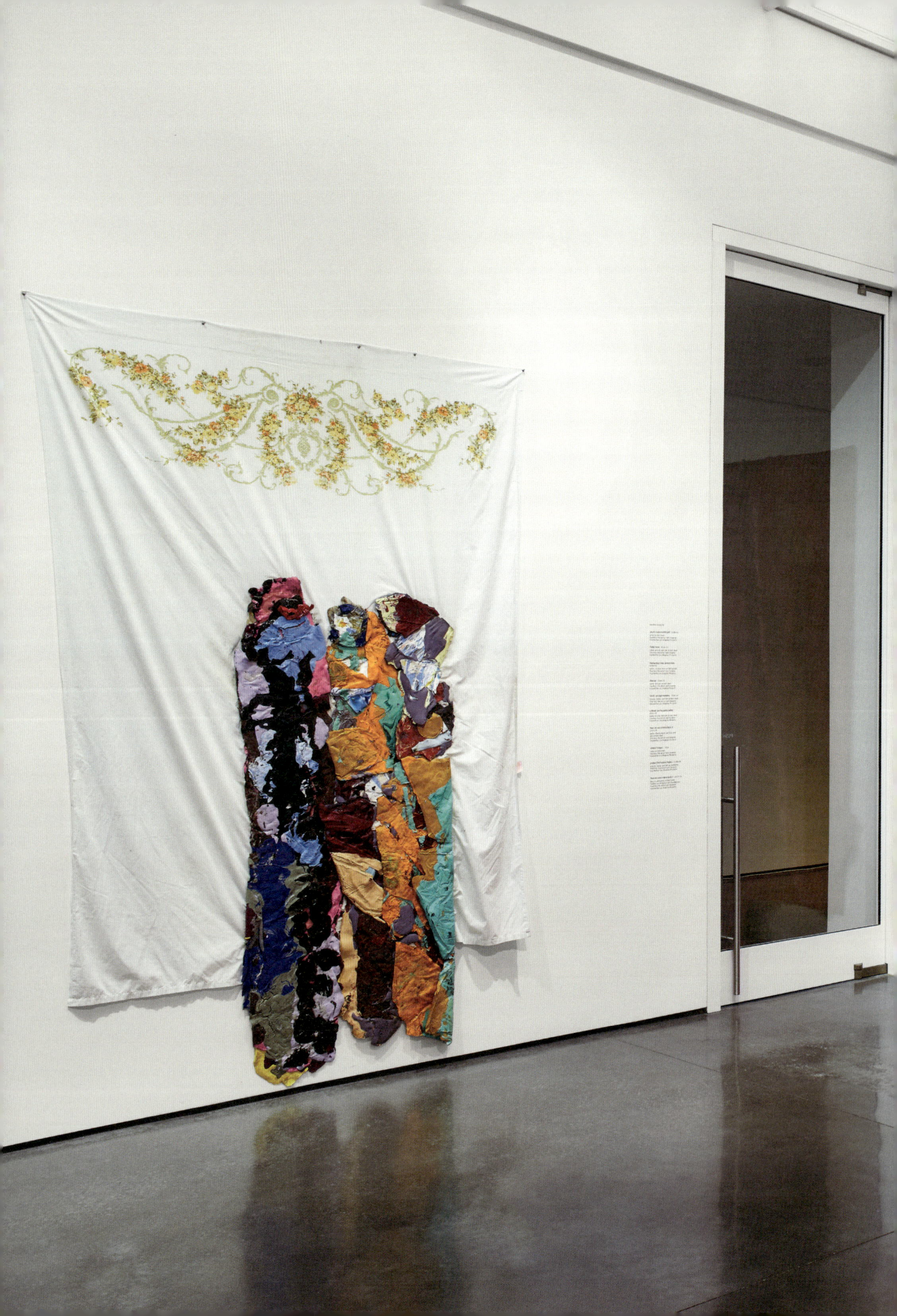

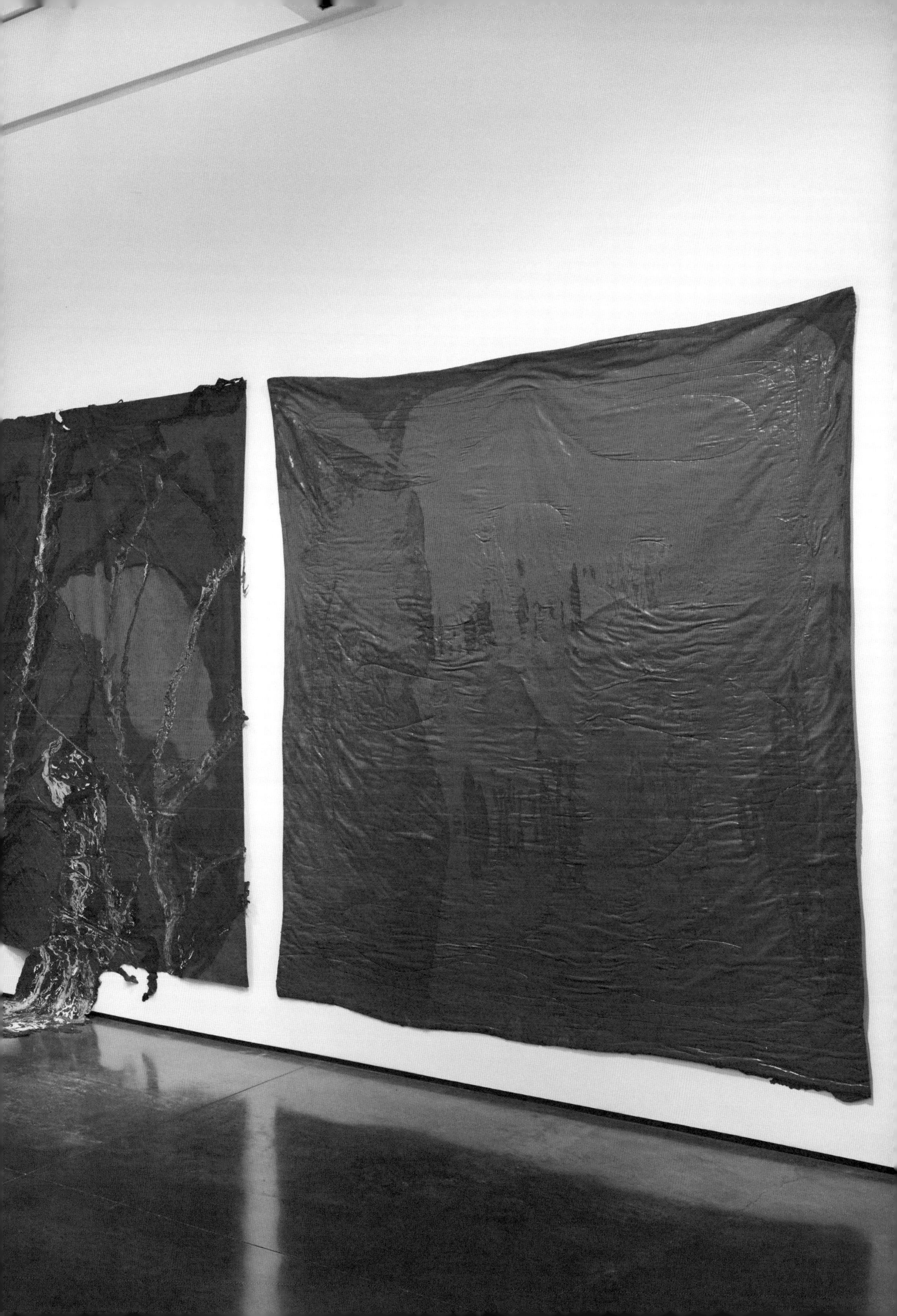

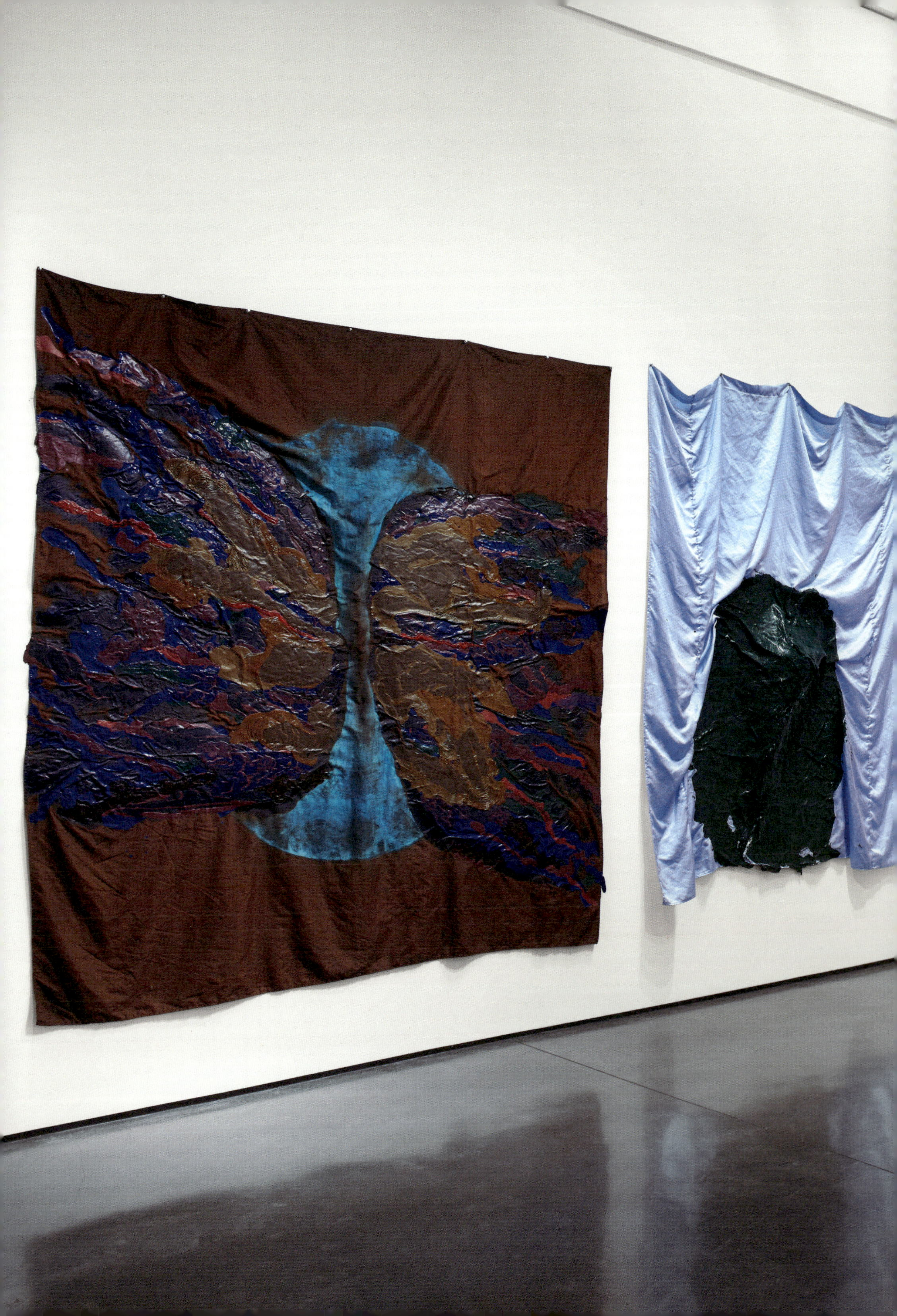

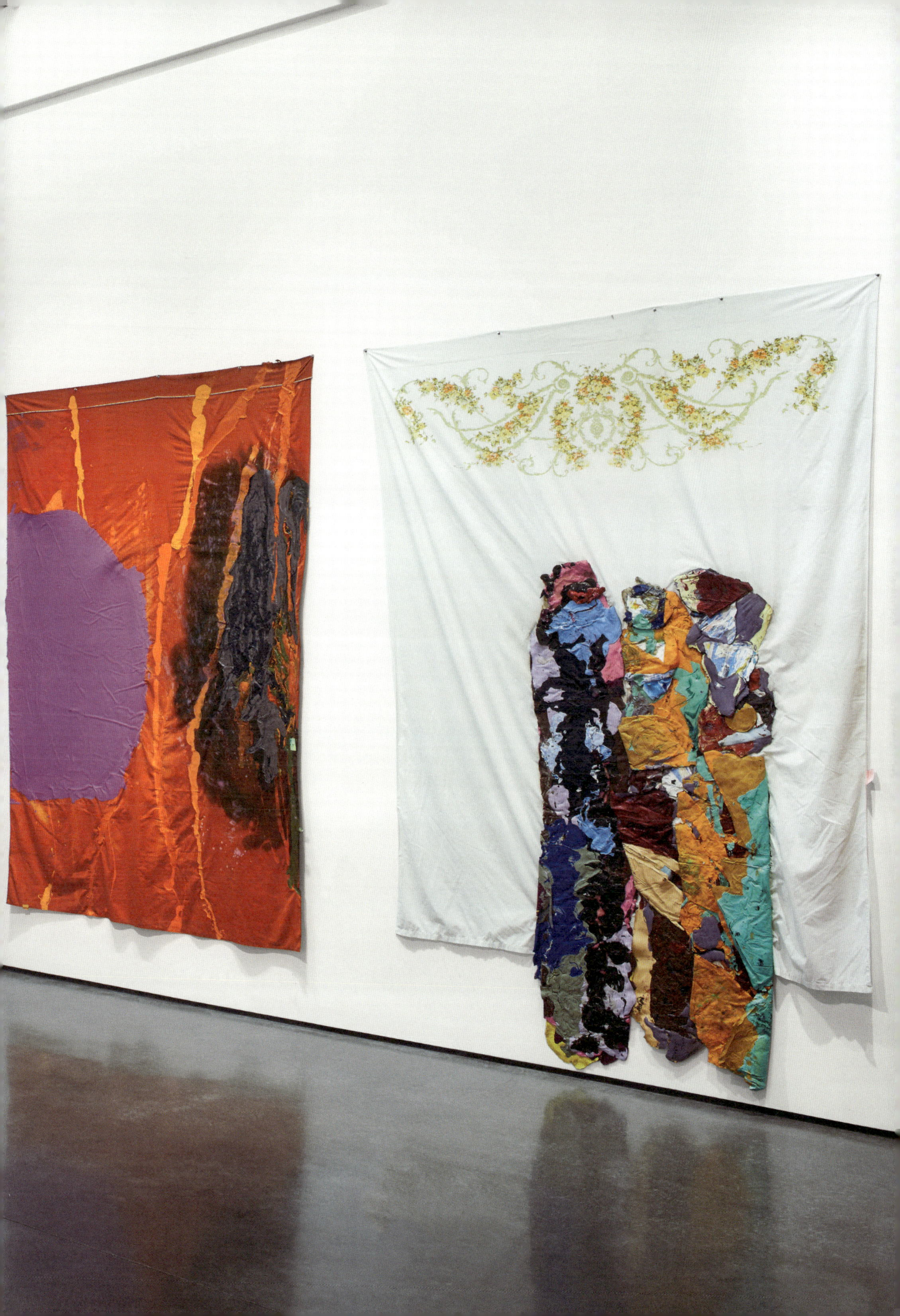

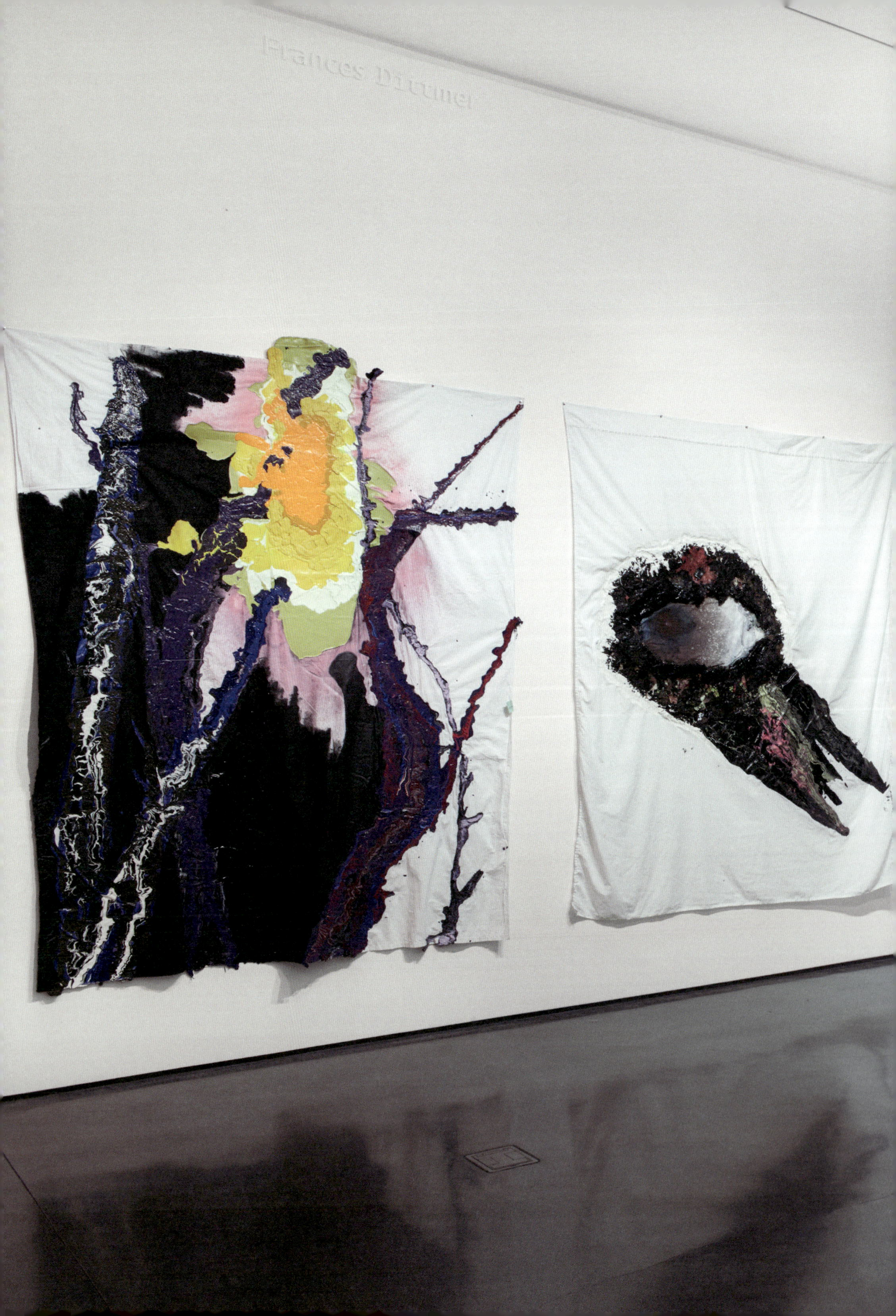
Frances Dittmer

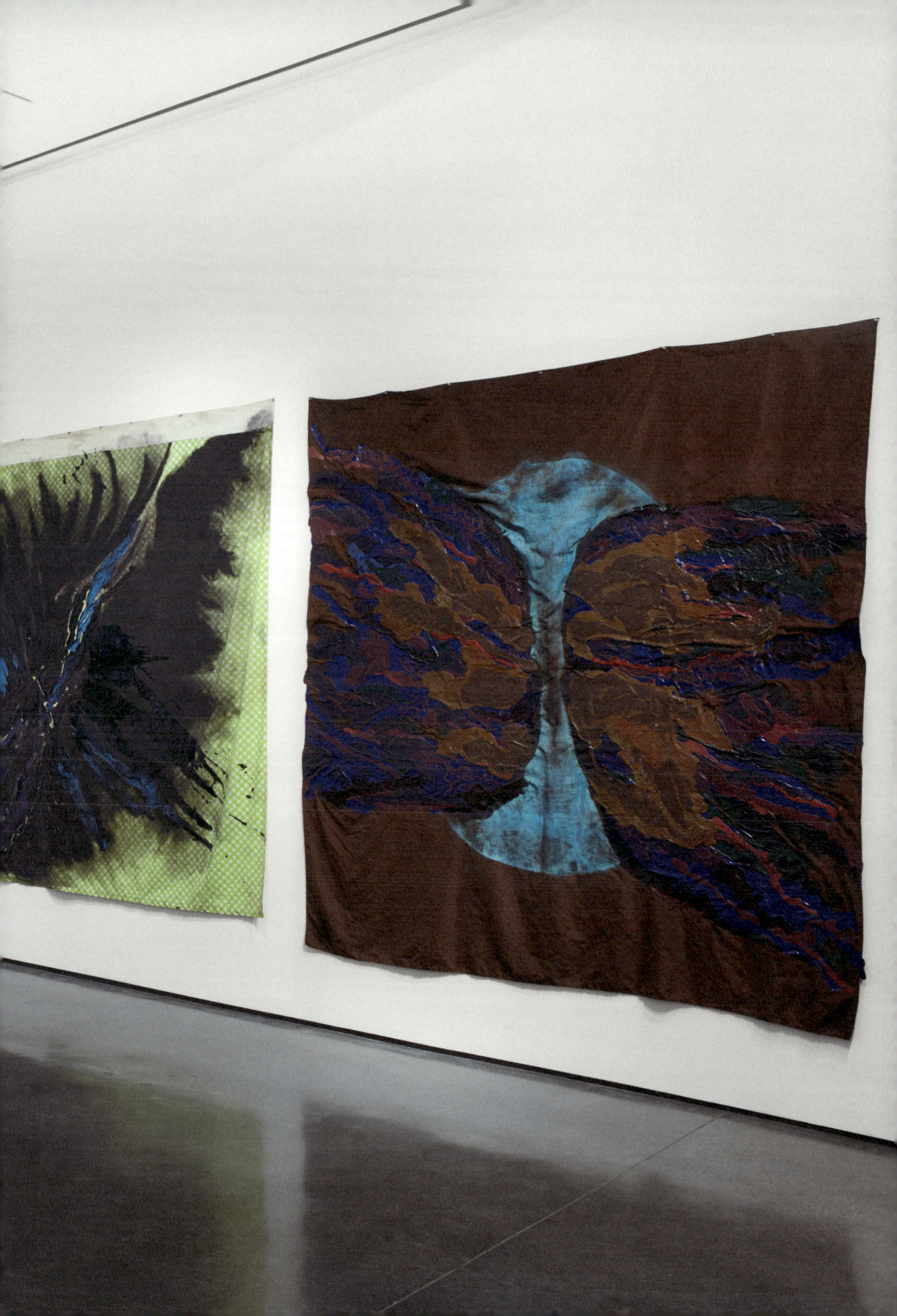

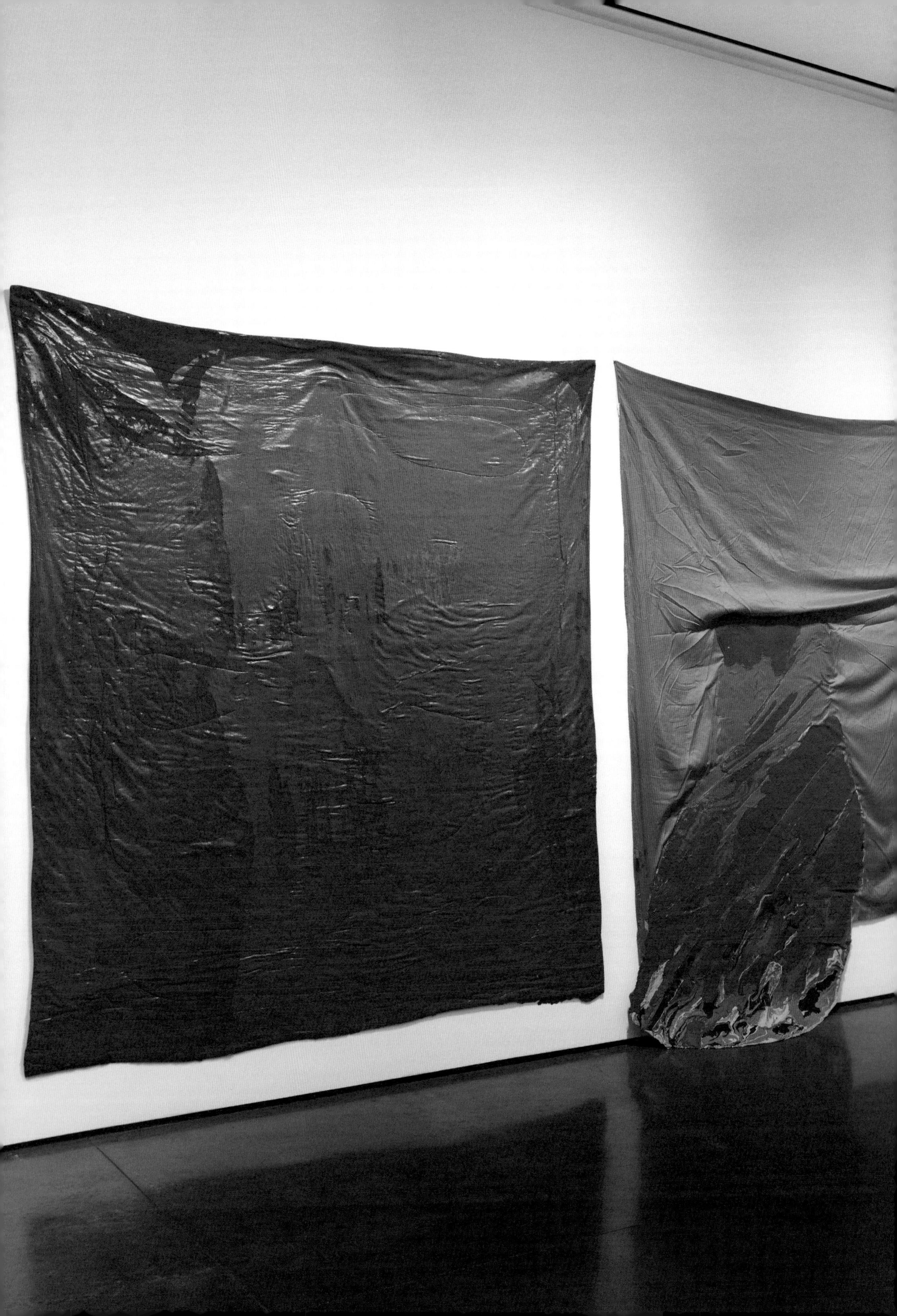

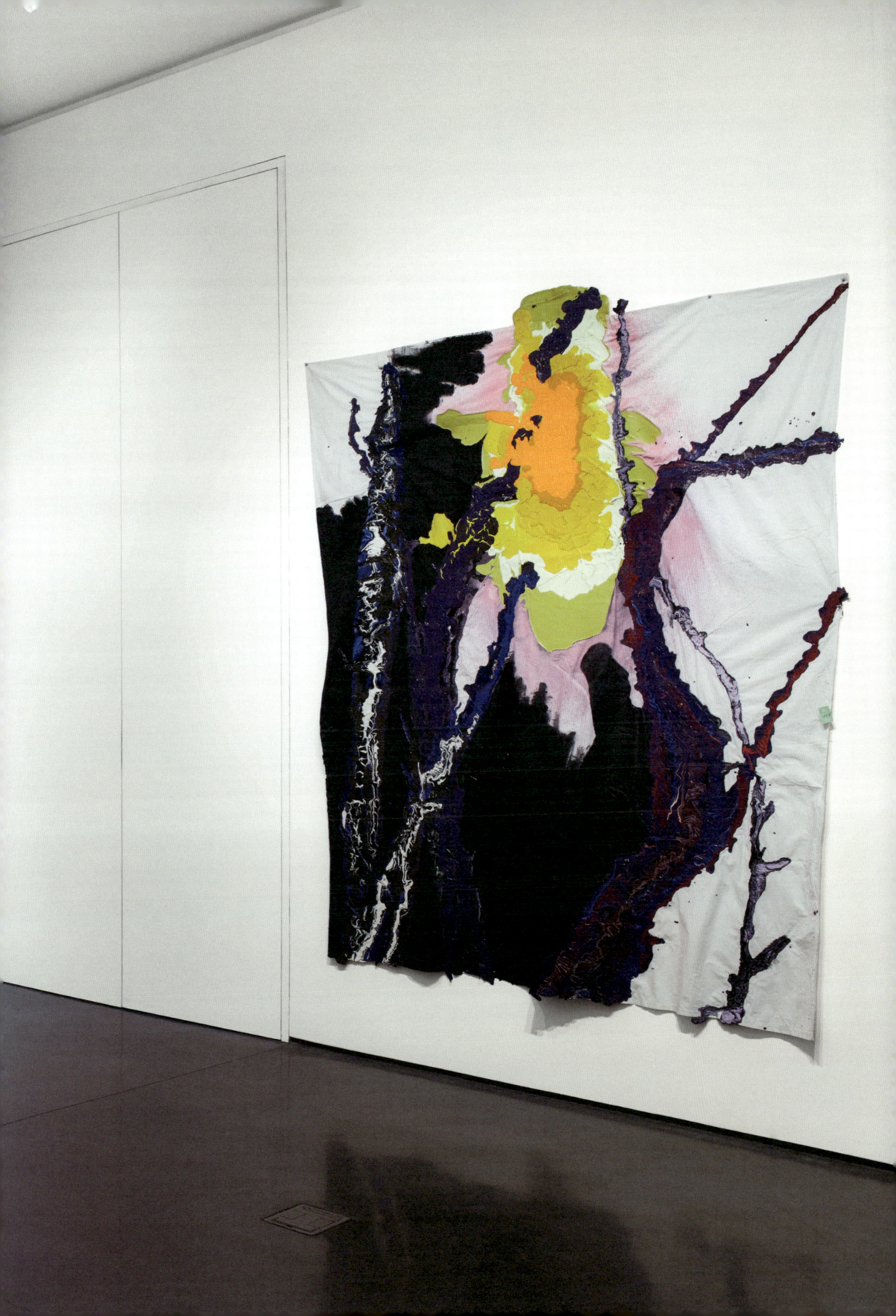

Contributors Biographies

Heidi Zuckerman is the AAM's Nancy and Bob Magoon CEO and Director. Zuckerman's curatorial projects include major one-person exhibitions as well as numerous pivotal group exhibitions. Previously, she served as the Phyllis Wattis MATRIX Curator and then the Chair of the Art Curatorial Department at the University of California, Berkeley Art Museum and Pacific Archive (1999–2005). Prior to this, she served as the Assistant Curator of 20th-Century Art at New York's Jewish Museum (1993–1998). Zuckerman's writing has appeared in numerous international exhibition catalogues and publications.

Thomas J. Lax is Associate Curator of Media and Performance Art at the Museum of Modern Art, New York. For the previous seven years, he worked at the Studio Museum in Harlem, where he organized over a dozen exhibitions as well as numerous screenings, performances, and public programs. Lax is a faculty member at the Institute for Curatorial Practice in Performance at Wesleyan University's Center for the Arts and received his BA from Brown University in Africana Studies and Art/Semiotics and an MA in Modern Art from Columbia University.

Exhibition Checklist

There are veins in these lands, I,
2007–13
Acrylic and latex on bedsheet
135 x 80 1/2 in (342.9 x 204.5 cm)
Collection of Kadist Art Foundation

Site #1: an origin narrative,
2008–13
Acrylic, latex, and ink on bedsheet
90 x 79 3/4 in (228.6 x 202.6 cm)

Site #3: stumps in plain sight,
2008–14
Latex on bedsheet
109 1/2 x 70 in (278.1 x 177.8 cm)

Untitled (for Francine Hughes),
2008–14
Acrylic, latex, and ink on comforter
100 x 84 in (254 x 213.4 cm)
Private collection

There are veins in these lands, II,
2010–14
Latex, flashe paint, acrylic, and ink on bedsheet
100 x 77 1/2 in (254 x 196.8 cm)

a Mouth: and the galaxy within,
2012–15
Latex, acrylic, and ink on bedsheet
92 x 76 in (233.7 x 193.04 cm)

Untitled (tongue), 2014
Latex on bedsheet
100 x 70 in (254 x 177.8 cm)

Blue Sun, 2014–15
Latex and ink on bedsheet
95 x 86 in (241.3 x 218.4 cm)

Purple Moon, 2014–15
Latex, acrylic, and ink on bedsheet
96 x 63 in (243.8 x 160 cm)

Wildseedling: it was already there,
2014–15
Latex, chicken wire on bedspread
92 x 74 in (233.7 x 187.9 cm)

All works courtesy the artist and Susanne Vielmetter Los Angeles Projects

List of Illustrations

$ 0.42, 2001
Oil on panel, photo, tangerine bag
15 x 34 in (38.1 x 86.4 cm)
Private collection
[p. 12; top]

Untitled, 2001
Mixed media on bedspread
90 x 70 in (228.6 x 177.8 cm)
Private collection
[p. 10]

Untitled, 2001
Mixed media on canvas
84 x 86 in (213.4 x 218.4 cm)
Private collection
[p. 9]

Untitled, 2001
Mixed media on carpet
79 x 173 in (200 x 439.4 cm)
Private collection
[p. 15; top]

Untitled (flag), 2001
Mixed media on canvas
97 x 107 in (246.4 x 271.8 cm)
Private collection
[p. 11; bottom]

Untitled (flag) I, 2001
Mixed media on canvas
96 x 147 in (243.8 x 373.4 cm)
Private collection
[p. 13]

Untitled (flag) II, 2001
Mixed media on canvas
69 x 89 in (175.3 x 226 cm)
Private collection
[p. 12; bottom]

Untitled (bald eagle), 2002
Carpet
60 x 96 in (152.4 x 243.8 cm)
Private collection
[p. 15; bottom]

Untitled (lollipop), 2002
Mixed media, latex on canvas
67 x 77 in (170.1 x 195.6 cm)
Private collection
[p. 11; top]

Unfinished (it's easier to get something new right than something old) for Laurie Nye and Martha Eknars, 2002–03
Oil on canvas
48 x 36 (121.9 x 91.4 cm)
Collection of Gaby and Wilhelm Schürmann, Germany
[p. 49]

in progress, 2003
Oil on wood
18 x 18 in (45.72 x 45.72 cm)
Collection of Gaby and Wilhelm Schürmann, Germany
[p. 44; bottom]

Untitled, 2003
Carpet and paper on canvas
160 x 110 in (406.4 x 278.4 cm)
Collection of Jeffrey Kerns, Los Angeles
[p. 14]

Untitled, 2003
Oil on canvas
18 x 18 in (45.72 x 45.72 cm)
Collection of Gaby and Wilhelm Schürmann, Germany
[p. 45; top]

Untitled, 2003
Oil on canvas
48 x 36 in (121.9 x 91.4 cm)
Collection of Gaby and Wilhelm Schürmann, Germany
[p. 47; top]

Apple (stretching and yawning) for G. Jones, 2004
Oil on wood
19 1/4 x 20 3/4 in (48.9 x 52.7 cm)
[p. 47; bottom]

Lily, 2004
Oil on wood
20 1/2 x 19 in (52 x 48.3 cm)
Private collection
[p. 48; bottom]

Untitled, 2004
Carpet, plastic coin, glue, nails
10 x 20 ft (3 x 6 m)
Museum Abteiberg, Mönchengladbach, Germany
[p. 18]

Untitled, 2004
Latex and charcoal on canvas
7 x 6 x 3 ft (2.1 x 1.8 x 0.9 m)
The Studio Museum in Harlem; Gift of Martin and Rebecca Eisenberg, Scarsdale, NY
[p. 52; top]

Untitled (Landscape), 2004
Latex on canvas
Approx. 10 x 8.5 ft (3 x 2.6 m)
Private collection
[p. 100]

Untitled (The Supreme Court Painting), 2004–06
Poured acrylic paint on cut canvas
18 x 18 ft (5.5 x 5.5 m)
[p. 82]

Ascension (From the church on the corner of Prospect Ave and Rodney Dr), 2005
Found carpet, plywood board
Carpet: 63 x 91 in (160 x 231 cm)
Board: 36 1/4 x 48 in (92 x 121.9 cm)
Collection of David Allan Grier, Los Angeles, CA
[p. 16]

Untitled, 2005
Blanket, thumb tacks
6 x 7 ft (1.8 x 2.1 m)
[p. 41]

Untitled, 2005
Carpet
11 1/2 x 14 x 8 ft (3.5 x 4.3 x 2.4 m)
Rubell Family Collection
[p. 19; top]

Untitled, 2005
Cotton sheet, paper, acrylic, charcoal, ink
77 x 85 in (195.5 x 215.9 cm)
Collection Dahlmann, Hamburg, Germany
[p. 102]

Untitled (for NTAG with love always), 2005
Poured latex on bedsheet, rocks
Approx. length 102 in (259 cm)
Collection of Nancy and Stanley Singer
[p. 101; top]

Untitled (In progress), 2005
Oil on wood
21 x 48 in (53.3 x 121.9 cm)
Collection of Jeffrey Kerns, Los Angeles
[p. 45; bottom]

Untitled (Landscape), 2005
Charcoal and acrylic on canvas
96 x 360 in (243.8 x 914.4 cm)
Private collection
[p. 52; bottom]

Installation view: *Untitled (The Capital Bldg.)*, 2005
Estro Galleria d'arte, Padova, Italy, February 26–April 30, 2005
Courtesy the artist, Estro Galleria d'arte, Padova, and Susanne Vielmetter Los Angeles Projects
[p. 83]

Untitled, 2005/06
Paper mounted on plastic tarp, acrylic latex, bedsheet
98 x 135 1/2 in (248.9 x 344.1 cm)
Private collection
[p. 97]

Untitled (sky), 2006
Latex on canvas
8 x 10 ft (2.4 x 3 m)
Private collection
[p. 99]

Untitled (Sky), 2006
Latex on canvas
94 x 202 in (238.7 x 513 cm)
Installation view: *Odes*, Susanne Vielmetter Los Angeles Projects, September 9–October 14, 2006.
Piece cut into multiple parts after the exhibition's conclusion and sold by the square foot. Multiple private collections
[p. 101; bottom]

Untitled, 2006–08
Acrylic on unstretched canvas, black vinyl, thread
Approx. 11 x 8 x 5 ft (3.3 x 2.4 x 1.5 m)
Collection of Orange County Museum of Art, Newport Beach, CA
[p. 56; bottom]

Untitled (flag) IV, 2006–08
Mixed media, acrylic on unstretched canvas, fabric, grommets
Approx. 9.5 x 11 x 1.5 ft (2.9 x 3.3 x 0.45 m)
Collection of MOCA, Los Angeles, CA
[p. 42]

Untitled (candles), 2006–10
Oil on wood
24 1/2 x 20 1/4 in (62.2 x 51.4 cm)
Collection of Joel Wachs
[p. 44; top]

a lemon, 2006–12
Oil on wood
24 x 28 in (60.9 x 71.1 cm)
Collection of Daniel Loeb, New York, NY
[p. 48; top]

Untitled (lungs), 2006–13
Acrylic, latex, ink on bedsheet
102 x 76 x 18 in (259 x 193 x 45.7 cm)
Private collection
[p. 39]

Untitled, 2007
Latex and acrylic on canvas
Diptych: 24 x 36 in (60.9 x 91.4 cm);
9 x 15 ft (2.7 x 4.5 m)
Private collection
[p. 57]

Untitled (flag) V, 2007–08
Two blankets, push pins
Diptych: each approx. 6 x 6 ft (1.8 x 1.8 m)
Collection of the artist
Courtesy the artist and Maccarone, NY
[p. 40]

There are veins in these lands, I, 2007–13
Acrylic and latex on bedsheet
135 x 80 1/2 in (342.9 x 204.5 cm)
Collection of Kadist Art Foundation
[p. 122]

Untitled, 2008
Latex paint, canvas
Three approx. 15 x 7 ft (4.5 x 2.1 m);
two approx. 15 x 8 ft (4.5 x 2.4 m)
Originally commissioned and produced
by ArtPace San Antonio
[p. 53–55, 56; top]

Untitled (for B. Traylor), I, 2008
Acrylic, latex, and ink on bedsheet
Approx. 84 x 48 in (213.4 x 121.9 cm)
Private collection
[p. 119]

Untitled (for B. Traylor), II, 2008
Acrylic, latex, ink on bedsheet
Approx. 72 x 48 in (182.9 x 121.9 cm)
[p. 118]

Untitled (after Bill Traylor) I, 2008
Acrylic, charcoal on canvas
40 1/4 x 36 1/2 in (102.2 x 92.7 cm)
[p. 80]

Untitled (after Bill Traylor) II, 2008
Acrylic, paper, charcoal on canvas
24 x 36 in (60.9 x 91.4 cm)
[p. 81]

Untitled (after Bill Traylor) III, 2008
Acrylic, latex, paper, charcoal on canvas
20 x 16 in (50.8 x 40.64 cm)
[p. 79]

Untitled (Part I), 2008
Acrylic, charcoal on brown paper
58 x 49 in (147.3 x 124.5 cm)
Collection of Edie Yvonne Firstenberg,
Los Angeles
[p. 51]

Untitled (Part II), 2008
Acrylic, charcoal on brown paper
48 x 59 in (121.9 x 149.8 cm)
Private collection
[p. 50]

Untitled, 2008–11
Latex on bedsheet
39 x 28 x 24 in (99 x 71.1 x 60.9 cm)
Collection of Blake Byrne, Los Angeles
[p. 92]

Site #1: an origin narrative, 2008–13
Acrylic, latex, and ink on bedsheet
90 x 79 3/4 in (228.6 x 202.6 cm)
[p. 114]

Site #3: stumps in plain sight, 2008–14
Latex on bedsheet
109 1/2 x 70 in (278.1 x 177.8 cm)
[p. 117]

Untitled (for Francine Hughes), 2008–14
Acrylic, latex, and ink on comforter
100 x 84 in (254 x 213.4 cm)
Private collection
[p. 123]

Untitled, 2009
Acrylic, latex, paper on canvas
Approx. 96 x 57 in (243.8 x 144.7 cm)
Private collection
[p. 58]

Untitled (4443 Prospect Ave.), 2009
Acrylic and latex on canvas
14 ft 6 in x 30 ft 6 in (4.4 x 9.3 m)
Installation view: *Sentimental Disappointment, Momentum 14: Rodney McMillian*, at ICA
Boston, MA, July 29–Nov 1, 2009
[p. 59]

a slow drip (from *The Clampetts*), 2010
Latex, paper, canvas, chicken wire
34 x 60 in (86.3 x 152.4 cm)
Collection of Axel and Barbara Haubrok,
Berlin, Germany
[p. 33; bottom]

There are veins in these lands, II, 2010–14
Latex, flashe paint, acrylic, and ink on
bedsheet
100 x 77 1/2 in (254 x 196.8 cm)
[p. 124]

Sleepy Time Down South (landscape with moon), 2011
Latex, acrylic, vinyl, paper, canvas
30 x 22 in (76.2 x 55.9 cm)
Collection of Bennie F. Johnson, Washington, DC
[p. 37; top]

Untitled, 2011
Carpet
15 x 13 ft (4.5 x 3.9 m)
[p. 17]

Untitled (from *The Clampetts*), I, 2011
Latex, paper, wire
26 x 15 in (66 x 38.1 cm)
Private collection of Fotene Demoulas & Tom Coté
[p. 32]

Untitled (from *The Clampetts*), II, 2011
Latex, paper, wire
24 x 16 in (60.9 x 40.6 cm)
Collection of Sasha Drosdick, Los Angeles, CA
[p. 33; top]

Untitled (Northern Lights), 2011
Acrylic, latex, vinyl, and ink on paper,
15 x 20 in (38.1 x 50.8 cm)
Collection of Ron Kreisel
[p. 35]

Untitled (zip), 2011
Bedsheet, latex, and thread
97 x 76 in (246.4 x 193 cm)
[p. 93]

The Vessels (a clear glass vase spray painted and painted again), 2011–14
Oil on panel
16 x 13 1/2 x 50 in (40.6 x 34.3 x 127 cm)
[p. 46; top]

25¢, 2012
Oil on wood panel
24 x 13 in (60.9 x 33 cm)
Collection of the artist
Courtesy the artist and Maccarone, NY
[p. 46; bottom]

Carpet Painting (Bedroom and TV Room), 2012
Carpet and ink
272 x 166 1/2 in (690.8 x 422.9 cm)
Collection of the artist
Courtesy the artist and Maccarone, NY
[p. 19; bottom]

Carpet Painting (Office and Ollie's Room), 2012
Carpet
197 x 94 x 5 in (500 x 238.7 x 12.7 cm)
Collection of the artist
Courtesy the artist and Maccarone, NY
[p. 20]

Installation view: *Prospect Ave*, 2012
Maccarone, New York, September 15–October 27, 2012
Courtesy the artist, Susanne Vielmetter Los Angeles Projects, and Maccarone, NY
[p. 60; bottom]

Representation of a Landscape as a Wall, 2012
Acrylic, latex, and ink on paper
14 x 48.6 ft (4.3 x 14.8 m)
Installation view: *Room to Live: Recent Acquisitions and Works from the Collection*, Museum of Contemporary Art, Los Angeles, CA, October 5, 2013–January 12, 2014
Collection of MOCA, Los Angeles, CA
[p. 60; top]

Untitled, 2012
Latex, acrylic, and vinyl on paper
22 x 30 in (55.9 x 76.2 cm)
The Studio Museum in Harlem; gift of the artist on the occasion of the Romare Bearden (1911–1988) Centennial and *The Bearden Project* at The Studio Museum in Harlem, November 10, 2011–October 21, 2012
[p. 36]

Untitled, 2012
Latex, paper, wire, plaster, burlap, and yarn
24 x 16 x 7 in (60.9 x 40.6 x 17.8 cm)
[p. 43; top]

Untitled Cloud #1, 2012
Latex on sheet
97 7/8 x 61 1/8 in (248.6 x 155.3 cm)
Collection of the artist
Courtesy the artist and Maccarone, NY
[p. 90]

Untitled Cloud #2, 2012
Tempera and latex on canvas
62 1/4 x 43 3/4 (158.1 x 111.1 cm)
Collection of the artist
Courtesy the artist and Maccarone, NY
[p. 89; bottom]

Untitled Cloud #3, 2012
Tempera and latex on canvas
71 x 94 1/2 in (180.3 x 240 cm)
Collection of the artist
Courtesy the artist and Maccarone, NY
[p. 86]

Untitled Cloud #4, 2012
Tempera and latex on canvas
58 x 70 1/2 in (147.3 x 179 cm)
Collection of the artist
Courtesy the artist and Maccarone, NY
[p. 87]

Untitled Cloud #5, 2012
Tempera and latex on canvas
60 1/2 x 70 in (153.7 x 177.8 cm)
Collection of the artist
Courtesy the artist and Maccarone, NY
[p. 88]

Untitled Cloud #6, 2012
Tempera and latex on canvas
23 x 40 1/2 in (58.4 x 102.9 cm)
Collection of the artist
Courtesy the artist and Maccarone, NY
[p. 89; top]

Untitled (flag VI), 2012
Burlap, thread, plastic, and latex
80 x 169 in (203.2 x 429.3 cm)
[p. 43; bottom]

Untitled Landscape #1, 2012
Latex, acrylic, and ink on canvas
135 x 166 1/2 in (342.9 x 422.9 cm)
Collection of the artist
Courtesy the artist and Maccarone, NY
[p. 84]

Untitled Landscape #2, 2012
Latex, acrylic, and ink on canvas
100 1/2 x 103 1/8 in
(255.3 x 261.9 cm)
Collection of the artist
Courtesy the artist and Maccarone, NY
[p. 91]

Untitled Landscape #3, 2012
Tempera and latex on canvas
103 1/2 x 147 1/2 in (262.9 x 374.6 cm)
Collection of the artist
Courtesy the artist and Maccarone, NY
[p. 85; bottom]

Untitled Landscape #4, 2012
Tempera and latex on canvas
103 1/2 x 147 1/2 in (262.9 x 374.6 cm)
Collection of the artist
Courtesy the artist and Maccarone, NY
[p. 85; top]

a Mouth: and the galaxy within, 2012–15
Latex, acrylic, and ink on bedsheet
92 x 76 in (233.7 x 193.04 cm)
[p. 116]

a kemmering, 2013
Mixed media on paper
42 1/2 x 32 1/2 x 10 1/2 (107.9 x
82.5 x 26.6 cm)
[p. 37; bottom]

Estuary, 2013
Acrylic and latex on canvas
73 1/5 x 48 in (186.7 x 121.9 cm)
Collection of Bennie Johnson,
Washington, DC
[p. 95]

Origins, 2013
Acrylic and latex on canvas
88 x 63 1/2 in (223.5 x 161.3 cm)
Collection of Carole Server and Oliver
Frankel, New York
[p. 98]

Untitled, 2013
Acrylic, latex, and thread on bedsheet
Approx. 96 x 72 in (243.8 x 182.8 cm)
[p. 38]

Untitled, 2013
Paint and paper on paper
22 x 14 in (55.8 x 35.5 cm)
Collection of Michael Price
[p. 31; top]

Untitled, 2013
Paint and paper on paper
14 x 20 in (35.5 x 50.8 cm)
Collection of Tina Perry-Whitney and
Ric Whitney, Los Angeles, CA
[p. 31; bottom]

untitled (from the nipple to the bottle...still), 2013
Mixed media on paper
44 1/2 x 22 x 2 in (113 x 55.8 x 5 cm)
Collection of Erin Leider-Pariser and
Paul Pariser, Aspen, CO
[p. 34]

From the Slop: it shines, 2014
Acrylic on canvas
53 1/4 x 66 x 1 3/4 in
(135.2 x 167.6 x 4.4 cm)
[p. 96]

should, I, 2014
Acrylic, ink, tempura, and cardstock
on paper
21 1/2 x 29 1/2 in (54.6 x 74.9 cm)
Private collection
[p. 94]

Untitled (tongue), 2014
Latex on bedsheet
100 x 70 in (254 x 177.8 cm)
[p. 120]

Blue Sun, 2014–15
Latex and ink on bedsheet
95 x 86 in (241.3 x 218.4 cm)
[p. 115]

Purple Moon, 2014–15
Latex, acrylic, and ink on bedsheet
96 x 63 in (243.8 x 160 cm)
[p. 121]

Wildseedling: it was already there, 2014–15
Latex, chicken wire on bedspread
92 x 74 in (233.7 x 187.9 cm)
[p. 113]

A seed is a star, 2015
Latex on bedsheet
119 x 101 in (302.3 x 256.5 cm)
[p. 125]

Unless otherwise noted, all works courtesy the artist and Susanne Vielmetter Los Angeles Projects.

Photo Credits:
Marc Bernier: 36; Lutz Bertram: 57; Todd Johnson: 53–55, 56 (top); Charles Meyer: 59; Gene Ogami: 41, 47–48, 50, 52, 58, 82, 101–2; Tony Prikryl: 134–41; Andres Ramirez: 35; Jeffrey Sturges: 19 (bottom), 20, 46 (bottom), 60 (bottom), 84–91; Michael Underwood: 31 (top), 51; Robert Wedemeyer: 17, 33–34, 37–40, 42–43, 44 (top), 46 (top), 48 (top), 56 (bottom), 79–81, 92–93, 95–96, 98, 113–25, cover

Staff

Administrative Staff

Heidi Zuckerman
Nancy and Bob Magoon CEO and Director
Michael Aberman
Design Director
John Barker
Development Officer
Sherry Black
Curatorial Associate and Archivist
Meagan Burger
Visitor Services Coordinator
Mary Daly
Café Assistant Manager
Julia DeRose
Education Assistant
Michelle Dezember
Learning Director
Allen Domingos
Culinary Partner
Julia Domingos
Culinary Partner
Courtenay Finn
Curator
Sara Fowler
Junior Graphic Designer
Jonathan Hagman
Chief Preparator
Kevin Haupt
Building Engineer and Facilities Manager
Annie Henninger
Education Program Manager
Karen Johnsen
Finance and Administrative Director
Raimundo Martinez
Facilities Assistant
Jeff Murcko
Communications Director
Amy Myles
Retail Manager
Grace Nims
Assistant Development Director
Elissa Pappalardo
Receptionist and Administrative Assistant
Madison Rupp
Development Assistant
Amelia Russo
Executive Coordinator for the Director
John-Paul Schaefer
Deputy Director
Caitlin Stanley
Special Events and Development Coordinator
Sarah Stephenson
Editor
Eric Tallman
Security Manager
Renee Thomas
HR Officer
Amanda Thompson
Public Relations and Marketing Assistant
Luis Yllanes
Director of Exhibitions and Registration

Installation Crew and Art Preparators

Seth Beckton
Charles Childress
John Cohorst
Jason Cook
James Gorman
Pete Hajdu
Takeo Hiromitsu
Ryan Jervis
Mara Tegethoff
Jed Woolley

Outreach Educators

Jennifer Johnson
Chelsea Richards

Shop Associates

Emilie Kay
Allison Menscher
Kevin Newland
Lois Triano
Patricia Witt

Café Service Associates

Jennifer Bentley
Cecilia Gonzalez
Valerie Valenzuela

Security Officers

Peter Feinzig
Siarhei Piatrovich
William Schneider
Gregg Yocom

Guides

Lee Azarcon
Jamie Beers
Barrett Black
Shannon Dick
Manny Doron
Mark Everhart
Phil Golden
Caitria Gunter
Josh Kirrinkol
Robert Lutz
Jessica Parsons
Shanna Reiley
Brittany Rhoads
Chelsea Richards
Ben Tomkins
Ines Vergara

Board of Trustees

National Council

This publication accompanies Rodney McMillian's exhibition *Landscape Paintings*, organized by the Aspen Art Museum, curated by Heidi Zuckerman, and presented at the Aspen Art Museum, March 27–June 28, 2015, and MoMA P.S.1 in 2016.

Published by Aspen Art Press
Aspen Art Museum
637 East Hyman Avenue
Aspen, CO 81611
United States
aspenartmuseum.org

Library of Congress Control Number: 2015934504

ISBN: 9780934324717

AAM exhibitions are made possible by the Marx Exhibition Fund. General exhibition support is provided by the Toby Devan Lewis Visiting Artist Fund. Rodney McMillian's *Landscape Paintings* is supported by Allison and Warren Kanders, and funded in part by the AAM National Council.

Support for this publication is provided by the Toby Devan Lewis Publications Fund.

Front Cover:
a Mouth: and the galaxy within, 2012–15. Latex, acrylic, and ink on bedsheet. 92 x 76 in (233.7 x 193.04 cm). Courtesy the artist and Susanne Vielmetter Los Angeles Projects. Photo: Robert Wedemeyer

Back Cover:
Purple Moon, 2014–15. Latex, acrylic, and ink on bedsheet. 96 x 63 in (243.8 x 160 cm). Courtesy the artist and Susanne Vielmetter Los Angeles Projects. Photo: Robert Wedemeyer

Curator
Heidi Zuckerman

Curatorial Associate
Sherry Black

Editor
Sarah Stephenson

Design Director
Michael Aberman

Catalogue Designer
Sara Fowler

Printer
The Avery Group at Shapco Printing, Inc., Minneapolis

Available through
Artbook, LLC
Distributed Art Publishers
155 Sixth Avenue, 2nd Floor
New York, NY 10013
artbook.com